Advanced Digital Image Steganography Using LSB, PVD, and EMD:

Emerging Research and Opportunities

Gandharba Swain
Koneru Lakshmaiah Education Foundation, India

A volume in the Advances in
Information Security, Privacy, and
Ethics (AISPE) Book Series

Published in the United States of America by
IGI Global
Information Science Reference (an imprint of IGI Global)
701 E. Chocolate Avenue
Hershey PA, USA 17033
Tel: 717-533-8845
Fax: 717-533-8661
E-mail: cust@igi-global.com
Web site: http://www.igi-global.com

Library of Congress Cataloging-in-Publication Data

Names: Swain, Gandharba, 1974- author.
Title: Advanced digital image steganography using LSB, PVD, and EMD : emerging research and opportunities / by Gandharba Swain.
Description: Hershey PA : Information Science Reference, [2019]
Identifiers: LCCN 2018029252| ISBN 9781522575160 (hardcover) | ISBN 9781522575177 (ebook)
Subjects: LCSH: Image steganography.
Classification: LCC TA1636 .S93 2019 | DDC 005.8/24--dc23 LC record available at https://lccn.loc.gov/2018029252

This book is published in the IGI Global book series Advances in Information Security, Privacy, and Ethics (AISPE) (ISSN: 1948-9730; eISSN: 1948-9749)

British Cataloguing in Publication Data
A Cataloguing in Publication record for this book is available from the British Library.

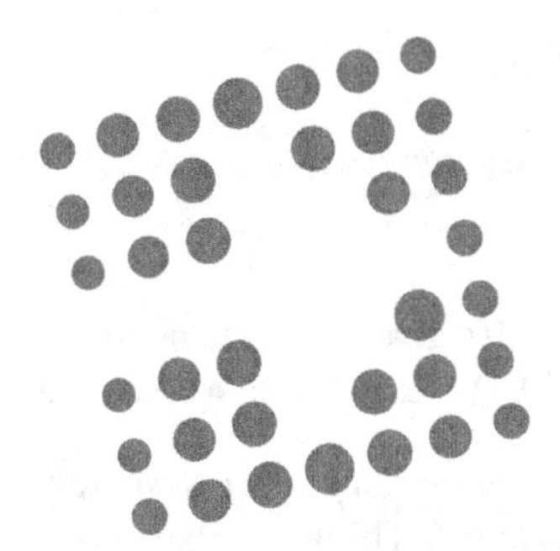

Advances in Information Security, Privacy, and Ethics (AISPE) Book Series

ISSN:1948-9730
EISSN:1948-9749

Editor-in-Chief: Manish Gupta, State University of New York, USA

MISSION

As digital technologies become more pervasive in everyday life and the Internet is utilized in ever increasing ways by both private and public entities, concern over digital threats becomes more prevalent.

The **Advances in Information Security, Privacy, & Ethics (AISPE) Book Series** provides cutting-edge research on the protection and misuse of information and technology across various industries and settings. Comprised of scholarly research on topics such as identity management, cryptography, system security, authentication, and data protection, this book series is ideal for reference by IT professionals, academicians, and upper-level students.

COVERAGE

- Electronic Mail Security
- Risk Management
- Tracking Cookies
- Data Storage of Minors
- Global Privacy Concerns
- Computer ethics
- Privacy Issues of Social Networking
- Privacy-Enhancing Technologies
- Technoethics
- Device Fingerprinting

IGI Global is currently accepting manuscripts for publication within this series. To submit a proposal for a volume in this series, please contact our Acquisition Editors at Acquisitions@igi-global.com or visit: http://www.igi-global.com/publish/.

The Advances in Information Security, Privacy, and Ethics (AISPE) Book Series (ISSN 1948-9730) is published by IGI Global, 701 E. Chocolate Avenue, Hershey, PA 17033-1240, USA, www.igi-global.com. This series is composed of titles available for purchase individually; each title is edited to be contextually exclusive from any other title within the series. For pricing and ordering information please visit http://www.igi-global.com/book-series/advances-information-security-privacy-ethics/37157. Postmaster: Send all address changes to above address.

Titles in this Series

For a list of additional titles in this series, please visit:
https://www.igi-global.com/book-series/advances-information-security-privacy-ethics/37157

Cybersecurity Education for Awareness and Compliance
Ismini Vasileiou (University of Plymouth, UK) and Steven Furnell (University of Plymouth, UK)
Information Science Reference • ©2019 • 306pp • H/C (ISBN: 9781522578475) • US $195.00

Detection and Mitigation of Insider Attacks in a Cloud Infrastructure Emerging Research ...
T. Gunasekhar (Koneru Lakshmaiah Education Foundation, India) K. Thirupathi Rao (Koneru Lakshmaiah Education Foundation, India) P. Sai Kiran (Koneru Lakshmaiah Education Foundation, India) V. Krishna Reddy (Koneru Lakshmaiah Education Foundation, India) and B. Thirumala Rao (Koneru Lakshmaiah Education Foundation, India)
Information Science Reference • ©2019 • 113pp • H/C (ISBN: 9781522579243) • US $165.00

Network Security and Its Impact on Business Strategy
Ionica Oncioiu (European Academy of the Regions, Belgium)
Business Science Reference • ©2019 • 289pp • H/C (ISBN: 9781522584551) • US $225.00

Exploring Security in Software Architecture and Design
Michael Felderer (University of Innsbruck, Austria) and Riccardo Scandariato (Chalmers University of Technology, Sweden & University of Gothenburg, Sweden)
Information Science Reference • ©2019 • 349pp • H/C (ISBN: 9781522563136) • US $215.00

Cryptographic Security Solutions for the Internet of Things
Mohammad Tariq Banday (University of Kashmir, India)
Information Science Reference • ©2019 • 367pp • H/C (ISBN: 9781522557425) • US $195.00

Advanced Methodologies and Technologies in System Security, Information Privacy, and...
Mehdi Khosrow-Pour, D.B.A. (Information Resources Management Association, USA)
Information Science Reference • ©2019 • 417pp • H/C (ISBN: 9781522574927) • US $285.00

For an entire list of titles in this series, please visit:
https://www.igi-global.com/book-series/advances-information-security-privacy-ethics/37157

701 East Chocolate Avenue, Hershey, PA 17033, USA
Tel: 717-533-8845 x100 • Fax: 717-533-8661
E-Mail: cust@igi-global.com • www.igi-global.com

Table of Contents

Preface

MOTIVATION FOR WRITING THE BOOK

A teacher should be a voracious reader. A researcher should be a voracious reader and a passionate thinker. The life of a researcher remains incomplete if he does not provide something to the rest of the world in the form of books or articles. Look at the following quote from Bhagavat Gita.

You came empty handed, and you will leave empty handed.

The meaning of this quote is that at the time of your birth you did not bring any wealth or wisdom and at the time of your death you will leave all your wealth and deeds. People will remember you for your deeds or you will be alive through your deeds. See another quote by Mahatma Gandhi.

A man is a product of his thoughts. What he thinks he becomes.

It means that a man can become anything as he thinks. Proper action plan and effort is required to become what he thinks.

ABOUT THE BOOK

This book on Digital Image Steganography is for researchers, graduate, and under graduate students those are doing their research or project work in this area. This book will orient the researchers and students to understand the concepts from scratch very quickly. Chapter 1 is an introduction about secret communication, and quality parameters of steganography techniques. Chapters 2 to 7 describe about the modern steganography techniques in spatial domain using the principles of substitution, pixel value differencing (PVD) and exploiting modification directions (EMD). This book possesses the following salient features.

- It provides an initial introductory knowledge on steganography and its importance.
- It provides a brief understanding of the other similar techniques like cryptography and watermarking.
- It describes in detail how the RS and PDH analysis are to be performed.
- The modern substitution and pixel value differencing principles are discussed very clearly.
- The hybrid approaches using substitution, PVD and EMD principles are also highlighted.
- At the end of every chapter the results are discussed to judge the efficacy of different techniques

Acknowledgment

Thanks to my parents who brought me to this wonderful world and my teachers who taught me to face the challenges in life. Thanks to my caring wife Anita and lovely daughter Poonam, because of their love and support I could write this book.

I thank to all the researchers whose papers I have referred in different chapters of this book. Without referring their papers this book cannot be possible.

Thanks to the editorial team of IGI Global for reminding me in time to submit the different chapters of this book. Thanks to Ms. Josie Dadeboe, assistant development editor of IGI Global for handling the publication of this book.

Chapter 1
Secret Communication Techniques

ABSTRACT

This chapter introduces the reader to cryptography, steganography, watermarking, and quality parameters of image steganography techniques. Cryptography is a technique for secret communication. Steganography is a technique for secret and unnoticeable communication. The watermarking techniques hide watermarks inside the digital media. There are four types of steganography techniques: (1) image steganography, (2) audio steganography, (3) video steganography, and (4) text steganography. The quality of image steganographic algorithms can be measured by three parameters like (1) hiding capacity, (2) distortion measure, and (3) security check.

INTRODUCTION

During the last few decades usage of Internet has grown tremendously. Now-a-days it is the most popular communication media. But the security of data during transit through internet has become a major challenge which needs to be addressed suitably. There are two main methods to address this challenge; (i) cryptography and (ii) steganography (Swain & Lenka, 2012a). In cryptography, the secret message is encrypted to cipher text, which is subsequently communicated to the receiver. Although an intruder cannot understand the communication, but can notice the communication. On the other hand, steganography hides the secret data inside a carrier file such that

DOI: 10.4018/978-1-5225-7516-0.ch001

it looks as if not hiding anything. So, the intruder can neither understand the communication nor suspect the communication. By using cryptography and steganography together, the security becomes two-fold. A good steganographic algorithm should possess higher hiding capacity, lesser distortion and undetectable by steganalytic attacks.

Cryptography

Cryptographic techniques are broadly categorized into two classes, (i) private key or symmetric key cryptography and (ii) public key or asymmetric key cryptography (Swain & Lenka, 2012a). In private key cryptography both sender and receiver share a common secret key. Sender encrypts the secret data using the encryption algorithm and the secret key, the receiver decrypts the cipher text using decryption algorithm and the secret key. The encryption/decryption algorithms are publicly available to the world but not the key. The only way to protect the secrecy is by maintaining the confidentiality of the secret key between the sender and the receiver. If the hacker captures the key the confidentiality will be lost. On the other hand, public key cryptographic techniques use two keys for communication. Suppose Alice is the sender and Bob is the receiver. Alice maintains two keys; (i) the public key, E_A and (ii) the private key, D_A. Alice shares his public key to everyone including Bob, but keeps his private key very secret. Bob also uses two keys; (i) the public key, E_B and (ii) the private key, D_B. Bob shares his public key to everyone including Alice, but keeps his private key secret. To send a secret message to Bob, Alice has to encrypt the message by using Bob's public key. This encrypted message can only be decrypted by Bob's private/secret key. Similarly, to send a secret message to Alice, Bob has to encrypt the message by using Alice's public key. This encrypted message can only be decrypted by Alice's private/secret key. Figure1 (a) represents how Bob sends message and Alice receives using symmetric key cryptography and Figure 1 (b) represents how Bob sends message and Alice receives message using public key cryptography.

Steganography

Steganography achieves secrecy in communication by maintaining the communication invisible. It injects the secret data inside a carrier file without showing any visual marks on it. The carrier files can be image, audio, video, and text files, as shown in Figure 2 (Swain & Lenka, 2014).

Figure 1. Cryptography

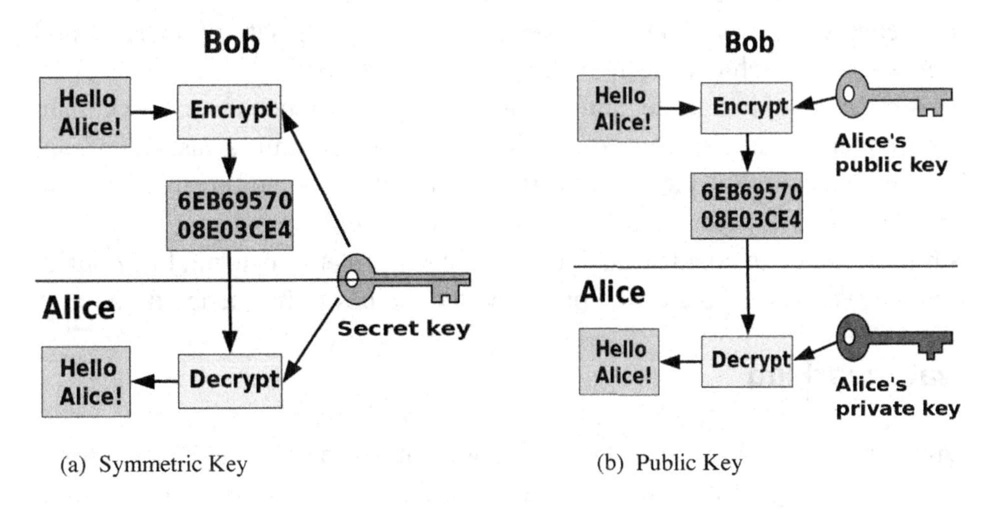

Figure 2. Image steganography techniques

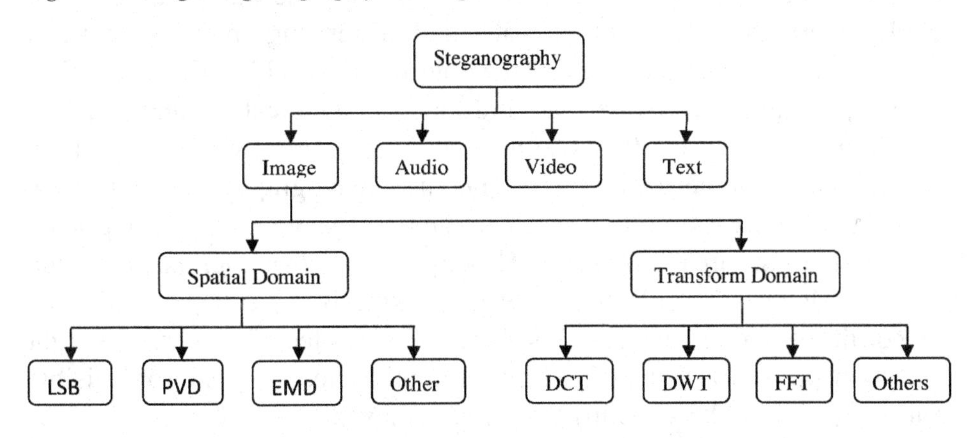

An image steganographic technique should inject the secret data inside the image in such a way that the changes in the image can't be noticed by ordinary human vision. The image which carries the hidden data in it is called as the stego-image. An audio steganographic technique should inject the secret data inside an audio file without altering the original rhythm of the audio. Similarly, a video steganographic technique should inject the secret data inside a video file without altering the rhythm and visual quality of the video file. A text steganographic technique injects the secret data inside a text file without changing the meaning of the text. Steganography and Cryptography are similar in the philosophy that both want to protect the secrecy of the data during transit. But the difference is in how they achieve this secrecy. Cryptography achieves it by making the data unreadable and Steganography achieves it by making the data unseen.

A majority of image steganography techniques are seen in spatial domain and frequency domain. Very few are in compressed domain. Least significant bit (LSB) substitution, pixel value differencing (PVD), exploiting modification directions (EMD) etc. are the most preferred techniques in spatial domain. Similarly, discrete cosine transform, discrete wavelet transform, fast Fourier transform etc. are some of the preferred techniques in frequency domain.

Watermarking

Digital watermarking techniques hide a watermark inside a media like video, audio, and image (Swain & Lenka, 2012a). The watermark is an information about the digital media itself. For example, to claim the ownership of a media the owner can inject some watermark in the media. The watermark can be a visible watermark or an invisible watermark depending on the context and application. In visible watermarking the watermark is visible on the image. For example, in Figure 3 the watermark is 2006, which indicates that the picture was captured in the year 2006. On the other hand, in invisible watermarking the watermark is hidden inside the media. The steganography techniques may be used to hide the watermark. Be clear that the objectives of steganography and watermarking are not the same. The objective of steganography is to hide the data; whereas the objective of watermarking is to keep an identifiable mark on the media. The applications of watermarking techniques are copyright protection, protection to unauthorized distribution etc. The visible or invisible watermarks should be very difficult to be removed.

COMBINING CRYPTOGRAPHY AND STEGANOGRAPHY

Both the techniques Cryptography and Steganography, their objective is secret communication. To attain dual security, we can use cryptography followed by steganography (Swain, & lenka, 2012a). That means at the sender we can first encrypt the plain text to cipher text and then embed the cipher text inside the image. On the other end at the receiver we first extract the cipher text from the image and then apply decryption technique to form the plain text. Figure 4 (a) and (b) represents the tasks at sender and receiver respectively.

Figure 3. A visible watermark

Figure 4. A model for crypto-stegano technique

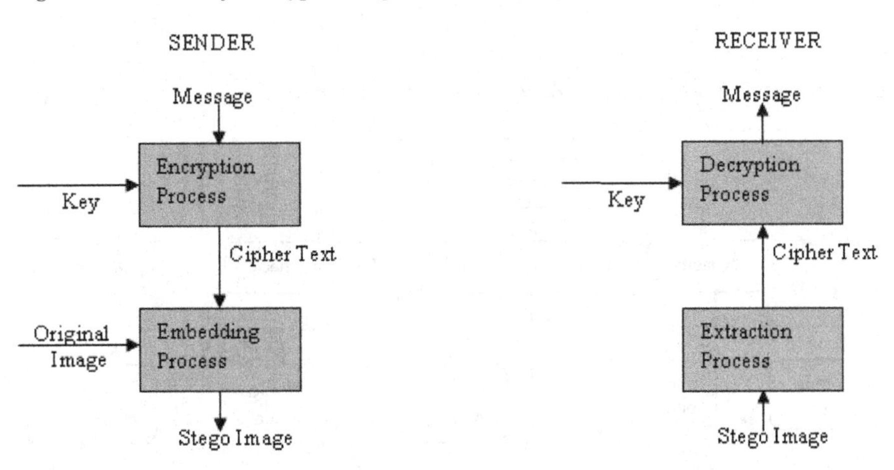

(a) Encryption and Embedding at sender (b) Extraction and Decryption at receiver

PERFORMANCE EVALUATION PARAMETERS

It has been found in the literature that an image steganography technique is weighed by three main parameters, Figure 5 (Pradhan, Sahu, Swain & Sekhar, 2016). The first parameter is the hiding capacity or embedding length. The hiding capacity can be for the image or for the pixels in an average. The hiding capacity of the image refers to the amount of data in bytes or kilo bytes that the image can conceal without showing any visual distortion. The hiding capacity per pixel is often termed as bits per pixel (bpp) (Swain, 2016b), it is the number of bits in an average that can be concealed inside a pixel without any visual distortion in the image.

The second parameter is the distortion measurement. It aims at quantifying the amount of distortion in the stego-image. There are many metrics to do this act. Mean square error (MSE) as represented by Eq. (1), is the average of the square of the pixel errors. The p_{ij} is a pixel corresponding to i^{th} row and j^{th} column in the original image, where as q_{ij} is a pixel corresponding to i^{th} row and j^{th} column in the stego-image. The m and n are the number of rows and columns in the image respectively. The root mean square error (RMSE) is the square root of the MSE, represented by Eq. (2). The widely used distortion estimation metric called peak signal-to-noise ratio (PSNR) is also based on MSE (Pradhan, Sahu, Swain, Sekhar, 2016), as shown in Eq. (3).

Figure 5. Image steganography evaluation parameters

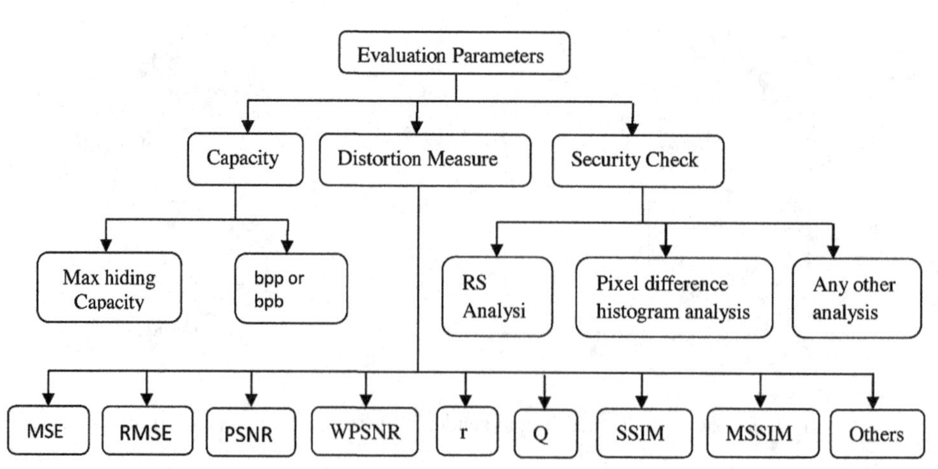

$$\mathrm{MSE} = \frac{1}{m \times n} \sum_{i=1}^{m} \sum_{j=1}^{n} \left(p_{ij} - q_{ij} \right)^2 \tag{1}$$

$$\mathrm{RMSE} = \sqrt{\frac{1}{m \times n} \sum_{i=1}^{m} \sum_{j=1}^{n} \left(p_{ij} - q_{ij} \right)^2} \tag{2}$$

$$\mathrm{PSNR} = 10 \times \log_{10} \frac{255 \times 255}{\mathrm{MSE}} \tag{3}$$

From PSNR another metric called weighted PSNR (WPSNR) (Pradhan, Sahu, Swain, Sekhar, 2016) has been derived as shown in Eq. (4), where the NVF value lies between 0 and 1. The NVF is based on $\sigma^2_{l(i,j)}$ which stands for the local variance centering a pixel at i^{th} row and j^{th} column, it is measured using Eq. (5).

$$\mathrm{WPSNR} = 10 \times \log_{10} \left(\frac{255}{\sqrt{\mathrm{MSE}} \times \mathrm{NVF}} \right)^2 \tag{4}$$

$$\mathrm{NVF}\,(i, j) = \frac{1}{1 + \sigma^2_{l(i,j)}} \tag{5}$$

Correlation (r), and Quality index (Q) (Swain, 2016b) are the metrics to estimate the similarity/dis-similarity between the original image and the stego image. Eq. (6) is used to measure the r, and eq. (7) is used to measure the Q value, where the $\overline{p}$ and $\overline{q}$ are the mean pixel value of original pixel and stego-pixel respectively, as shown in Eq. (8) and Eq. (9) respectively.

$$r = \frac{\sum_{i=1}^{m} \sum_{j=1}^{n} \left(p_{ij} - \overline{p} \right) \times \left(q_{ij} - \overline{q} \right)}{\sqrt{\left(\sum_{i=1}^{m} \sum_{j=1}^{n} \left(p_{ij} - \overline{p} \right)^2 \right) \times \left(\sum_{i=1}^{m} \sum_{j=1}^{n} \left(q_{ij} - \overline{q} \right)^2 \right)}} \tag{6}$$

$$Q = \frac{4\sigma_{xy}\overline{p}\overline{q}}{\left(\sigma_x^2 + \sigma_y^2\right)\left[\left(\overline{p}\right)^2 + \left(\overline{q}\right)^2\right]} \tag{7}$$

$$\overline{p} = \frac{1}{m \times n}\sum_{i=1}^{m}\sum_{j=1}^{n} p_{ij} \tag{8}$$

$$\overline{q} = \frac{1}{m \times n}\sum_{i=1}^{m}\sum_{j=1}^{n} q_{ij} \tag{9}$$

The other symbols used in estimation of Q and r are represented by Eq. (10), Eq. (11), and Eq. (12).

$$\sigma_x^2 = \frac{1}{m \times n - 1}\sum_{i=1}^{m}\sum_{j=1}^{n}\left(p_{ij} - \overline{p}\right)^2 \tag{10}$$

$$\sigma_y^2 = \frac{1}{m \times n - 1}\sum_{i=1}^{m}\sum_{j=1}^{n}\left(q_{ij} - \overline{q}\right)^2 \tag{11}$$

$$\sigma_{xy} = \frac{1}{m \times n - 1}\sum_{i=1}^{m}\sum_{j=1}^{n}\left(p_{ij} - \overline{p}\right)\left(q_{ij} - \overline{q}\right) \tag{12}$$

Another metric called as the structural similarity (SSIM) is defined in Eq. (13). The original image is divided into B blocks each of size 8×8 pixels. For the block mean pixel value ($\overline{p}$) and standard deviation (σ_x^2) is calculated. Then for stego-image also the mean pixel value ($\overline{q}$) and standard deviation (σ_y^2) is calculated. The covariance (σ_{xy}) between the original image and stego-image is calculated. Finally, SSIM is computed as in Eq. (13). Here c_1 is a constant used to avoid instability, when ($\overline{p}^2 + \overline{q}^2$) is very close to zero. Similarly, c_2 is a constant used to avoid instability, when ($\sigma_x^2 + \sigma_y^2$) is very close to zero. The c_1 value can be chosen as $(K_1L)^2$, where L is 255 for gray image and $K_1 \ll 1$. Similarly, c_2 value can be chosen as $(K_2L)^2$, where $K_2 \ll 1$. Note that when $c_1 = 0$ and $c_2 = 0$, SSIM is equal to quality index Q. Thus, Q is a special case of SSIM (Pradhan, Sahu, Swain, Sekhar, 2016).

$$\mathrm{SSIM} = \frac{\left(2\bar{p}\bar{q} + c_1\right)\left(2\sigma_{xy} + c_2\right)}{\left(\bar{p}^2 + \bar{q}^2 + c_1\right)\left(\sigma_x^2 + \sigma_y^2 + c_2\right)} \tag{13}$$

For all the B blocks of the image SSIM is computed and then the mean SSIM (MSSIM) is calculated to evaluate the overall quality of the image, as in Eq. (14).

$$\mathrm{MSSIM} = \frac{1}{B}\sum_{i=1}^{B} \mathrm{SSIM}_i \tag{14}$$

K-L divergence, Manhattan distance, and Euclidian distance are the other type of metrics to estimate the similarity/difference in histograms of cover image and its stego-image. Suppose h1 is the histogram of cover image and h2 is the histogram of stego-image. Then we can define the K-L divergence from h1 to h2 as $d1$ using Eq. (15) and K-L divergence from h2 to h1 as $d2$ using Eq. (16). Then we take an average of these two values. It will be 0 if cover image is same as the stego-image.

$$d1 = \sum_{i=0}^{255} h1(i) * \log \frac{h1(i)}{h2(i)} \tag{15}$$

$$d2 = \sum_{i=0}^{255} h2(i) * \log \frac{h2(i)}{h1(i)} \tag{16}$$

Similarly, the Manhattan distance MD(h1, h2) is measured using Eq. (17), and Euclidian distance ED(h1, h2) are measured Eq. (18) (Pradhan, Sahu, Swain & Sekhar, 2016).

$$MD(h1, h2) = \sum_{i=0}^{255} \left| h1(i) - h2(i) \right| \tag{17}$$

$$ED(h1, h2) = \sqrt{\sum_{i=0}^{255} \left\{ h1(i) - h2(i) \right\}^2} \tag{18}$$

SECURITY ANALYSIS

The security analysis talks about the attack resistance of the steganographic technique. Least significant bit (LSB) substitution is the very simplest and familiar image steganography technique. The substitution can be done up to 3 LSBs to increase the hiding capacity. The weakness of LSB substitution is that it is detected by RS analysis (Fridrich, Goljian & Du, 2001; Pradhan, Sahu, Swain & Sekhar, 2016; Swain & Lenka, 2015). So many improved LSB substitution techniques have been proposed to address this issue to some extent (Swain, Kumar, Pradhan, & Lenka, 2010; Swain, & Lenka, 2012b; Swain, & Lenka, 2012c; Swain, 2016a). The first and traditional pixel value differencing (PVD) was proposed in (Wu & Tsai, 2003). The prime goal of this technique was that smooth regions of the image will hide lesser number of secret bits, whereas edge regions of an image will hide a greater number of secret bits. The weakness of PVD steganography is that it is detected by pixel difference histogram (PDH) analysis (Zhang & Wang, 2004). Improved PVD techniques like adaptive PVD (Swain, 2016b) and multidirectional PVD (Pradhan, Sekhar & Swain, 2016a) can survive from PDH analysis. LSB substitution techniques have more hiding capacity and PVD techniques have less distortion. To extract both the benefits, LSB substitution and PVD have been combined in (Khodaei, & Faez, 2012; Swain, 2014; Swain, 2016c; Pradhan, Sekhar & Swain, 2016b). Techniques using both LSB substitution and PVD approaches will be accepted as secured if they are neither detected by RS analysis nor detected by PDH analysis.

RS Analysis

In traditional LSB substitution steganography, the LSB of a pixel is replaced by a secret data bit. To achieve larger embedding capacity, we can extend this substitution up to 3 LSBs. Look at the Table 1 below. There are four pixels with values 30, 31, 32 and 33. Their binary pixel values and after substituting the LSB by 0/1 the stego pixel values are given in this table. From Table 1, we can observe that if the LSB of original pixel is same as the secret data bit, then no change occurs. But if the LSB of original pixel is not same as the secret data bit, then the pixel value changes from 2n to 2n + 1 or from 2n + 1 to 2n. It can also be identified that a change from 2n to 2n – 1 or from 2n + 1 to 2n + 2 does not occur. For example, 30 changes to 31, it never changes to 29. Similarly, 31 changes to 30, it never changes to 32. This mystery is captured by RS analysis.

The RS analysis is based on this type of statistical measures. It is done in the following manner. Define a function F_1: 2n ↔2n+1. It defines two transformations, (i) from value 2n to value 2n + 1, and (ii) from value 2n + 1 to value 2n. Similarly, define another function F_{-1}: 2n ↔2n -1. It defines other two transformations, (i) from value 2n to value 2n – 1, and (ii) from value 2n + 1 to value 2n + 2 (Pradhan, Sahu, Swain, Sekhar, 2016; Swain & Lenka, 2015). The image, say M is divided into a number of equal size blocks. Suppose such a block is G whose pixels are $X_1, X_2, X_3, \ldots, X_n$. Then

Table 1. Pixel values and stego pixel values

Pixel Value (Decimal)	Pixel Value (Binary)	Embedded Bit	Stego Pixel Value (Binary)	Stego Pixel Value (Decimal)
30 =2xn, for n=15	00011110	0	00011110	30=2xn
		1	00011111	31=2xn+1
31 =2xn+1, for n=15	00011111	0	00011110	30=2xn
		1	00011111	31=2xn+1
32 =2xn, for n=16	00100000	0	00100000	32=2xn
		1	00100001	33=2xn+1
33 =2xn+1, for n=16	00100001	0	00100000	32=2xn
		1	00100001	33=2xn+1

use the function $f(X_1, X_2, X_3, \ldots, X_n) = \sum_{i=1}^{n-1} \left| X_{i+1} - X_i \right|$ to measure the smoothness of G. For example, suppose we have an image of size 20×20, total 400 pixels. We divided it into 100 blocks, each block with 4 pixels. Then apply F_1 to all the blocks of M and define the two parameters R_m and S_m using Eq. (19) and Eq. (20) respectively. Similarly, apply $F\text{-}_1$ to all the blocks of M and define the two parameters R_{-m} and S_{-m} using Eq. (21) and Eq. (22) respectively.

$$R_m = \frac{\text{No of blocks satisfying the condition } f\left(F_1\left(G\right)\right) > f\left(G\right)}{\text{Total number of blocks}} \tag{19}$$

$$S_m = \frac{\text{No of blocks satisfying the condition } f\left(F_1\left(G\right)\right) < f\left(G\right)}{\text{Total number of blocks}} \tag{20}$$

$$R_{-m} = \frac{\text{No of blocks satisfying the condition } f\left(F\_1\left(G\right)\right) > f\left(G\right)}{\text{Total number of blocks}} \tag{21}$$

$$S_{-m} = \frac{\text{No of blocks satisfying the condition } f\left(F_{-1}\left(G\right)\right) < f\left(G\right)}{\text{Total number of blocks}} \tag{22}$$

By applying F_1 and F_{-1} on an original cover image, we can notice that the relation $R_m \approx R_{-m} > S_m \approx S_{-m}$ will be satisfied. But, by applying F_1 and F_{-1} on a stego-image another relation R_{-m} - $S_{-m} > R_m$ - S_m will be satisfied.

The RS graphs are plotted in the following way. Take the original image, say M. Take atleast four stego-images, say C_1, C_2, C_3 and C_4 such that the amount of secret data hidden in C_{i+1} is greater than the amount of secret data hidden in C_i, for i=1, 2 and 3. Suppose the four parameters estimated for cover image are R_{m0}, R_{-m0}, S_{m0} and S_{-m0}. For the stego image C_1 the parameters are R_{m1}, R_{-m1}, S_{m1} and S_{-m1}. For the stego image C_2 the parameters are R_{m2}, R_{-m2}, S_{m2} and S_{-m2}. For the stego image C_3 the parameters are R_{m3}, R_{-m3}, S_{m3} and S_{-m3}. For the stego image C_4 the parameters are R_{m4}, R_{-m4}, S_{m4} and S_{-m4}. Suppose we have utilized the hiding capacities 20% in C_1, 40% in C_2, 60% in C_3 and 80% in C_4. In cover image M, the hiding capacity is 0% utilized i.e. we have hided 0% of the actual hiding capacity.

Now plot a curve/line between the two sets, X coordinate points (0, 20, 40, 60, 80) and Y coordinate points (R_{m0}, R_{m1}, R_{-m2}, R_{m3}, R_{m4}). This graph is indicated by the curve R_m.

Plot a curve/line between the two sets, X coordinate points (0, 20, 40, 60, 80) and Y coordinate points (R_{-m0}, R_{-m1}, R_{-m2}, R_{-m3}, R_{-m4}). This graph is indicated by the curve R_{-m}.

Plot a curve/line between the two sets, X coordinate points (0, 20, 40, 60, 80) and Y coordinate points (S_{m0}, S_{m1}, S_{m2}, S_{m3}, S_{m4}). This graph is indicated by the curve S_m.

Plot a curve/line between the two sets, X coordinate points (0, 20, 40, 60, 80) and Y coordinate points (S_{-m0}, S_{-m1}, S_{-m2}, S_{-m3}, S_{-m4}). This graph is indicated by the curve S_{-m}.

Figure 6 (a) is the RS analysis for traditional LSB substitution and Figure 6 (b) is the RS analysis for adaptive PVD in (Swain, 2016b). Figure 6 (b), satisfies $R_m \approx R_{-m} > S_m \approx S_{-m}$, so this adaptive PVD technique is not vulnerable to RS analysis, But Figure 6(a) satisfies, $R_{-m} - S_{-m} > R_m - S_m$, so traditional LSB substitution technique is vulnerable to RS analysis.

PDH Analysis

Consider every two consecutive pixels of the image as a block. For a block calculate the difference value between the two pixels. This difference values will be in between -255 to +255 including 0. So, there are a total of 511 distinct difference values. Calculate the frequency of each of these difference values. Plot a graph with the pixel difference value on X-axis and frequency on Y-axis. This curve obtained is the PDH (Pradhan, Sahu, Swain & Sekhar, 2016; Swain, 2016b). Table 2 represents the pixel values of a sample 10×10 gray image. There are 100 pixels. Table 3 represents the 50 pixel value differences. Table 4 represents the pixel value differences and their corresponding frequencies. Figure 7 represents the PDH for this sample image. The pixel value differences for this sample image are from -9 to +8. But in real images like Lena, Baboon etc. the pixel value differences will be from -255 to +255.

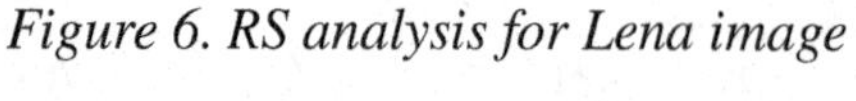

Figure 6. RS analysis for Lena image

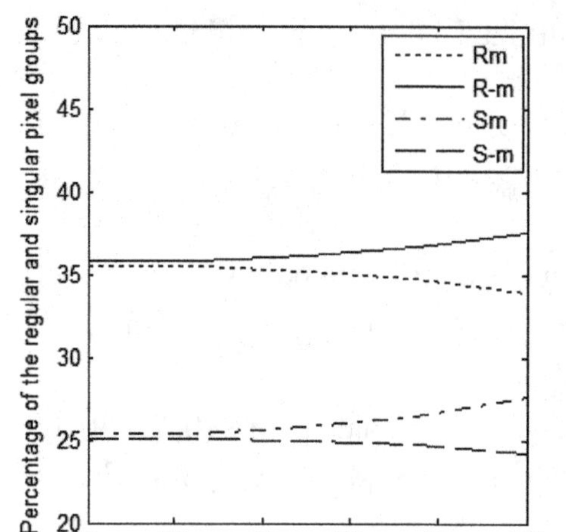

(a) 1-bit LSB substitution scheme

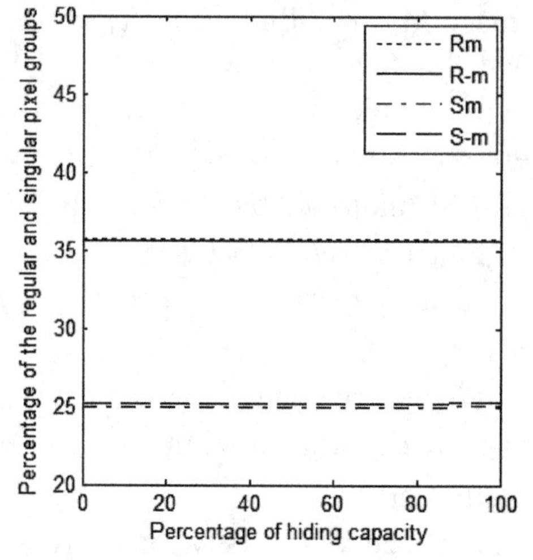

(b) Adaptive PVD scheme (Swain, 2016b)

Table 2. Pixel values of a sample 10×10 image

157	157	159	154	158	154	155	158	153	157
158	158	156	155	157	158	155	159	158	152
160	157	156	153	156	161	156	155	162	155
154	158	156	155	154	160	159	155	158	152
151	160	157	156	156	155	155	159	155	155
158	159	155	156	154	162	157	155	157	158
153	155	158	157	155	157	153	156	155	160
159	158	154	157	155	156	155	153	153	157
154	156	157	159	161	157	159	158	159	160
159	156	161	153	159	159	160	159	160	156

Look at Figure 8(a), the dotted line curve is the PDH for the stego Lena image and the solid line is that of the original Lena image for the PVD scheme proposed in (Wu & Tsai, 2003). The curve for the original image is smooth in nature and the curve of the stego-image is zig-zag in nature. This zig-zag nature, also called as step effect is an evidence of data hiding. For the seven-way PVD proposed in (Pradhan, Sekhar & Swain, 2016a) the step effects are reduced, (Figure 8(b)) and for the adaptive PVD technique proposed in (Swain, 2016b) the step effects do not at all exist, (Figure 8(c)). Thus, this adaptive

Table 3. Pixel differences

0	5	4	-3	-4
0	1	-1	-4	6
3	3	-5	1	7
-4	1	-6	4	6
-9	1	1	-4	0
-1	-1	-8	2	-1
-2	1	-2	-3	-5
1	-3	-1	2	-4
-2	-2	4	1	-1
3	8	0	1	4

Table 4. Pixel differences and frequencies

Pixel Difference values	-9	-8	-7	-6	-5	-4	-3	-2	-1	0	1	2	3	4	5	6	7	8
Frequencies / Occurrences	1	1	0	1	2	5	3	4	6	4	9	2	3	4	1	2	1	1

Figure 7. Pixel difference histogram for the 10×10 sample image

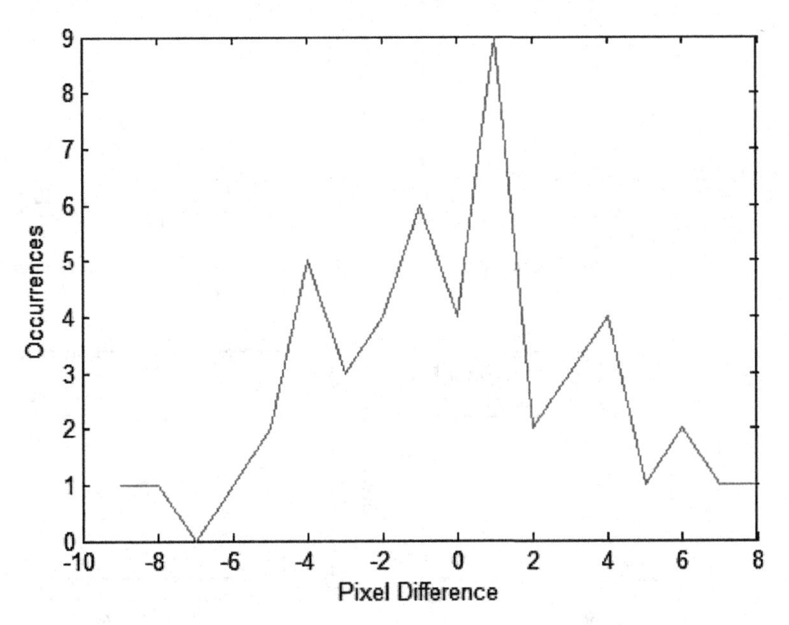

PVD steganography proposed in (Swain, 2016b) is not detected by PDH analysis. Some techniques those uses both LSB and PVD are also detected by PDH analysis. For example, Khodaei & Faez's LSB+PVD technique (Khodaei & Faez, 2012), shown in Figure 8(d) is detected by PDH analysis.

The LSB substitution techniques can't be detected by PDH analysis, see Figure 9(a) and (b). Similarly, the PVD techniques can't be detected by RS analysis, see Figure 6(b).

CONCLUSION

Cryptography is a technique for secret communication, which is visible, but not understandable to the intruder. Steganography is a technique for secret communication, which is not visible to the intruder. By using cryptography with steganography, the security becomes two-fold. A good steganographic

Figure 8. PDH analysis for PVD techniques

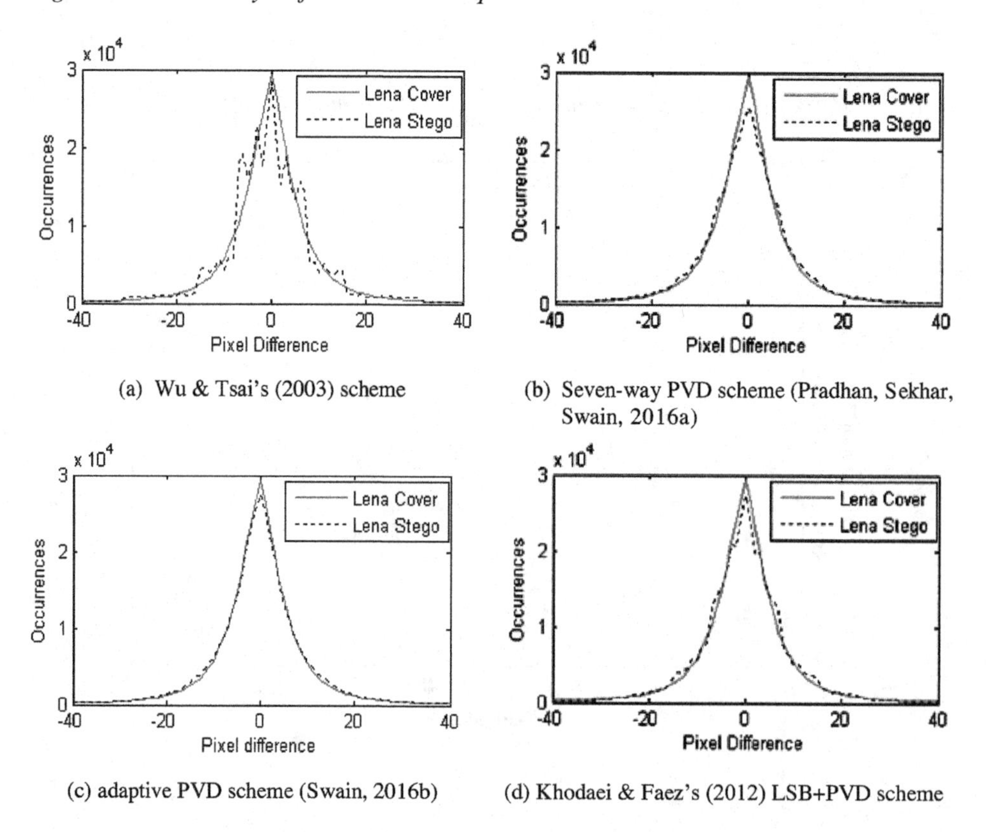

(a) Wu & Tsai's (2003) scheme

(b) Seven-way PVD scheme (Pradhan, Sekhar, Swain, 2016a)

(c) adaptive PVD scheme (Swain, 2016b)

(d) Khodaei & Faez's (2012) LSB+PVD scheme

Figure 9. PDH analysis for LSB substitution schemes

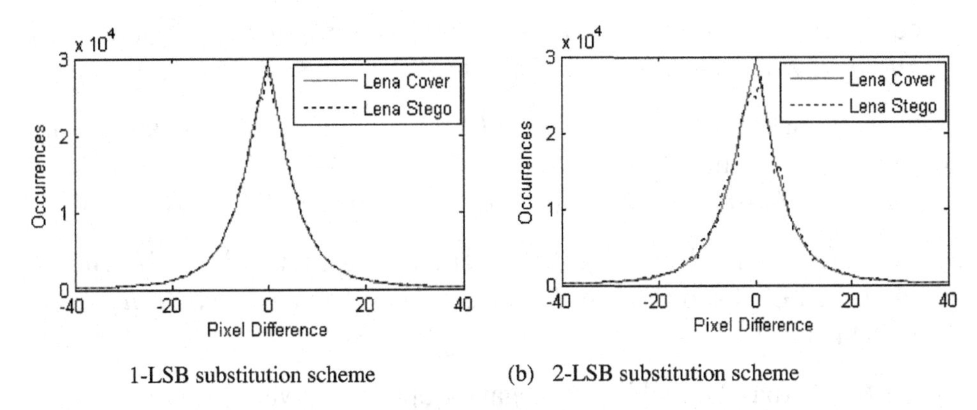

1-LSB substitution scheme (b) 2-LSB substitution scheme

algorithm should possess higher hiding capacity, lesser distortion and undetectable by steganalytic attacks. The security of least significant bit (LSB) substitution techniques are to be analyzed by RS analysis and the security of pixel value differencing (PVD) steganography techniques are to be analyzed by pixel difference histogram (PDH) analysis. The hybrid techniques those are using both LSB substitution and PVD are to be analyzed by both RS analysis and PDH analysis. The practical ways how to perform the RS analysis and PDH analysis have been described in a procedural fashion.

REFERENCES

Fridrich, J., Goljian, M., & Du, R. (2001). Detecting LSB steganography in color and gray-scale images. *Magazine of IEEE Multimedia Special Issue on Security*, *8*(4), 22–28. doi:10.1109/93.959097

Khodaei, M., & Faez, K. (2012). New adaptive steganographic method using least-significant-bit substitution and pixel-value differencing. *IET Image Processing*, *6*(6), 677–686. doi:10.1049/iet-ipr.2011.0059

Pradhan, A., Sahu, A. K., Swain, G., & Sekhar, K. R. (2016). Performance evaluation parameters of image steganography techniques. *Proceedings of IEEE International Conference on Research Advances in Integrated Navigation Systems*, 1-8. 10.1109/RAINS.2016.7764399

Pradhan, A., Sekhar, K. R., & Swain, G. (2016a). Digital image steganography based on seven way pixel value differencing. *Indian Journal of Science and Technology*, *9*(37), 1–11. doi:10.17485/ijst/2016/v9i37/88557

Pradhan, A., Sekhar, K. R., & Swain, G. (2016b). Digital image steganography combining LSB substitution with five way PVD in 2×3 pixel blocks. *International Journal of Pharmacy and Technology*, *8*(4), 22051–22061.

Swain, G. (2014). Digital image steganography using nine-pixel differencing and modified LSB substitution. *Indian Journal of Science and Technology*, *7*(9), 1444–1450.

Swain, G. (2016a). Digital image steganography using variable length group of bits substitution. *Procedia Computer Science*, *85*, 31–38. doi:10.1016/j.procs.2016.05.173

Swain, G. (2016b). Adaptive pixel value differencing steganography using both vertical and horizontal edges. *Multimedia Tools and Applications*, *75*(21), 13541–13556. doi:10.100711042-015-2937-2

Swain, G. (2016c). A steganographic method combining LSB substitution and PVD in a block. *Procedia Computer Science*, *85*, 39–44. doi:10.1016/j.procs.2016.05.174

Swain, G., Kumar, D. R., Pradhan, A., & Lenka, S. K. (2010). A technique for secure communication using message dependent steganography. *International Journal of Computer and Communication Technology*, *2*(2-4), 177–181.

Swain, G., & Lenka, S. K. (2012a). A Quick review on network security and steganography. *International Journal of Electronics and Computer Science Engineering*, *1*(2), 426–435.

Swain, G., & Lenka, S. K. (2012b). A dynamic approach to image steganography using the three least significant bits and extended hill cipher. *Advanced Materials Research*, *403*, 842–849.

Swain, G., & Lenka, S. K. (2012c). A robust image steganography technique using dynamic embedding with two least significant bits. *Advanced Materials Research*, 403–408, 835–841.

Swain, G., & Lenka, S. K. (2014). Classification of spatial domain image steganography techniques: A study. *International Journal of Computer Science & Engineering Technology*, *4*(3), 219–232.

Swain, G., & Lenka, S. K. (2015). A novel steganography technique by mapping words with LSB array. *International Journal of Signal and Imaging Systems Engineering*, *8*(1), 115–122. doi:10.1504/IJSISE.2015.067052

Wu, D. C., & Tsai, W. H. (2003). A steganographic method for images by pixel value differencing. *Pattern Recognition Letters*, *24*(9), 1613–1626. doi:10.1016/S0167-8655(02)00402-6

Zhang, X., & Wang, S. (2004). Vulnerability of pixel-value differencing steganography to histogram analysis and modification for enhanced security. *Pattern Recognition Letters*, *25*(3), 331–339. doi:10.1016/j.patrec.2003.10.014

Chapter 2
Steganography Using Substitution Principle

ABSTRACT

In this chapter, the author describes the various substitution-based image steganography techniques. Basically, there are four categories of substitution techniques: (1) least significant bit (LSB) substitution, (2) LSB array-based substitution, (3) group of bits substitution (GBS), and (4) adaptive LSB substitution. The LSB substitution-based techniques are very much insecure (detectable by RS analysis), so LSB array, GBS, and adaptive LSB substitution techniques are proposed in literature. If substitution principle is used in a steganography technique, then it must be evaluated by RS analysis.

INTRODUCTION

The first category of substitution technique in digital image steganography is the least significant bit (LSB) substitution. It is the very simplest technique. The substitution can be done up to 4 least significant bits. As it is attacked by RS analysis (Fridrich, Goljian, & Du, 2001), so enhanced versions of substitution schemes have been proposed in different forms. The technique, message dependent LSB substitution (Swain & Lenka, 2012a), randomizes the embedding in three LSBs to improve the security. The technique in (Swain & Lenka, 2012b) performs LSB embedding based on indicator with RGB images.

DOI: 10.4018/978-1-5225-7516-0.ch002

The second category of substitution technique embeds in LSB array (Swain & Lenka, 2012a; Swain & Lenka, 2015). The LSBs of the pixels can be formed to be an array of bits and the binary data can be mapped into this array and be placed in appropriate location with minimum distortion.

The third category of substitution is group of bits substitution (GBS) (Swain, 2016; Sahu, & Swain, 2017). The principle in GBS is that "a group of bits of a pixel are replaced by another group of bits (these are not secret data bits) to conceal 1 or 2 bits of data". There are two techniques described, (i) 1-bit GBS algorithm, and (ii) 2-bit GBS substitution.

The fourth category of substitution techniques are adaptive LSB substitution techniques (Liao, Wen & Zhang, 2011; Swain, 2014). These techniques find the pixel difference value and based on this value the number of bits to be embedded is decided.

LSB SUBSTITUTION

Simple LSB Substitution

In digital image steganography the simplest data hiding technique is least significant bit (LSB) substitution. For a gray image one pixel is represented in 8-bits. For a color image one pixel is represented in 24 bits. For every byte the right most bit is the LSB and left most bit is the most significant bit (MSB). LSB substitution means substitution of the LSBs by one data bit. For example, if my secret data is of 99 bits length then I can be able to hide in 99 pixels of a gray image or 33 pixels of a color image. When using a color image, the red, green and blue color components, each can hide 1 bit in their LSB position. For example, suppose in the following three pixels of a color image shown in Figure 1 (a), I want to hide the character A whose binary value is 10000001. Then the stego-pixels are given on Figure 1 (b).

In this example, we can see that out of 8 bytes we have touched; only 3 bits are changed from 0 to 1 or 1 to 0. In general, only 50% of the bits will be changed. In one-bit LSB substitution we hide only one bit in a byte. So, bit rate is 1. Bit rate means number of bits hidden per byte of the image. To improve the bit rate, substitution can be performed up to 3 least significant bits in a byte of the image, so that the bit rate can be increased up to 3.

Figure 1. Original and stego pixels

Original pixels
(00100111 11101001 11001000)
(00100111 11001000 11101001)
(11001000 00100111 11101001)

(a) Three original pixels

Stego-pixels
(0010011**1** 1110100**0** 1100100**0**)
(0010011**0** 1100100**0** 1110100**0**)
(1100100**0** 0010011**1** 11101001)

(b)Three stego pixels

Message Bit Dependent LSB Substitution

This technique was proposed by Swain & Lenka (2012a). Here the main idea is that the embedding locations in the next pixel are dependent on the pattern of bits hidden in the present pixel. So, we call it as message bit dependent LSB substitution. The three LSBs are explored but only two bits are hidden. The embedding is done by the following four clauses.

1. If in the present pixel the data bits hidden are 00, then in the next pixel the 7th and 8th bit positions will be used to hide the next two data bits. The 8th bit means the first LSB, the 7th bit means the second LSB and the 6th bit means the third LSB.
2. If in the present pixel the data bits hidden are 01, then in the next pixel the 8th and 7th bit positions will be used to hide the next two data bits.
3. If in the present pixel the data bits hidden are 10, then in the next pixel the 6th and 7th bit positions will be used to hide the next two data bits.
4. If in the present pixel the data bits hidden are 11, then in the next pixel the 7th and 6th bit positions will be used to hide the next two data bits.

For an example suppose we have the pixels by number 1, 2, 3 etc. We have the data 11001001 00011010 01100110 10011111. We can hide in the manner as shown in Figure 2. To start the process let us substitute the first two bits in 7th and 8th bit positions of the first pixel, for subsequent pixels it is as per the algorithm.

The data retrieval is the reverse of embedding. From the first pixel the 7th and 8th bits are retrieved. For the subsequent pixels, retrieval is performed by the following four clauses.

Figure 2. Message bit dependent embedding

Cover image byte numbers	Operation	At Locations
1	hide 11	7th and 8th
2	hide 00	7th and 6th
3	hide 10	7th and 8th
4	hide 01	6th and 7th
5	hide 00	8th and 7th
6	hide 01	7th and 8th
7	hide 10	8th and 7th
8	Hide 10	6th and 7th
9	hide 01	6th and 7th
10	hide 10	8th and 7th
11	hide 01	6th and 7th
12	hide 10	8th and 7th
13	hide 10	6th and 7th
14	hide 01	6th and 7th
15	hide 11	8th and 7th
16	hide 11	7th and 6th
etc...		

1. If from the present pixel the bits retrieved are 11, then from the next pixel we have to retrieve from the 7th and 6th bit locations.
2. If from the present pixel the bits retrieved are 10, then from the next pixel we have to retrieve from the 6th and 7th bit locations.
3. If from the present pixel the bits retrieved are 01, then from the next pixel we have to retrieve from the 8th and 7th bit locations.
4. If from the present pixel the bits retrieved are 00, then from the next pixel we have to retrieve from the 7th and 8th bit locations.

RGB INDICATOR BASED LSB SUBSTITUTION

This technique was proposed by Swain & Lenka (2012b). Here RGB stands for Red, Green, and Blue channels of a color image pixel. One of these three channels can be used as indicator to indicate the data hiding in other two channels. The embedding algorithm is as discussed by the following six steps.

1. Divide the image into 8 blocks; say they are B_0, B_1, B_2, B_3, B_4, B_5, B_6, and B_7.
2. Divide the secret binary message into 8 blocks in the following manner. The binary message comprises of so many bytes. Each byte is 8 bits. For i=0 to 7 keep together the ith bits of all the bytes, it becomes message block M_i. Here the 0th bit is the MSB and 7th bit is the LSB.
3. Enter the sub key K_1, this sub key is for the allocation of message blocks to image blocks for possible embedding. This is a string of digits with a length of 8, formed by the digits 0 through 7, such that each digit occurs only once in the string. For example a sub key K_1 = 05432167 means message block M_0 is to be allocated to image block B_0, message block M_5 is to be allocated to image block B_1, message block M_4 is to be allocated to image block B_2, message block M_3 is to be allocated to image block B_3, message block M_2 is to be allocated to image block B_4, message block M_1 is to be allocated to image block B_5, message block M_6 is to be allocated to image block B_6, and message block M_7 is to be allocated to image block B_7.
4. The second sub key K_2, which tells about the indicator channels of all the 8 different image blocks, is to be calculated from the image blocks. From each block one indicator channel is calculated. One of the red, green and blue channels will be the indicator channel, whose sum over all the pixels in that block is the maximum. For example, suppose sum1, sum2 and sum3 are the sum of red, green and blue channels of different pixels in a block respectively. If the largest is sum2, then green channel (G) is the indicator channel and red (R) and blue (B) channels are the data channels. Suppose R is the indicator channel in image block B_0, B is the indicator channel in image block B_1, B is the indicator channel in image block B_2, R is the indicator channel in image block B_3, G is the indicator channel in image block B_4, B is the indicator channel in image block B_5, G is the indicator channel in image block B_6 and R is the indicator channel in image block B_7, then the sequence is RBBRGBGR. R corresponds to 0, G corresponds to 1 and B corresponds to 2. Thus, the sequence is 02201210, which is the sub key K_2. Thus, our key K= K_1 K_2 = 05432167 02201210, which is to be hidden in some reserved area of the image along with the length of the blocks, so that receiver has to use it for retrieval of the message.

5. Now the different message blocks are allocated to different image blocks and in each image block the indicator is decided. Now the embedding in a block is done as follows.
   a. Take the next pixel of the image block. Take 4 bits of the secret binary message.
   b. Compare 4 LSBs of channel1 with 4 bits of secret binary message, if the difference is less than or equal to 7 then embed these 4 secret binary message bits at those 4 LSBs of channel1. Take next 4 bits of secret binary message, go to step(c). Otherwise (if the difference is greater than 7) with the same 4 bits of secret binary message go to step(c).
   c. Compare 4 least significant bits of channel2 with 4 bits of secret binary message, if the difference is less than or equal to 7 then embed these 4 secret binary message bits at those 4 LSBs of channel2. Otherwise do not embed in channel2, and those 4 secret binary message bits are to be considered for the next pixel.
   d. Go to step (a).
6. For a pixel if embedding is done as per step (b) only, i.e. data is embedded in channel1 only, then the two LSBs of its indicator will be set to 00. If for a pixel embedding is done as per step(c) only i.e., data is embedded in channel2 only, then the two LSBs of its indicator will be set to 01. If for a pixel embedding is done as per both the steps (b) and (c) i.e., 4 bits embedded in channel1 and 4 bits embedded in channel2, then the two LSBs of indicator will be set to 10. If in a pixel data is embedded neither in channel1 nor in channel2, then the last two LSBs of its indicator will be set to 11.

As an example, suppose we have the three pixels as in Figure 3 and the Green channel is the indicator channel. Suppose the secret binary message stream is: 0010 1010 0000 1111 0011. In pixel1 channel1 is 10010110 = 150, if the four bits: 0010 are embedded it becomes 10010010 = 146, the difference between 150 and 146 is less than 7, so embedded. Now channel2 of pixel1 is 00011110=30, the next 4 secret binary message bits are 1010, if these four bits are embedded it becomes 00011010 = 26, the difference is less than 7, so embedded. The last two bits of indicator of pixel1 are made 10.

In pixel2 channel1 is 00001111=15, the next 4 secret binary message bits are 0000, if embedded it becomes 00000000=0, and the difference is more than 7, so not embedded. Then check the channel2 of pixel2. It is 11000100=196, the secret binary message bits are 0000, if embedded it becomes 11000000

= 192, and the difference is less than 7, so embedded in channel2 of pixel2. Last two bits of indicator are changed to 01.

In pixel3 channel1 is 10111101 = 189, the next 4 secret binary message bits are 1111, if embedded, it becomes 10111111 = 191, and the difference is less than 7, so embedded. The channel2 of pixel3 is 11001100 = 204, the next 4 bits of secret binary message is 0011, if embedded the channel value becomes 11000011 = 195, the difference is more than 7, so not embedded. Thus, the last two bits of indicator become 00. After embedding the pixels are also shown in table 1 (lower part).

The message retrieval is the opposite of the embedding algorithm and is done by the following five steps.

1. Retrieve the sub key K_1, sub key K_2, and the length of the blocks from the reserved location in the image.
2. Suppose K_1= 05432167 and K_2= 02201210. In K_2, 0 means Red, 1 means Green and 2 means Blue. Thus K_2 = 02201210, means Red is the indicator channel in image block B_0, Blue is the indicator channel in image block B_1, Blue is the indicator channel in image block B_2, Red is the indicator channel in image block B_3, Green is the indicator in image block B_4, Blue is the indicator channel in image block B_5, Green is the

Figure 3. Example of embedding

	Before Embedding		
	Red (Channel1)	Green **(Indicator Channel)**	Blue (Channel2)
Pixel1	1001**0110**	100011<u>11</u>	0001**1110**
Pixel2	00001111	010101<u>00</u>	1100**0100**
Pixel3	1011**1101**	111100<u>00</u>	11001100
	After Embedding		
	Red (Channel1)	Green **(Indicator Channel)**	Blue (Channel2)
Pixel1	1001**0010**	100011**<u>10</u>**	0001**1010**
Pixel2	00001010	010101**<u>01</u>**	1100**0000**
Pixel3	1011**1111**	111100**<u>00</u>**	11001100

indicator channel in image block B_6 and Red is the indicator channel in image block B_7.

3. For each block identify the channel1 and channel2 as the indicator channel is identified. If Red is the indicator channel, then Green is channel1 and Blue is channel2. If Green is the indicator channel, then Red is channel1 and Blue is channel2. If Blue is the indicator channel, then Red is channel1 and Green is channel2.
4. Declare the variables $DATA_i$ for i=0 to 7. For i=0 to 7 do the following. Take the image Block B_i. Start from the first pixel. Continue till the number of bits extracted is equal to the message block length.
   a. Read the indicator of the pixel.
   b. If the last two bits of indicator are 00, retrieve the 4 LSBs of channel1 and append to the variable $DATA_i$.
   c. If the last two bits of indicator are 01, retrieve the 4 LSBs of channel2 and append to the variable $DATA_i$.
   d. If the last two bits of indicator are 10, retrieve the 4 LSBs of channel1 and channel2 and append to the variable $DATA_i$.
   e. If the last two bits of indicator are 11, neither retrieve from channel1 nor retrieve from channel2 of that pixel.
   f. Take the Next pixel, Go to 4(a).
5. Concatenate all the cipher blocks, $DATA_1$ to $DATA_7$ to get the DATA.

LSB ARRAY BASED SUBSTITUTION

Binary Message Embedding in LSB Array

This technique was proposed by Swain & Lenka (2012c). In this technique the message is hidden in the LSB array. The embedding algorithm is described by the following steps.

1. Create the LSB0 array by keeping together all the 8th bits (LSBs) of the pixels. Create LSB1 array by keeping together all the 7th bits of the pixels. Similarly, create the LSB2 array by keeping together all the 6th bits of the pixels and create LSB3 array by keeping together all the 5th bits of the pixels.
2. Divide the binary message into 4 blocks, say block0, block1, block2, and block3. Slide block0 on LSB0 array and hide at a place where minimum

distortion or maximum match occurs. Note down the start index in the array where hiding is done, say it is index0. Similarly hide block1 in LSB1 array, block2 in LSB2 array and block3 in LSB3 array. Find the respective start indices index1, index2, and index3.
3. Embed these four indices and the block lengths in the reserved pixels which are to be used at receiver for retrieval of message.

The retrieval process is as discussed below.

1. From the stego image the four arrays LSB0, LSB1, LSB2 and LSB3 are formed as was done from the original image at receiver.
2. Retrieve index0, index1, index2 and index3 from the reserved pixels.
3. Retrieve block0 from LSB array from the location starting with index0. Retrieve block1 from LSB1 array from the location starting with index1. Retrieve block2 from LSB2 array from the location starting with index2. Retrieve block3 from LSB3 array from the location starting with index3. Concatenate all these 4 blocks, thus we get the message.

Binary Word Embedding in LSB Array

This technique was proposed by Swain & Lenka (2015). In this technique the binary words are hidden in the LSB array at maximum match or minimum distortion areas. The embedding algorithm is described by the following steps.

1. Create the four different arrays, LSB0, LSB1, LSB2, and LSB3. The LSB0 is created by taking only 1 LSB from each pixel. LSB1 array is created by taking 2 LSBs from each pixel. Similarly, LSB2 array is created by taking 3 LSBs from the pixels and LSB3 array is created by taking 4 LSBs from each pixel. Depending upon the length of our secret message one of these 4 arrays is to be chosen for embedding. If our message is very long, we prefer LSB3 array and if the message is too short, we prefer LSB0 array.
2. Every binary word (word converted to binary) is slided over the chosen array and hidden in maximum match or minimum distortion area. The start indices are noted down. Suppose the indices are index1, index2, …, indexn.
3. Suppose the lengths of the words are denoted as length1, length2, length3,…, lengthn. Arrange length1, index1, length2, index2, …, lengthn, indexn as another array, E.

4. Encrypt E and then compress. After compression, say it is E_1. Find the length of E_1. Embed E_1 in some reserved area using 2-bit LSB substitution.

The retrieval process is as discussed below.

1. Formulate the selected array, i.e. LSB0 or LSB1 or LSB2 or LSB3
2. Retrieve the array E_1 from the two least significant bit locations of the reserved area. Decompress it, then decrypt it, thus we got E.
3. Calculate length1, index1, length2, indexe2,..., lengthn, indexn from E.
4. Retrieve the words from the selected array with the help of these indices and lengths of the different words and formulate the message.

The following example illustrates the embedding algorithm in detail. Suppose the message is: "*With the huge growth of computer network and the latest advances in digital technologies, a huge amount of digital data is exchanged over various types of networks.*". It is to be hidden in Lena image which is 768 kilobytes in length, Figure 4. We choose LSB3 array. The message comprises of 27 words. These words are mapped into the LSB3 array, and hidden at maximum match locations. The matching data is presented in Figure 5. Now a new array called length-index array E is created, which consists of the word lengths and indices. It is: 32, 9701, 24, 44148, 32, 38571, 48, 54631, ..., 64, 88443. Now E is encrypted and then compressed, say it is E_1. This E_1 is shown in Figure 6. The length of E_1 is: 43576 bits (5447 bytes). This E_1 is now embedded in some reserved area using 2 LSB substitution.

GROUP OF BITS SUBSTITUTION

The 1-Bit GBS Algorithm

This technique was proposed by Swain (2016). The data hiding is performed in the following manner. The cover image and secret data both are converted to binary. The length of the binary secret data is represented in 20 bits. These 20 bits are concatenated at the beginning of the secret binary data. Now the whole thing binary length plus secret data, say message is to be hidden in the binary cover image. One message bit needs to be hidden in a byte of binary cover image. Assume that the length of binary image is N bytes and the length

Figure 4. Lena image 512×512 (color)

Figure 5. Matching information of the words

Word No	Word Content	Word length	Matched %	Matched Index
1	With	32	84.38	9701
2	the	24	91.67	44148
3	huge	32	87.50	38571
4	growth	48	79.17	54631
5	of	16	100.00	140856
6	computer	56	79.69	123524
7	network	56	83.93	51274
8	and	24	91.67	22203
9	the	24	91.67	51092
10	latest	48	81.25	39716
11	advances	64	76.56	95642
12	in	16	100.00	17257
13	digital	56	83.93	118836
14	Technologies,	104	71.15	62889
15	a	8	100.00	3086
16	huge	32	87.50	161947
17	amount	48	81.25	104355
18	of	16	100.00	213669
19	digital	56	76.79	42889
20	data	32	87.50	161947
21	is	16	100.00	11702
22	exchanged	72	75.00	146382
23	over	32	90.62	56265
24	various	56	80.36	69628
25	types	40	87.50	238247
26	of	16	93.75	35022
27	networks	64	75.00	88443

Figure 6. Encrypted and Compressed Length-Index array, E_1


```
xœQÛÀ0ZIT÷_¬¤wýHäåÅî$à4Qhtô\Ý
¢ÙŰ¯h(‡ÝÁí^S11Õ3y½±ÍÖ˜¡ýŠ50àn«
ZêG‘Ëè312bžÎ›S³FS˜[ßÓ—ˆÕ$ÄÐUF™+/Îò
Kbã²róÆ¨+ëÆ1e"Î)aßk~->Â^7må Àœ)Ë¨Ý
8üÀ¶°7Eu†8°·Ï7µê’M#¯§^kO8g«G
B□föX•′3Œ¿jB•.£D¦Ýæ+Ô¿v½nµ¶fyhqå`N
<m]êø¤à¯¢İas[k3¯žÔM¼pÎ ŒÎãçGg;rêÿ“
WéF}H±Ïm;ƒ>nÖö¨³¾Íb½µ½¥ÐÍšYÞUAÎàœ
IïÐ›—+Z÷*xµ»¹□□Gz.“bŒz\
```


of *message* is n bits. For embedding to take place the condition $n \leq N$ should be satisfied. Data hiding is achieved in the following steps.

Step 1: For i=1 to N, say A_i is a byte of the cover image. For i= 1 to n, say b_i is a bit of the message.

Step 2: If the condition $n \leq N$ is satisfied the steps 3 is applied for message hiding, otherwise embedding cannot be done.

Step 3: For i= 1 to n the following procedure is repeated for n times

The byte A_i is represented by its constituent bits as $d_1d_2d_3d_4d_5d_6d_7d_8$. Furthermore, D_1, $D_2, D_3, D_4, D_5, D_6,$ and D_7 are derived from A_i.

$$D_1 = d_1d_2d_3d_4d_5d_6d_7d_8,$$

$$D_2 = d_2d_3d_4d_5d_6d_7d_8,$$

$$D_3 = d_3d_4d_5d_6d_7d_8,$$

$$D_4 = d_4d_5d_6d_7d_8,$$

$$D_5 = d_5d_6d_7d_8,$$

$D_6 = d_6d_7d_8$, and

$D_7 = d_7d_8$.

If the D_1 value is either 11111111 or 00000000; use 1-bit LSB substitution. The stego value of D_1 will be one of the four values from the list {11111111, 11111110, 00000000, 00000001}.

Otherwise if D_1 value is either 01111111 or 10000000;

And if b_i is 0, the stego value of D_1 is 01111111. If b_i is 1, the stego value of D_1 is 10000000.

Otherwise if D_2 is 0111111 or 1000000;

And if b_i is 0, the stego value of D_2 is 0111111. If b_i is 1, the stego value of D_2 is 1000000.

Otherwise if D_3 is either 011111 or 100000;

And if b_i is 0, the stego value of D_3 is 011111. If b_i is 1, the stego value of D_3 is 100000.

Otherwise if D_4 is either 01111 or 10000;

And if b_i is 0, the stego value of D_4 is 01111. If b_i is 1, the stego value of D_4 is 10000.

Otherwise if D_5 is either 0111 or 1000;

And if b_i is 0, the stego value of D_5 is 0111. If b_i is 1, the stego value of D_5 is 1000.

Otherwise if D_6 is either 011 or 100;

And if b_i is 0, the stego value of D_6 is 011. If b_i is 1, the stego value of D_6 is 100.

Otherwise if D_7 is either 01 or 10;

And if b_i is 0, the stego value of D_7 is 01. If b_i is 1, the stego value of D_7 is 10.

The message retrieval is done in the following manner. Suppose that B is the binary stego image from which the message m has to be retrieved.

Step 1: Initially m is empty and counter, c is 1.

Step 2: For stego image, B every byte is denoted as B_i, for i= 1 to N. Initialize i=1

Step 3: B_i is represented as $d_1d_2d_3d_4d_5d_6d_7d_8$. Furthermore, D_1, $D_2, D_3, D_4, D_5, D_6,$ and D_7 are derived from B_i.

$D_1 = d_1d_2d_3d_4d_5d_6d_7d_8$,

$D_2 = d_2d_3d_4d_5d_6d_7d_8$,

$D_3 = d_3d_4d_5d_6d_7d_8$,

$D_4 = d_4d_5d_6d_7d_8$,

$D_5 = d_5d_6d_7d_8$,

$D_6 = d_6d_7d_8$, and

$D_7 = d_7d_8$.

If the D_1 is in the list {11111111, 00000000, 11111110, 00000001}, then the retrieved bit d_8 is concatenated to m.

Otherwise if D_1 = 01111111 or 10000000, the retrieved bit is 0 or 1 respectively. It is concatenated to m.

Otherwise if D_2 = 0111111 or 1000000, the retrieved bit is 0 or 1 respectively. It is concatenated to m.

Otherwise if D_3 = 011111 or 100000, the retrieved bit is 0 or 1 respectively. It is concatenated to m.

Otherwise if D_4 = 01111 or 10000, the retrieved bit is 0 or 1 respectively. It is concatenated to m.

Otherwise if D_5 = 0111 or 1000, the retrieved bit is 0 or 1 respectively. It is concatenated to m.

Otherwise if D_6 = 011 or 100, the retrieved bit is 0 or 1 respectively. It is concatenated to m.

Otherwise if D_7 = 01 or 10, the retrieved bit is 0 or 1 respectively. It is concatenated to m.

Step 4: Increment both c and i values by 1. If $c \leq 20$ then jump to step3, otherwise jump to step5.

Step 5: Take out the 20 bits from m leaving m as empty and find their decimal equivalent and multiply it by 7. Thus, we get the length of hidden data in bits. Let it be n. Again step 3 is repeated for i= 21 to n. Then we accumulate n-20 bits in m. Convert this n-20 bits to characters. It is the hidden data.

The 2-Bit GBS Algorithm (Swain, 2016)

This technique was proposed by Swain (2016). The data hiding is performed in the following manner. The cover image and secret data both are converted to binary. The length of the binary secret data is represented in 20 bits. These 20 bits are concatenated at the beginning of the secret binary data. Now the whole thing binary length plus secret data, say message is to be hidden in the binary cover image. Two message bits need to be hidden in a byte of binary cover image. Assume that the length of binary image is N bytes and the length of *message* is n bits. For embedding to take place the condition $\frac{n}{2} \leq N$ should be satisfied. Data hiding is achieved in the following steps.

Step 1: For i=1 to N, say A_i is a byte of the cover image. For i= 1 to n, say b_i is a bit of the message.

Step 2: If the condition $\frac{n}{2} \leq N$ is satisfied the steps 3 is applied for message hiding, otherwise embedding cannot be done.

Step 3: For k= 1 to $\frac{n}{2}$ the following procedure is repeated for $\frac{n}{2}$ times. Define i=2×k-1

The byte A_k is represented by its constituent bits as $d_1d_2d_3d_4d_5d_6d_7d_8$. Furthermore, D_1, D_2, D_3, D_4, D_5, D_6, , and D_7 are derived from A_i.

$$D_1 = d_1d_2d_3d_4d_5d_6d_7d_8,$$

$$D_2 = d_2d_3d_4d_5d_6d_7d_8,$$

$D_3 = d_3d_4d_5d_6d_7d_8$,

$D_4 = d_4d_5d_6d_7d_8$,

$D_5 = d_5d_6d_7d_8$,

$D_6 = d_6d_7d_8$, and

$D_7 = d_7d_8$.

If D_1 value is either 11111111 or 00000000; use 2-bit LSB substitution. The stego value of D_1 will be one value from the list {11111100, 11111101, 11111110, 11111111, 00000000, 00000001, 00000010, 00000011}

Otherwise if D_1 is 01111111 or 10000000;

For b_ib_{i+1} values 00, 01, 10 and 11 the stego values of D_1 are 01111111, 01111110, 10000001, and 10000000 respectively.

Otherwise if D_2 is 0111111 or 1000000;

For b_ib_{i+1} values 00, 01, 10 and 11 the stego values of D_2 are 0111111, 0111110, 1000001, and 1000000 respectively.

Otherwise if D_3 is 011111 or 100000;

For b_ib_{i+1} values 00, 01, 10 and 11 the stego values of D_3 are 011111, 011110, 100001, and 100000 respectively.

Otherwise if D_4 is 01111 or 10000;

For b_ib_{i+1} values 00, 01, 10 and 11 the stego values of D_4 are 01111, 01110, 10001, and 10000 respectively.

Otherwise if D_5 is 0111 or 1000;

For b_ib_{i+1} values 00, 01, 10 and 11 the stego values of D_5 are 0111, 0110, 1001, and 1000 respectively.

Otherwise if D_6 is 011 or 100;

For b_ib_{i+1} values 00, 01, 10 and 11 the stego values of D_5 are 011, 010, 101, and 100 respectively.

Otherwise if D_7 is 01 or 10;

For b_ib_{i+1} values 00, 01, 10 and 11 the stego values of D_5 are 11, 10, 01, and 00 respectively.

The message retrieval is done in the following manner. Suppose that B is the binary stego image from which the message m has to be retrieved

Step 1: Initially m is empty and counter, c=1.

Step 2: For stego image, B every byte is denoted as B_i, for i= 1 to N. Initialize i=1.

Step 3: B_i is represented as $d_1d_2d_3d_4d_5d_6d_7d_8$. Furthermore, D_1, D_2, D_3, D_4, D_5, D_6, and D_7 are derived from B_i.

$$D_1 = d_1d_2d_3d_4d_5d_6d_7d_8,$$

$$D_2 = d_2d_3d_4d_5d_6d_7d_8,$$

$$D_3 = d_3d_4d_5d_6d_7d_8,$$

$$D_4 = d_4d_5d_6d_7d_8,$$

$$D_5 = d_5d_6d_7d_8,$$

$$D_6 = d_6d_7d_8, \text{ and}$$

$$D_7 = d_7d_8.$$

If the value of D_1 belongs to the list {11111100, 11111101, 11111110, 11111111, 00000000, 00000001, 00000010, 00000011} then the retrieved bits d_7d_8 are concatenated to m.

Otherwise for D_1 being 01111111, 01111110, 10000001, 10000000, the retrieved bits are 00, 01, 10 and 11 respectively. The retrieved value is concatenated to m.

Otherwise for D_2 being 0111111, 0111110, 1000001, 1000000, the retrieved bits are 00, 01, 10 and 11 respectively. The retrieved value is concatenated to m.

Otherwise for D_3 being 011111, 011110, 100001, 100000, the retrieved bits are 00, 01, 10 and 11 respectively. The retrieved value is concatenated to m.

Otherwise for D_4 being 01111, 01110, 10001, 10000, the retrieved bits are 00, 01, 10 and 11 respectively. The retrieved value is concatenated to m.

Otherwise for D_5 being 0111, 0110, 1001, 1000, the retrieved bits are 00, 01, 10 and 11 respectively. The retrieved value is concatenated to m.

Otherwise for D_6 being 011, 010, 101, 100, the retrieved bits are 00, 01, 10 and 11 respectively. The retrieved value is concatenated to m.

Otherwise for D_7 being 11, 10, 01, 00, the retrieved bits are 00, 01, 10 and 11 respectively. The retrieved value is concatenated to m.

Step 4: Increment c by 2 and if $c \leq 20$ then, increment i by 1 and jump to step3, otherwise jump to step5.

Step 5: Take out the 20 bits from m leaving m as empty and find their decimal equivalent and multiply it by 7. Thus, we get the length of hidden data in bits. Let it be n. Again, for i= 11 to $\frac{n}{2}$ repeat step3. Then we accumulate n-20 bits in m. Convert this n-20 bits to characters. It is the hidden data.

Like this 1-bit and 2-bit GBS 3-bit GBS also proposed in (Sahu, & Swain, 2017). It hides 3 bits in a pixel by decreasing the PSNR.

GBS AND LSB COMPARISON

In Table 1 the 1-bit GBS algorithm is compared with 1-bit LSB algorithm. Similarly, in Table 2 the 2-bit GBS algorithm is compared with 2-bit LSB algorithm. Eight sample images are used for this purpose, Figure 7. There are four comparison parameters, namely, PSNR, hiding capacity, quality index, and bit rate. From Table 1 it can be observed that the performance of 1-bit GBS is same as the performance of 1-bit LSB algorithm. The additional advantage of 1-bit GBS algorithm is in resistance to security attack, which is discussed in the next section. From Table 2 it can be observed that the performance of 2-bit GBS is better in terms of PSNR as the performance of 2-bit LSB algorithm. The additional advantage of 2-bit GBS algorithm is in resistance to security attack, which is discussed in the next section.

GBS SECURITY ANALYSIS

The security analysis of GBS and LSB substitution algorithms are compared in this section. The PDH analysis (Pradhan, Sahu, Swain, & Sekhar, 2016) of two sample images like Lena and Baboon, it is shown in Figure 8 and Figure 9 respectively. For 2-bit LSB substitution algorithm the step effects in PDH are higher than that of 2-bit GBS algorithm. This implies that the security of 2-bit GBS algorithm is improved. Thus, GBS algorithms do well in PDH analysis. But the RS analysis can be able to capture both the LSB and GBS algorithms.

Figure 7. (a)-(h) Test Images

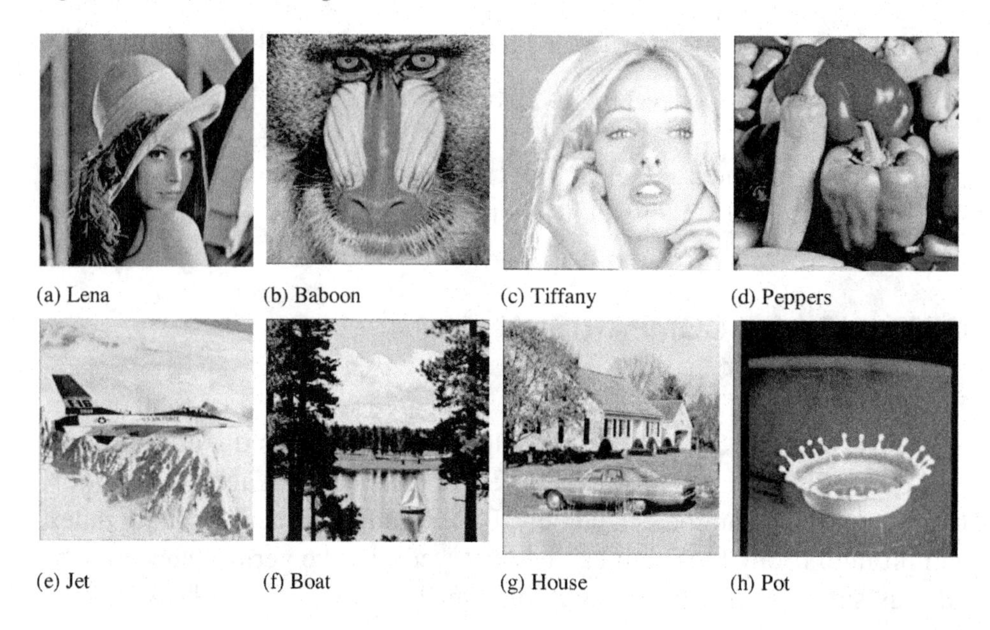

(a) Lena (b) Baboon (c) Tiffany (d) Peppers

(e) Jet (f) Boat (g) House (h) Pot

Table 1. Comparison between 1-bit LSB substitution and 1-bit GBS

Images 512×512 (Color)	1-Bit LSB Substitution Algorithm				Proposed 1-Bit GBS Algorithm			
	PSNR	Capacity	Q	Bit Rate	PSNR	Capacity	Q	Bit Rate
Lena	51.65	786432	0.9999	1.0	51.63	786432	0.9999	1.0
Baboon	51.64	786432	0.9999	1.0	51.64	786432	0.9999	1.0
Tiffany	51.70	786432	0.9998	1.0	51.71	786432	0.9998	1.0
Peppers	51.64	786432	0.9999	1.0	51.62	786432	0.9999	1.0
Jet	51.64	786432	0.9998	1.0	51.65	786432	0.9998	1.0
Boat	51.64	786432	0.9999	1.0	51.64	786432	0.9999	1.0
House	51.64	786432	0.9999	1.0	51.64	786432	0.9999	1.0
Pot	51.64	786432	0.9999	1.0	51.63	786432	0.9999	1.0
Average	51.65	786432	0.9999	1.0	51.64	786432	0.9999	1.0

Table 2. Comparison between 2-bit LSB substitution and 2-bit GBS

Images 512×512 (Color)	2-Bit LSB Substitution Algorithm				Proposed 2-Bit GBS Algorithm			
	PSNR	Capacity	Q	Bit Rate	PSNR	Capacity	Q	Bit Rate
Lena	47.57	1572864	0.9998	2.0	49.90	1572864	0.9999	2.0
Baboon	47.57	1572864	0.9998	2.0	49.88	1572864	0.9998	2.0
Tiffany	47.44	1572864	0.9996	2.0	49.33	1572864	0.9997	2.0
Peppers	47.50	1572864	0.9998	2.0	49.70	1572864	0.9999	2.0
Jet	47.56	1572864	0.9997	2.0	49.86	1572864	0.9998	2.0
Boat	47.53	1572864	0.9998	2.0	49.85	1572864	0.9999	2.0
House	47.59	1572864	0.9998	2.0	49.87	1572864	0.9998	2.0
Pot	47.51	1572864	0.9998	2.0	49.71	1572864	0.9999	2.0
Average	47.53	1572864	0.9998	2.0	49.76	1572864	0.9998	2.0

CONCLUSION

A steganographic approach, if uses the principle of substitution, then its security must be evaluated by RS steganalysis. As traditional LSB substitution is vulnerable to RS analysis, so various attempts are done to improve upon it and enhanced versions of it are proposed. The word matching on LSB array is a very bright idea among all the above techniques. It is not attackable by RS steganalysis.

Figure 8. PDHs for Lena image

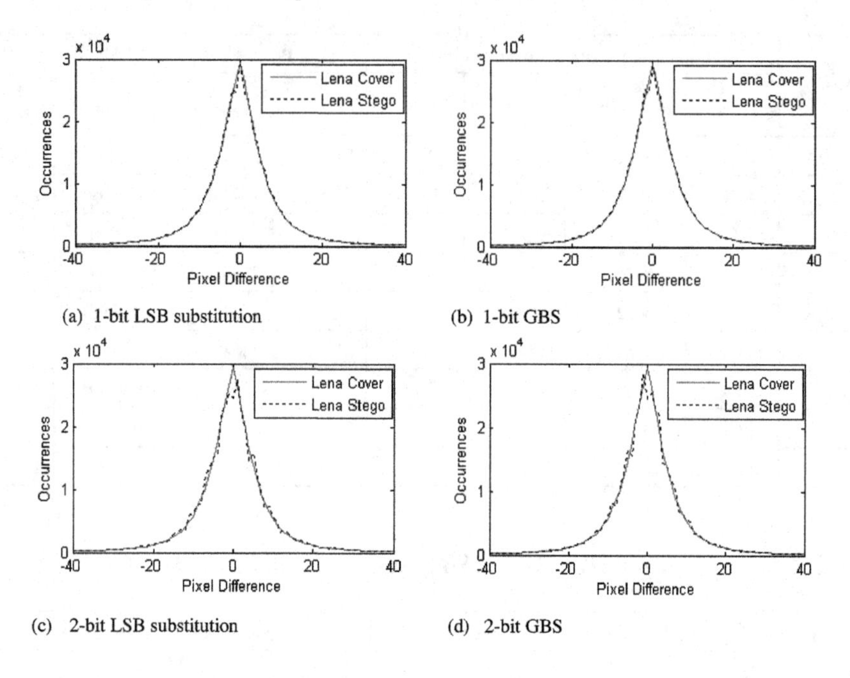

(a) 1-bit LSB substitution

(b) 1-bit GBS

(c) 2-bit LSB substitution

(d) 2-bit GBS

Figure 9. PDHs for Baboon image

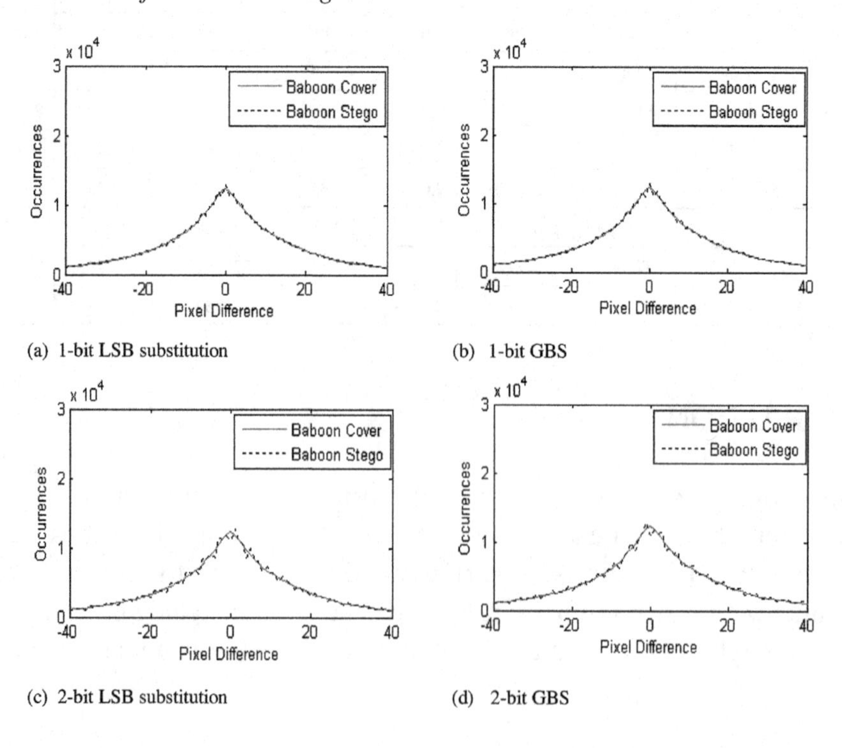

(a) 1-bit LSB substitution

(b) 1-bit GBS

(c) 2-bit LSB substitution

(d) 2-bit GBS

The GBS algorithms discussed here are very different kind of substitution algorithms. These types of algorithms were not seen in literature earlier. The results are comparable with 1-bit and 2-bit LSB substitution techniques. The PDH analysis results are quite better as compared to LSB substitution techniques. Moreover, the GBS algorithms do not qualify in RS analysis.

REFERENCES

Fridrich, J., Goljian, M., & Du, R. (2001). Detecting LSB steganography in color and gray-scale images. *Magazine of IEEE Multimedia Special Issue on Security*, *8*(4), 22–28. doi:10.1109/93.959097

Liao, X., Wen, Q. Y., & Zhang, J. (2011). A steganographic method for digital images with four-pixel differencing and modified LSB Substitution. *Journal of Visual Communication and Image Representation*, *22*(1), 1–8. doi:10.1016/j.jvcir.2010.08.007

Pradhan, A., Sahu, A. K., Swain, G., & Sekhar, K. R. (2016). Performance evaluation parameters of image steganography techniques. *Proceedings of IEEE International Conference on Research Advances in Integrated Navigation Systems*, 1-8. 10.1109/RAINS.2016.7764399

Sahu, A. K., & Swain, G. (2017). Information hiding using group of bits substitution. *International Journal on Communications Antenna and Propagation*, *7*(2), 162–167. doi:10.15866/irecap.v7i2.11675

Swain, G. (2014). Digital image steganography using nine-pixel differencing and modified LSB substitution. *Indian Journal of Science and Technology*, *7*(9), 1444–1450.

Swain, G. (2016). Digital image steganography using variable length group of bits substitution. *Procedia Computer Science*, *85*, 31–38. doi:10.1016/j.procs.2016.05.173

Swain, G., & Lenka, S. K. (2012a). A technique for secret communication by using a new block cipher with dynamic steganography. *International Journal of Security and Its Applications*, *6*(2), 1–12.

Swain, G., & Lenka, S.K. (2012b). A novel approach to RGB channel based image steganography technique. *International Arab Journal of e-Technology*, *2*(4),181-186.

Swain, G., & Lenka, S. K. (2012c). LSB array based image steganography technique by exploring the four least significant bits. *Communications in Computer and Information Science*, *270*, 479–488. doi:10.1007/978-3-642-29216-3_52

Swain, G., & Lenka, S. K. (2015). A novel steganography technique by mapping words with LSB array. *International Journal of Signal and Imaging Systems Engineering*, *8*(1), 115–122. doi:10.1504/IJSISE.2015.067052

Chapter 3
Pixel Value Differencing Steganography

ABSTRACT

In this chapter, the author describes the different categories of pixel value differencing (PVD) techniques and their performances. The main goal in PVD technique is to find the pixel value difference. If it is large, hide the larger number of bits; otherwise, hide the lesser number of bits. The traditional PVD techniques operates on 2, 4, and 8 pixel blocks to calculate the pixel value difference and then take the embedding decision. The traditional PVD techniques use a range table to decide the embedding capacity in a block. The adaptive PVD techniques do not use any range table and calculate the embedding capacity dynamically for every block based on the pixel values of that block. Most of the traditional PVD techniques are attacked by pixel difference histogram (PDH) analysis, but adaptive PVD techniques are tolerant to PDH analysis.

INTRODUCTION

The prime idea in PVD technique is that smooth regions should hide lesser number of bits and edge regions should hide a greater number of bits, so that the distortion will not be noticed. Thus, the pixel value differences are utilized to find the embedding capacity of a pixel block based on a range table.

DOI: 10.4018/978-1-5225-7516-0.ch003

There are two types of PVD techniques, (i) non-adaptive table PVD techniques (Wu & Tsai, 2003; Zhang & Wang, 2004; Chang, Chang, Huang & Tu, 2008, Lee, Lee, Chen, Chang, Su & Chang, 2012; Balasubramanian, Selvakumar & Geetha, 2014; Pradhan, Sekhar, & Swain, 2016), and adaptive PVD techniques (Luo, Huang & Huang, 2011; Swain, 2016; Pradhan, Sekhar & Swain, 2017). The non-adaptive PVD techniques utilize a fixed range table for all the pixel blocks to take embedding decision. The adaptive PVD techniques calculate the lower bound and upper bound for every block separately based on the correlation of the pixel values in a block. Based on these lower and upper bounds embedding length is decided.

TRADITIONAL PVD

One Way PVD

Wu & Tsai (2003) discovered a new paradigm, i.e. "edge regions of an image can hide a greater number of bits as compared to smooth regions". They came up with a steganographic algorithm known as PVD. The embedding algorithm in PVD is as described below.

The pixels of the image are raster scanned and a pair of adjacent pixels (P_i, P_{i+1}) are termed as a block. For such a block the difference value $d = ($ P_{i+1} - P_i) is found. A range table like Table 1 is considered. This d value belongs to one of the ranges R_i whose width is $W_i = (u_i - l_i + 1)$. Here, l_i and u_i are the lower and upper bounds of the range R_i. The number of bits that can be hidden in this block is n_i. Now n_i bits of data are taken from the binary data stream and converted to decimal value b. The new difference value is calculated by hiding b in this block as in Eq. (1).

$$d' = \begin{cases} l_i + b, & \text{if } d \geq 0, \\ -l_i - b, & \text{if } d < 0 \end{cases} \quad (1)$$

Now $m = d'$ - d is calculated. If d is an odd number the stego block is $(p_i - m/2, p_{i+1} + m/2)$. If d is an even number the stego block is $(p_i - m/2, p_{i+1} + m/2)$.

The extraction algorithm is as below. The pixels of the stego-image are raster scanned and a pair of adjacent pixels (P_i^*, P_{i+1}^*) are termed as a block. For such a block the difference value $d = (P_{i+1}^* - P_i^*)$. The same range table i.e. Table 1 is considered. This d value belongs to one of the ranges R_i whose width is $W_i = (u_i - l_i + 1)$. Here, l_i and u_i are the lower and upper bounds of the range R_i.The number of bits that can be extracted from this block is n_i. An example of embedding is as shown in Figure 1. The block is (50, 65). The difference value is 15; it lies in the range {8, 23}. So lower bound is 8 and n value is 4. Suppose the four bits of data to be hidden is 1010, its decimal value is 10. As $d \geq 0$, the new value of difference, $d' = 8+10 = 18$. Now $m = d' - d = 3$. As d is odd the new value for the block is $\left(50 - \frac{3}{2}, 65 + \frac{3}{2}\right)$ = (48, 66).

As per the observation by Zhang and Wang (Zhang & Wang, 2004) this PVD technique is detected by PDH analysis. In PDH of stego-images the zig-zg nature is observed.

Chang et al. (2008) and Lee et al. (2012) extended this PVD idea into 2×2 pixel blocks to improve upon the performance. But they did not prove that their techniques qualify through PDH analysis. Balasubramanian et al. (2014) proposed octonary PVD to improve the performance further and to qualify from PDH analysis.

Table 1. The range table

Range	Width	No. of Bits
$R_1 \in \{0, 7\}$	$W_1 = 8$	$n_1 = 3$
$R_2 \in \{8, 15\}$	$W_2 = 8$	$n_2 = 3$
$R_3 \in \{16, 31\}$	$W_3 = 16$	$n_3 = 4$
$R_4 \in \{32, 63\}$	$W_4 = 32$	$n_4 = 5$
$R_5 \in \{64, 127\}$	$W_5 = 64$	$n_5 = 6$
$R_6 \in \{128, 255\}$	$W_6 = 128$	$n_6 = 7$

Figure 1. Example of PVD

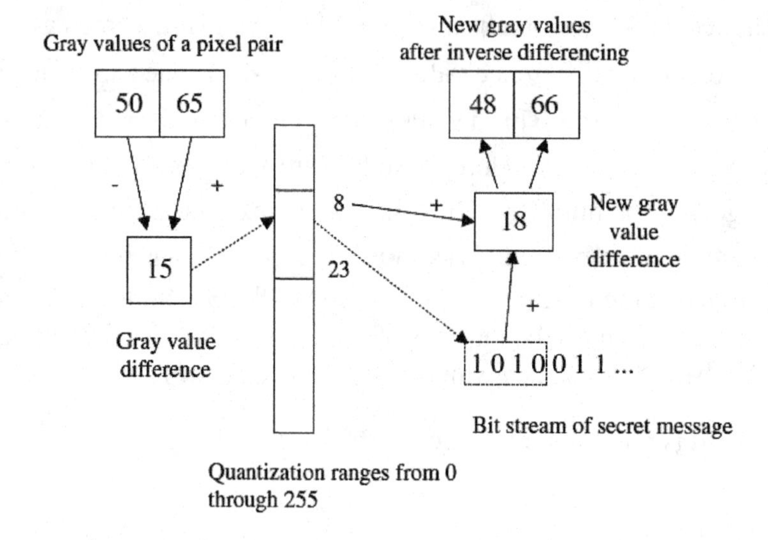

The Seven Way PVD

This technique was proposed by Pradhan, Sekhar & Swain (2016). For data embedding the image is raster scanned and divided into 3×3 non-overlapping blocks, a sample block is shown in Figure 2.

Seven pairs are formed out of these nine pixels. Those are $P_0=(p_{22}, p_{23})$, $P_1=(p_{22}, p_{13})$, $P_2=(p_{22}, p_{12})$, $P_3=(p_{22}, p_{11})$, $P_4=(p_{22}, p_{21})$, $P_5=(p_{22}, p_{31})$, $P_6=(p_{22}, p_{32})$. The pixel p_{33} is excluded from these pairs. The 7 pixel value differences, $d_0 = p_{23} - p_{22}$, $d_1=p_{13}-p_{22}$, $d_2=p_{12}-p_{22}$, $d_3=p_{11}-p_{22}$, $d_4=p_{21}-p_{22}$, $d_5=p_{31}-p_{22}$, $d_6=p_{32}-p_{22}$ are computed. Here also we can refer Table 1 as the range Table. For i=0 to 6, the d_i value lies in range R_{ki}, the width

Figure 2. A 3×3 sample block

p_{11}	p_{12}	p_{13}
p_{21}	p_{22}	p_{23}
p_{31}	p_{32}	p_{33}

$w_{ki} = u_{ki} - l_{ki} + 1$, wherein u_{ki} and l_{ki} are upper and lower bounds. The embedding length for each d_i is, $n_i = \log_2 w_{ki}$. For each d_i, n_i data bits from the binary data stream is taken and converted to the decimal equivalent b_i and then $d_i^{'}$ is calculated following the Eq. (2).

$$d_i^{'} = \begin{cases} l_{ki} + b_i, & \text{if } d_i \geq 0, \\ -l_{ki} - b_i, & \text{if } d_i < 0 \end{cases} \tag{2}$$

Now for i=0 to 6, $m_i = d_i^{'} - d_i$ is calculated. After data embedding the new pairs are calculated as in Eq. (3).

$$P_0^{'} = \begin{cases} (p_{22} - m_0 / 2, \ p_{23} + m_0 / 2), & \text{if } d_0 \text{ is even}, \\ (p_{22} - m_0 / 2, \ p_{23} + m_0 / 2), & \text{if } d_0 \text{ is odd} \end{cases}$$

$$P_1^{'} = \begin{cases} (p_{22} - m_1 / 2, \ p_{13} + m_1 / 2), & \text{if } d_1 \text{ is even}, \\ (p_{22} - m_1 / 2, \ p_{13} + m_1 / 2), & \text{if } d_1 \text{ is odd} \end{cases}$$

$$P_2^{'} = \begin{cases} (p_{22} - m_2 / 2, \ p_{12} + m_2 / 2), & \text{if } d_2 \text{ is even}, \\ (p_{22} - m_2 / 2, \ p_{12} + m_2 / 2), & \text{if } d_2 \text{ is odd} \end{cases}$$

$$P_3^{'}. = \begin{cases} (p_{22} - m_3 / 2, \ p_{11} + m_3 / 2), & \text{if } d_3 \text{ is even}, \\ (p_{22} - m_3 / 2, \ p_{11} + m_3 / 2), & \text{if } d_3 \text{ is odd} \end{cases} \tag{3}$$

$$P_4^{'} = \begin{cases} (p_{22} - m_4 / 2, \ p_{21} + m_4 / 2), & \text{if } d_4 \text{ is even}, \\ (p_{22} - m_4 / 2, \ p_{21} + m_4 / 2), & \text{if } d_4 \text{ is odd} \end{cases}$$

$$= \begin{cases} (p_{22} - m_5 / 2, \ p_{31} + m_5 / 2), & \text{if } d_5 \text{ is even}, \\ (p_{22} - m_5 / 2, \ p_{31} + m_5 / 2), & \text{if } d_5 \text{ is odd} \end{cases}$$

$$P_6^{'} = \begin{cases} (p_{22} - m_6 / 2, \ p_{32} + m_6 / 2), & \text{if } d_6 \text{ is even}, \\ (p_{22} - m_6 / 2, \ p_{32} + m_6 / 2), & \text{if } d_6 \text{ is odd} \end{cases}$$

In these new pairs, p_{22} has obtained seven new values, they need to converge into a single value. Suppose the seven pairs for i=0 to 6 are (x_i, y_i). The x_i value is unified to x as in Eq. (4).

$$x = (x_0 + x_1 + x_2 + x_3 + x_4 + x_5 + x_6)/7 \quad (4)$$

When x_i value is changed to x, the y_i values are also changed to $y_i' = y_i + x - x_i$.

For i=0 to 6, if the new pairs (x, y_i') falls in range {0, 255}, the block is marked as ok by embedding 1 to LSB of p_{33}. For i=0 to 6, if the new pairs (x, y_i') falls out of the range {0, 255}, the block is marked as unsuitable by embedding 0 to LSB of p_{33} and undoing the embedding.

The data retrieval is done in the following way, by forming the blocks as was done in embedding. Suppose Figure 2 is a stego block. If LSB of p_{33} is 0, the block is ignored. If LSB of p_{33} is 1, then 7 difference values d_i^*, for i=0 to 6 are computed. Suppose d_i^* lies in ranges R_{ki} whose width is w_{ki}, the embedding bit length, $n_i^* = \log_2 w_{ki}$ is calculated. The decimal value of the n_i^* embedded bits is calculated as $b_i^* = \left|d_i^*\right| - l_{ki}$.

The blocks which suffered with FOBP in 7 PVD may be used for 2-pixel block PVD to slightly enhance the embedding capacity.

Results and Comparisons

In Table 2 the comparison of the seven-way PVD with Wu & Tasai's one-way PVD is performed. The comparison is done by averaging the results over a sample of 8 images, shown in Figure 3. From the results, shown in Table 2, it can be observed that with a slight reduction in PSNR, the increase in hiding capacity is almost 50% for seven-way and seven+one way-PVD. The average bit rate of one-way PVD is 1.53, where as in seven-way PVD it is 2.37 and in seven-way+one-way it is 2.39.

The PDH analysis of the seven-way PVD is compared with Wu & Tsai's PVD in Figures 4-5 for Lena and Baboon images. In Wu & Tsai (Figure 4.a & Figure 5.a) the step effects are visible, so this method is detected. In seven-way PVD, Figures 4.b-c & Figures 5.b-c step effects are not visible. The second advantage of seven-way PVD is that it has higher embedding capacity as compared to Wu & Tsai's method.

The RS diagrams for the seven-way PVD and seven-way+one-way PVD schemes are shown in Figure 6 and Figure 7 for Lena and Baboon images

Figure 3. (a)-(h) Test images

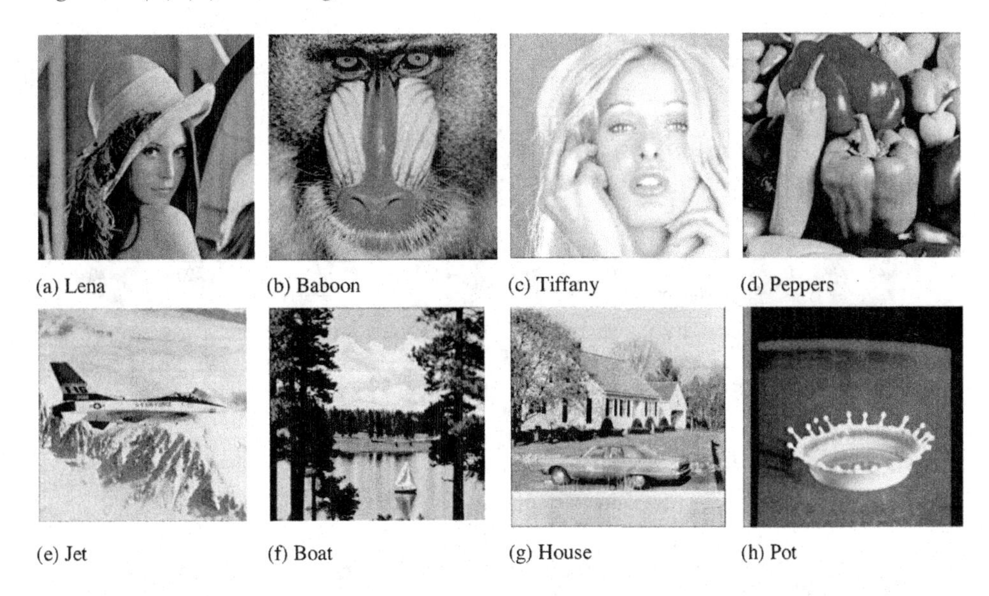

(a) Lena (b) Baboon (c) Tiffany (d) Peppers

(e) Jet (f) Boat (g) House (h) Pot

Table 2. Comparison of the results

Images 512×512 (Color)	One-Way PVD (Wu & Tsai, 2003)				Seven-Way PVD (Pradhan, Sekhar & Swain, 2016)				Seven-Way + One-Way PVD (Pradhan, Sekhar & Swain, 2016)			
	PSNR	Capacity	Q	Bit Rate	PSNR	Capacity	Q	Bit Rate	PSNR	Capacity	Q	Bit Rate
Lena	43.63	1232606	0.9995	1.56	41.73	1896662	0.9993	2.41	41.73	1901149	0.9993	2.41
Baboon	38.33	1403491	0.9984	1.78	33.79	2226806	0.9957	2.83	33.77	2243218	0.9957	2.85
Tiffany	44.07	954070	0.9992	1.21	41.23	1400756	0.9986	1.78	41.30	1450799	0.9986	1.84
Peppers	43.07	1174751	0.9996	1.49	40.42	1778072	0.9993	2.26	40.20	1806166	0.9992	2.29
Jet	43.95	1220544	0.9993	1.55	42.09	1906254	0.9989	2.42	41.98	1909595	0.9989	2.42
Boat	41.30	1278971	0.9994	1.62	37.89	1972086	0.9988	2.50	37.91	1991005	0.9988	2.53
House	41.22	1256404	0.9991	1.59	38.97	1972223	0.9986	2.50	38.98	1977403	0.9986	2.51
Pot	43.95	1163700	0.9997	1.47	42.37	1795551	0.9996	2.28	42.40	1803635	0.9996	2.29
Average	42.44	1210567	0.9992	1.53	39.81	1868551	0.9986	2.37	39.78	1885371	0.9985	2.39

respectively. The curves for R_m and R_{-m} are straight lines and almost overlap with each other. Similarly, the curves for S_m and S_{-m} are straight lines and almost overlap with each other. Thus, the relation $R_m \cong R_{-m} > S_m \cong S_{-m}$ is satisfied. This ensures that the RS analysis cannot detect the seven-way steganography schemes.

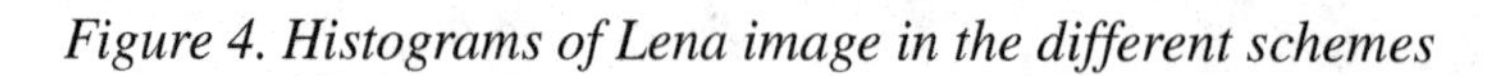
Figure 4. Histograms of Lena image in the different schemes

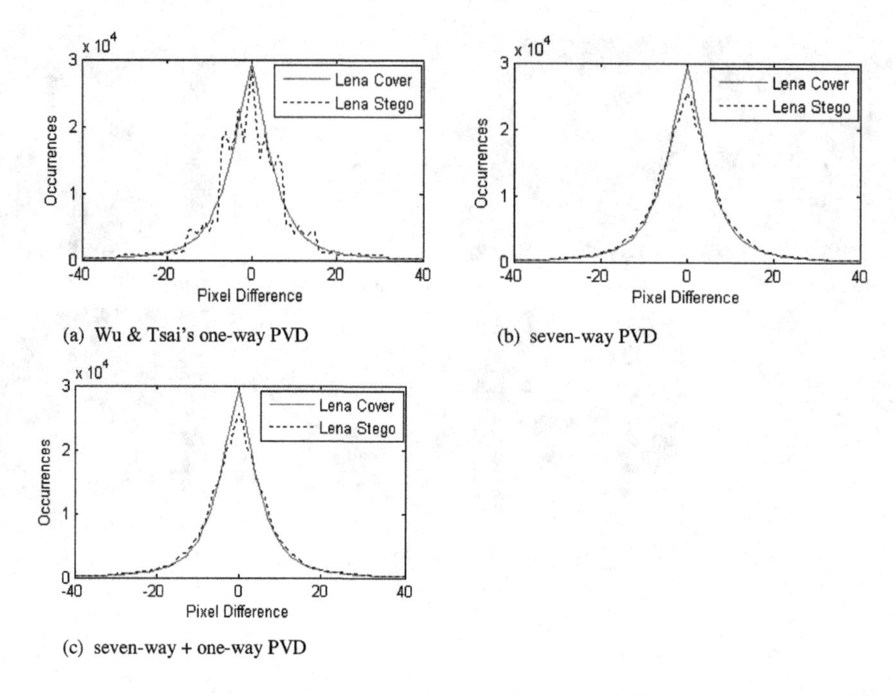

(a) Wu & Tsai's one-way PVD

(b) seven-way PVD

(c) seven-way + one-way PVD

Figure 5. Histograms of Baboon image in the different schemes

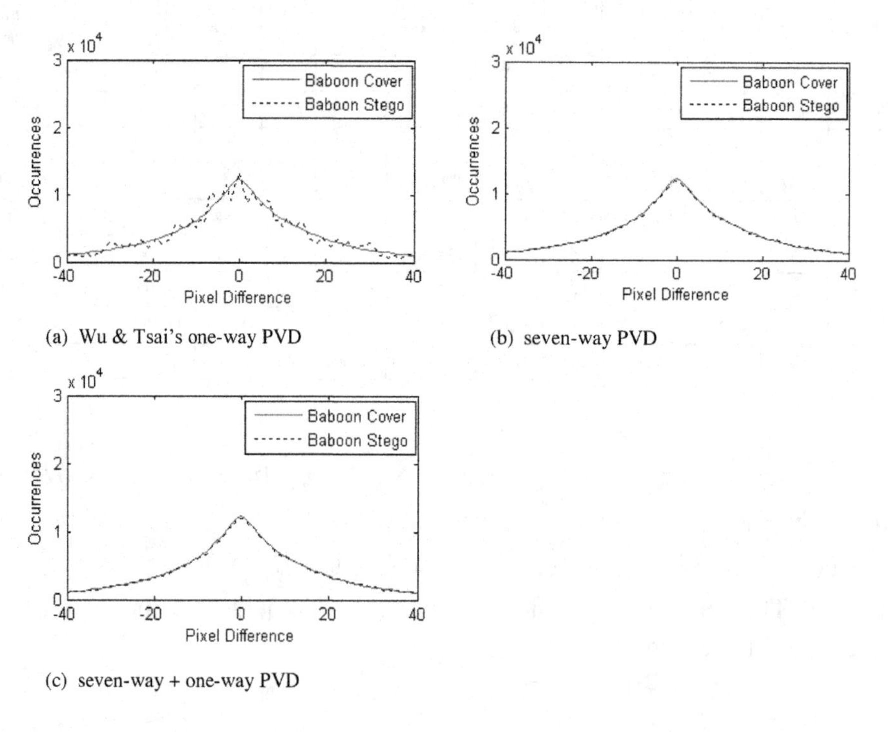

(a) Wu & Tsai's one-way PVD

(b) seven-way PVD

(c) seven-way + one-way PVD

Figure 6. RS diagrams for Lena image

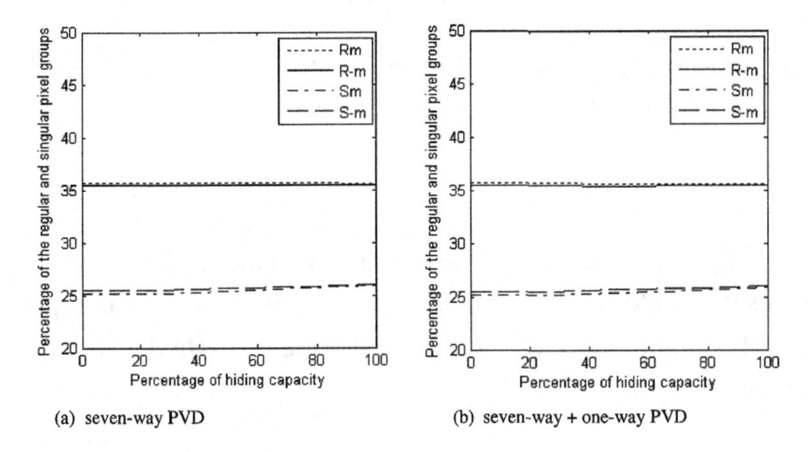

(a) seven-way PVD (b) seven-way + one-way PVD

Figure 7. RS diagrams for Baboon image in proposed scheme

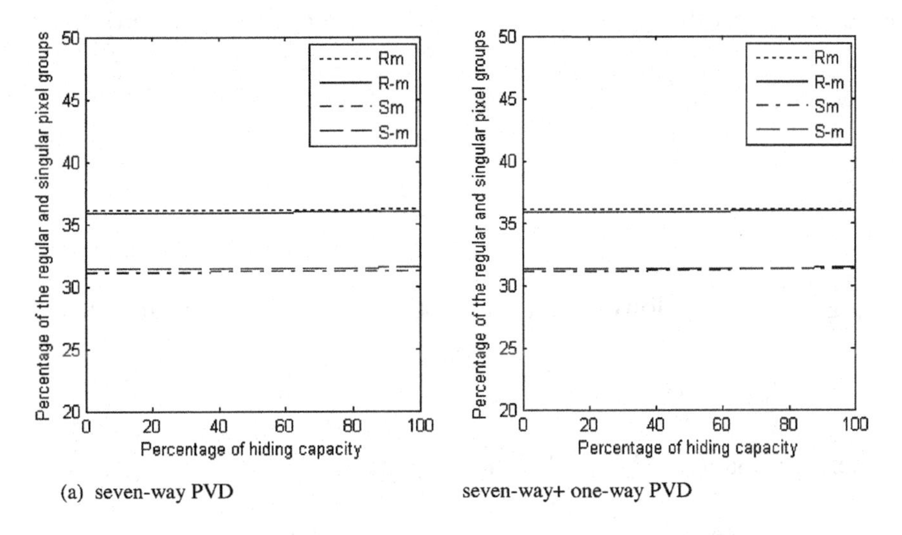

(a) seven-way PVD seven-way+ one-way PVD

ADAPTIVE PVD

Luo et al. (2011) initiated the adaptive PVD technique in 1×3 pixel blocks. The range table need not be fixed for all the pixel blocks. The lower bound and upper bound of ranges for different blocks can be varied based on correlation of the pixels in that block. Swain (2016) has extended this concept to 2×2 pixel blocks and 3×3 pixel blocks. These extended techniques perform better.

Adaptive PVD With 2×2 Pixel Blocks

This technique was proposed by Swain (2016). The embedding algorithm follows the below steps.

Step 1

The cover image is raster scanned and partitioned into 2×2 non-overlapping blocks. A sample block is in Figure 8(a), the pixels are named as g_{x1}, g_r, g_b, and g_{x2}. The target pixels g_{x1} and g_{x2} will hide the data depending on the other two neighbors.

Step 2

Four difference values d_1, d_2, d_3, and d_4 are calculated using Eq. (5).

$$d_1 = g_{x1} - g_r ,\ d_2 = g_{x1} - g_b ,\ d_3 = g_{x2} - g_r ,\ d_4 = g_{x2} - g_b \tag{5}$$

Step 3

For target pixel g_{x1}, lower and upper bounds, l_1 and u_1 are calculated.

Case 1: If $d_1 > 0$ and $d_2 > 0$

Then $l_1 = \max(g_r + 1,\ g_b + 1)$, and $u_1 = 255$

Case 2: If $d_1 \leq 0$ and $d_2 \leq 0$

Then $l_1 = 0$, and $u_1 = \min(g_r,\ g_b)$

Case 3: If $d_1 > 0$ and $d_2 \leq 0$

Then $l_1 = g_r + 1$, and $u_1 = g_b$

Case 4: If $d_1 \leq 0$ and $d_2 > 0$

Then $l_1 = g_b + 1$, and $u_1 = g_r$

Similarly, For target pixel g_{x2}, lower and upper bounds, l_2 and u_2 are calculated

Case 5: If $d_3 > 0$ and $d_4 > 0$

Then $l_2 = \max(g_r + 1,\ g_b + 1)$, and $u_2 = 255$

Case 6: If $d_3 \leq 0$ and $d_4 \leq 0$

Then $l_2 = 0$, and $u_2 = \min(g_r,\ g_b)$

Case 7: If $d_3 > 0$ and $d_4 \leq 0$

Then $l_2 = g_r + 1$, and $u_2 = g_b$

Case 8: If $d_3 \leq 0$ and $d_4 > 0$

Then $l_2 = g_b + 1$, and $u_2 = g_r$

Step 4

Based on l_1 and u_1, g_{x1} can hide n_1 number of bits. Similarly based on l_2 and u_2, g_{x2} can hide n_2 number of bits. These are calculated using Eq. (6).

$$n_1 = \text{floor}\left(\log_2 \left|u_1 - l_1 + 1\right|\right),\ n_2 = \text{floor}\left(\log_2 \left|u_2 - l_2 + 1\right|\right) \tag{6}$$

Step 5

For $n_1 > 0$, the decimal equivalent of n_1 binary bits (b_1) can be hidden in g_{x1} and the stego value is g^*_{x1}. Similarly, for $n_2 > 0$, the decimal equivalent of n_2 binary bits (b_2) can be hidden in g_{x2} and the stego value is g^*_{x2}. These values are calculated using Eq. (7) and Eq. (8).

$$g^*_{x1} = \underset{e}{\text{argmin}}\left\{\left|e - g_{x1}\right| \mid \left|e - g_r\right| \equiv b_1 \left(\text{mod} 2^{n_1}\right), e \in \left[l_1, u_1\right]\right\} \tag{7}$$

$$g^*_{x2} = \underset{e}{\text{argmin}}\left\{\left|e - g_{x2}\right| \mid \left|e - g_r\right| \equiv b_2 \left(\text{mod} 2^{n_2}\right), e \in \left[l_2, u_2\right]\right\} \quad (8)$$

For data extraction also, the stego image is raster scanned and partitioned into 2×2 non-overlapping blocks. A sample block is in Figure 8(b). The differences $d_1 = g^*_{x1} - g^*_r$, $d_2 = g^*_{x1} - g^*_b$, $d_3 = g^*_{x2} - g^*_r$, and $d_4 = g^*_{x2} - g^*_b$ are calculated. Using step 3 and 4 of embedding the number of bits to be extracted from g^*_{x1} and g^*_{x2} are n_1 and n_2 as below in Eq. (9).

$$n_1 = \text{floor}\left(\log_2 \left|u_1 - l_1 + 1\right|\right), \text{ and } n_2 = \text{floor}\left(\log_2 \left|u_2 - l_2 + 1\right|\right) \quad (9)$$

The decimal equivalent of n_1 bits of data to be extracted from g^*_{x1} is b_1 and the decimal equivalent of n_2 bits of data to be extracted from g^*_{x2} is b_2. These are calculated using Eq. (10)

$$b_1 \equiv \left|g^*_{x1} - g^*_r\right| \left(\text{mod} 2^{n_1}\right),\ b_2 \equiv \left|g^*_{x2} - g^*_r\right| \left(\text{mod} 2^{n_2}\right) \quad (10)$$

Now b_1 is converted to n_1 binary bits and b_2 is converted to n_2 binary bits.

Adaptive PVD With 3×3 Pixel Blocks

This technique was proposed by Swain (2016) The embedding algorithm is described in the following steps.

Figure 8. 2×2 Pixel blocks

g_{x1}	g_r
g_b	g_{x2}

(a) Original block

g^*_{x1}	g^*_r
g^*_b	g^*_{x2}

(b) Stego block

Step 1

The cover image is raster scanned and partitioned into 3×3 overlapped blocks. A sample block is in Figure 9. The 3rd row and 3rd column of a block can be used as 1st row and 1st column for other blocks. The pixel named as g_x is used as target pixel, and it's upper, left, right, and bottom neighbor pixel values are, g_u, g_l, g_r and g_b respectively.

Step 2

For a block, four difference values d_1, d_2, d_3, and d_4 are calculated using Eq. (11).

$$d_1 = g_x - g_l \, , \; d_2 = g_r - g_x \, , \; d_3 = g_x - g_u \, , \; d_4 = g_b - g_x \qquad (11)$$

For some threshold value T, if $| d_1 | \le T$, $| d_2 | \le T$, $| d_3 | \le T$, and $| d_4 | \le T$, then this block is abandoned for embedding. Otherwise, the target pixel is capable of carrying data. A chosen value for T is 10.

Step 3

If $| d_1 | > T$ and/or $| d_2 | > T$, then the lower bound l_h, and the upper bound u_h of the horizontal range R_h can be calculated by applying the following twelve cases. Otherwise set $l_h = 0$ and $u_h = 0$.

Case 1: if $(g_x < g_l \,\&\, g_x < g_r)$ and $(| d_1 | > T \,\&\, | d_2 | > T)$

Then, $l_h = 0$ and $u_h = \min\left(g_l - T - 1,\; g_r - T - 1\right)$

Case 2: if $(g_x < g_l \;\&\; g_x < g_r)$ and $(| d_1 | > T \;\&\; | d_2 | \le T)$

Then, $l_h = \max(g_r - T, 0)$ and $u_h = \min\left(g_l - T - 1,\; g_r - 1\right)$

Case 3: if $(g_x < g_l \;\&\; g_x < g_r)$ and $(| d_1 | \le T \;\&\; | d_2 | > T)$

Then, $l_h = \max(g_l - T, 0)$ and $u_h = \min\left(g_r - T - 1,\; g_l - 1\right)$

Figure 9. Nine overlapped 3×3 blocks

Ind	g_u	Ind	g_u	Ind	g_u	
g_l	g_x	g_r /g_l	g_x	g_r /g_l	g_x	g_r
Ind	g_b/g_u	Ind	g_b/g_u	Ind	g_b/g_u	
g_l	g_x	g_r /g_l	g_x	g_r /g_l	g_x	g_r
Ind	g_b/g_u	Ind	g_b/g_u	Ind	g_b/g_u	
g_l	g_x	g_r /g_l	g_x	g_r /g_l	g_x	g_r
	g_b		g_b		g_b	

Case 4: if $(g_x > g_l \;\&\; g_x > g_r)$ and $(|d_1| > T \;\&\; |d_2| > T)$

Then, $l_h = \max\left(g_l + T + 1,\; g_r + T + 1\right)$ and $u_h = 255$

Case 5: if $(g_x > g_l \;\&\; g_x > g_r)$ and $(|d_1| > T \;\&\; |d_2| \le T)$

Then, $l_h = \max\left(g_l + T + 1,\; g_r + 1\right)$ and $u_h = \min\left(g_r + T, 255\right)$

Case 6: if $(g_x > g_l \;\&\; g_x > g_r)$ and $(|d_1| \le T \;\&\; |d_2| > T)$

Then, $l_h = \max\left(g_l + 1,\; g_r + T + 1\right)$ and $u_h = \min\left(g_l + T, 255\right)$

Case 7: if $(g_l \ge g_x \ge g_r)$ and $(|d_1| > T \;\&\; |d_2| > T)$

Then, $l_h = g_r + T + 1,$ and $u_h = g_l - T - 1$

Case 8: if $(g_l \ge g_x \ge g_r)$ and $(|d_1| > T \;\&\; |d_2| \le T)$

Then, $l_h = g_r,$ and $u_h = \min(g_r + T, g_l - T - 1)$

Case 9: if $(g_l \ge g_x \ge g_r)$ and $(|d_1| \le T \;\&\; |d_2| > T)$

Then, $l_h = \max(g_r + T + 1,\; g_l - T)$ and $u_h = g_l$

Case 10: if $(g_l \le g_x \le g_r)$ and $(|d_1| > T \;\&\; |d_2| > T)$

Then, $l_h = g_l + T + 1$, and $u_h = g_r - T - 1$

Case 11: if $(g_l \le g_x \le g_r)$ and $(|d_1| > T \;\&\; |d_2| \le T)$

Then, $l_h = \max(g_r - T, g_l + T + 1)$ and $u_h = g_r$

Case 12: if $(g_l \le g_x \le g_r)$ and $(|d_1| \le T \;\&\; |d_2| > T)$

Then, $l_h = g_l$ and $u_h = \max(g_r - T - 1, g_l + T)$

Step 4

If $|d_3| > T$ and/or $|d_4| > T$, then the lower bound l_v, and the upper bound u_v of the vertical range R_v can be calculated by applying the following twelve cases. Otherwise set $l_v = 0$ and $u_v = 0$.

Case 13: if $(g_x < g_u \;\&\; g_x < g_b)$ and $(|d_3| > T \;\&\; |d_4| > T)$

Then, $l_v = 0$ and $u_v = \min(g_u - T - 1,\ g_b - T - 1)$

Case 14: if $(g_x < g_u \;\&\; g_x < g_b)$ and $(|d_3| > T \;\&\; |d_4| \le T)$

Then, $l_v = \max(g_b - T, 0)$ and $u_v = \min(g_u - T - 1,\ g_b - 1)$

Case 15: if $(g_x < g_u \;\&\; g_x < g_b)$ and $(|d_3| \le T \;\&\; |d_4| > T)$

Then, $l_v = \max(g_u - T, 0)$ and $u_v = \min(g_b - T - 1,\ g_u - 1)$

Case 16: if $(g_x > g_u \;\&\; g_x > g_b)$ and $(|d_3| > T \;\&\; |d_4| > T)$

Then, $l_v = \max(g_u + T + 1,\ g_b + T + 1)$ and $u_v = 255$

Case 17: if $(g_x > g_u \;\&\; g_x > g_b)$ and $(|d_3| > T \;\&\; |d_4| \le T)$

Then, $l_v = \max(g_u + T + 1,\ g_b + 1)$ and $u_v = \min(g_b + T, 255)$

Case 18: if $(g_x > g_u \;\&\; g_x > g_b)$ and $(|d_3| \le T \;\&\; |d_4| > T)$

Then, $l_v = \max(g_u + 1,\ g_b + T + 1)$ and $u_v = \min(g_u + T, 255)$

Case 19: if $(g_u \geq g_x \geq g_b)$ and $(|d_3| > T\ \&\ |d_4| > T)$

Then, $l_v = g_b + T + 1$, and $u_v = g_u - T - 1$

Case 20: if $(g_u \geq g_x \geq g_b)$ and $(|d_3| > T\ \&\ |d_4| \leq T)$

Then, $l_v = g_r$, and $u_v = \min(g_b + T, g_u - T - 1)$

Case 21: if $(g_u \geq g_x \geq g_b)$ and $(|d_3| \leq T\ \&\ |d_4| > T)$

Then, $l_v = \max(g_b + T + 1,\ g_u - T)$ and $u_v = g_u$

Case 22: if $(g_u \leq g_x \leq g_b)$ and $(|d_3| > T\ \&\ |d_4| > T)$

Then, $l_v = g_u + T + 1$, and $u_v = g_b - T - 1$

Case 23: if $(g_u \leq g_x \leq g_b)$ and $(|d_3| > T\ \&\ |d_4| \leq T)$

Then, $l_v = \max(g_b - T, g_u + T + 1)$ and $u_v = g_b$

Case 24: if $(g_u \leq g_x \leq g_b)$ and $(|d_3| \leq T\ \&\ |d_4| > T)$

Then, $l_v = g_u$ and $u_v = \max(g_b - T - 1, g_u + T)$

Step 5

Now the final lower bound, l_f and the final upper bound, u_f can be calculated from l_h, u_h, l_v, and u_v in the following manner. And a normalized pixel value g_f can also be calculated. Furthermore, a flag value is calculated in the following manner.

Case 1: If $l_h = 0\ \&\ u_h = 0$,

Then $l_f = l_v$, $u_f = u_v$, $g_f = g_u$, and flag=1

Case 2: If $l_v = 0$ & $u_v = 0$,

Then $l_f = l_h$, $u_f = u_h$, $g_f = g_l$, and flag=0

Case 3: (If the above case 1 and case 2 fails) & $|u_h - l_h| \geq |u_v - l_v|$,

Then $l_f = l_v$, $u_f = u_v$, $g_f = g_u$, and flag=1

Case 4: (If the above case 1 and case 2 fails) & $|u_h - l_h| < |u_v - l_v|$,

Then $l_f = l_h$, $u_f = u_h$, $g_f = g_l$, and flag=0

Step 6

The number of bits, n to be embedded in the target pixel g_x can be calculated as in Eq. (12).

$$n = \text{floor}\left(\log_2 |u_f - l_f + 1|\right) \tag{12}$$

Step 7

If n > 0, take n secret message bits and convert to integer value b, and then calculate the new value of target pixel g_x as in Eq. (13).

$$g_x' = \underset{e}{\text{argmin}}\{|e - g_x| \,|\, |e - g_f| \equiv b \left(\text{mod} 2^n\right) \tag{13}$$

The upper-left neighbor pixel of g_x is g_{ul}. If flag=0 then the LSB bit of g_{ul} is set to 0. If flag=1 then the LSB bit of g_{ul} is set to 1. This LSB bit of g_{ul} will be used as indicator during extraction.

The data extraction is done by raster scanning the image and partitioning into 3×3 overlapped pixel blocks. The 3rd row and 3rd column of a block can be used as 1st row and 1st column for other blocks. For a block the central pixel g_x^* is the target stego-pixel from where the data is to be extracted and let its upper, left, right, and bottom neighbor pixel values are g_u^*, g_l^*, g_r^*, and g_b^* respectively.

Four differences $d_1^* = g_x^* - g_l^*$, $d_2^* = g_r^* - g_x^*$, $d_3^* = g_x^* - g_u^*$, and $d_4^* = g_b^* - g_x^*$ are calculated. If $|d_1^*| \le T$, $|d_2^*| \le T$, $|d_3^*| \le T$, and $|d_4^*| \le T$, then this block is abandoned for extraction, and try for the next block. Otherwise, using steps 3 and 4 of embedding algorithm the values, l_h, u_h, l_v., and u_v are computed. Suppose g_{ul}^* is the upper-left neighbor pixel of g_x^*. If the LSB bit of g_{ul}^* is 0, then set $l_f = l_h$, $u_f = u_h$ and $g_f = g_l$. Otherwise if the LSB bit of g_{ul}^* is 1, then set $l_f = l_v$, $u_f = u_v$ and $g_f = g_u$. Now calculate the number of bits embedded in the target stego-pixel g_x^* using Eq. (14).

$$n = \text{floor}\left(\log_2 |u_f - l_f + 1|\right) \tag{14}$$

And the integer value b is calculated as in Eq. (15)

$$b \equiv \left|g_x^* - g_f\right| \left(\text{mod}\, 2^n\right) \tag{15}$$

Finally, this b value is converted into n bit binary.

Results and Comparison

The experimental results of the adaptive PVD techniques are compared with one-way PVD (Wu & Tsai, 2003) in Table 3. The PSNR and hiding capacity of the 3×3 pixel block adaptive technique (Swain, 2016) is not better than one-way PVD. Although the PSNR of 2×2 pixel block adaptive (Swain, 2016) PVD is lesser than that of one-way PVD, but the hiding capacity is improved. The main advantages of adaptive PVD technique are that these are resistant to PDH analysis. The security of these techniques is evaluated by tools like, (i) RS steganalysis, and (ii) PDH steganalysis (Pradhan, Sahu, Swain & Sekhar, 2016).

The PDH analysis of the adaptive PVD schemes is shown in Figure 10 and Figure 11 for two sample images. The solid line curve is the PDH of original image and dotted line curves are the PDH of the stego-image. It can be observed from the graphs that in the PDH of stego-images there are no step effects. So the adaptive PVD techniques are resistant to PDH analysis.

Figure 12 and Figure 13 represents the RS diagrams for the adaptive PVD schemes for Lena and Baboon images respectively. The curves for R_m and R_{-m} are straight lines and almost overlap with each other. And the curves

Table 3. Comparison of the results

Images 512×512 (Color)	One-Way PVD (Wu and Tsai, 2003)				Swain's (2016) Adaptive Technique for 3×3 pixel Blocks, With T=10				Swain's (2016) Adaptive Technique for 2×2 Pixel Blocks			
	PSNR	Maximum Capacity	r	Bit Rate	PSNR	Maximum Capacity	r	Bit Rate	PSNR	Maximum Capacity	r	Bit Rate
Lena	53.76	1232606	0.9999	1.56	50.57	116831	0.9998	0.15	46.17	1341192	0.9996	1.71
Baboon	44.21	1403491	0.9996	1.78	49.56	481201	0.9999	0.61	48.49	1489945	0.9998	1.89
Peppers	51.79	1174751	0.9999	1.49	50.27	180578	0.9999	0.23	47.06	1350251	0.9998	1.72
Jet	53.93	1220544	0.9999	1.55	50.45	112053	0.9998	0.14	46.18	1267690	0.9995	1.61
Boat	49.10	1278971	0.9999	1.62	49.98	289397	0.9999	0.37	47.29	1424967	0.9998	1.81
House	51.10	1256404	0.9999	1.59	50.20	210858	0.9999	0.27	44.73	1339985	0.9996	1.70
Average	50.64	1261127	0.9998	1.59	50.17	231819	0.9998	0.29	46.65	1369005	0.9997	1.74

Figure 10. Pixel difference histogram for Lena image

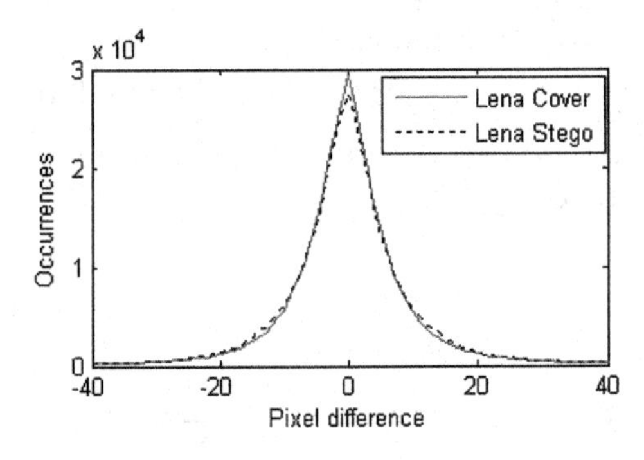

(a) Adaptive PVD with 2×2 pixel block

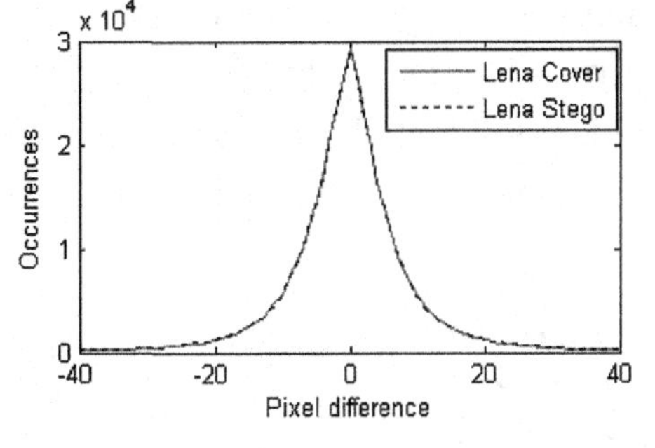

(b) Adaptive PVD with 3×3 pixel block

Figure 11. Pixel difference histogram for baboon image

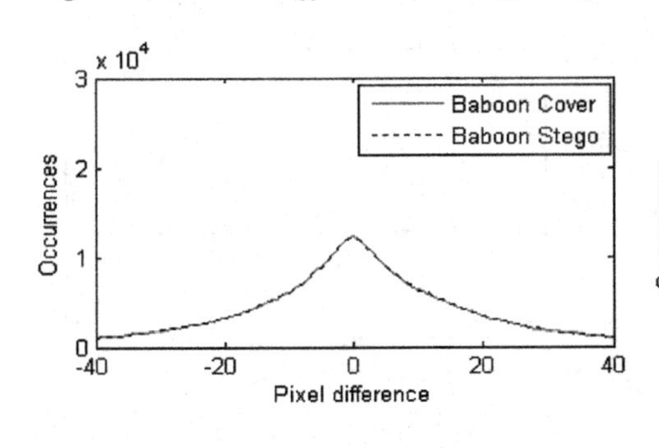

(a) Adaptive PVD with 2×2 pixel block

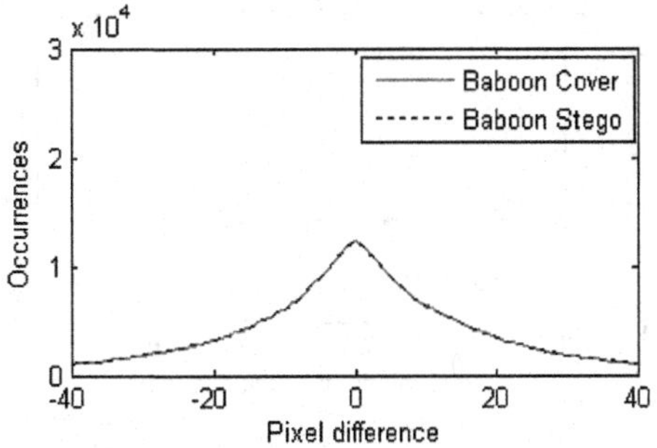

(b) Adaptive PVD with 3×3 pixel block

for S_m and S_{-m} are straight lines and almost overlap with each other. Thus, the relation $R_m \cong R_{-m} > S_m \cong S_{-m}$ is true. This confirms that the RS analysis cannot detect the adaptive PVD schemes.

ADAPTIVE PVD TECHNIQUE WITH OPTIMIZED RESULTS

The idea of adaptive PVD described in (Pradhan, Sekhar & Swain, 2017) produces the improved results using 2×3 and 3×2 pixel blocks. The results are found to be optimal as compared to other adaptive PVD techniques.

Adaptive PVD Technique With 2×3 Pixel Blocks

The data embedding is performed by traversing the image in raster scan order and splitting the image into blocks of size 2×3 pixels. A sample block is given in Figure 14(a). The four corner pixels, g_1, g_2, g_3, and g_4 are used to hide confidential message bits, based on the two center pixels g_u, and g_b. The embedding scheme is narrated in the steps below.

Figure 12. RS analysis with Lena Image

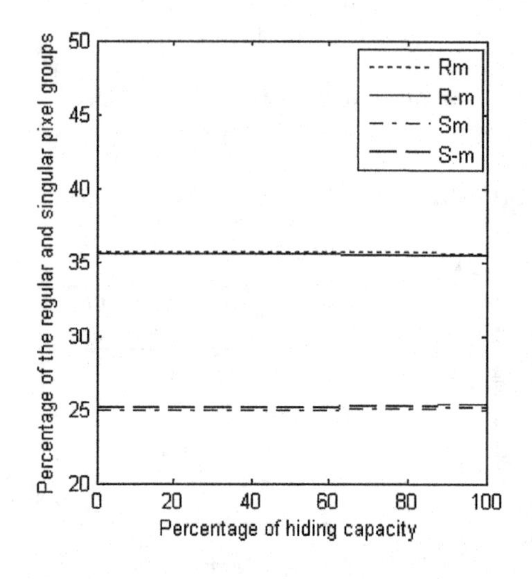

(a) Adaptive PVD with 2×2 pixel block

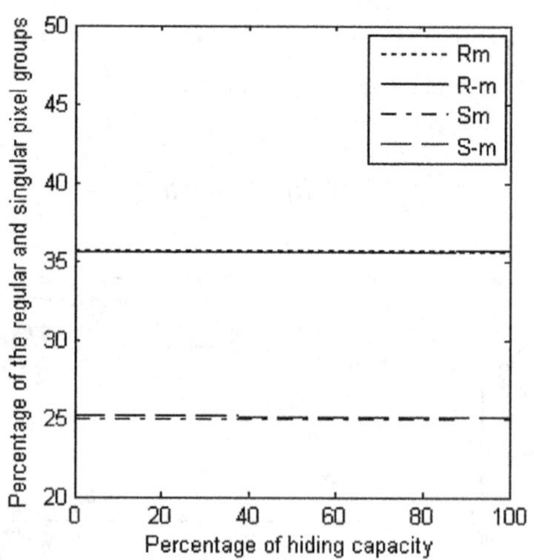

(b) Adaptive PVD with 3×3 pixel block

Figure 13. RS analysis with Baboon Image

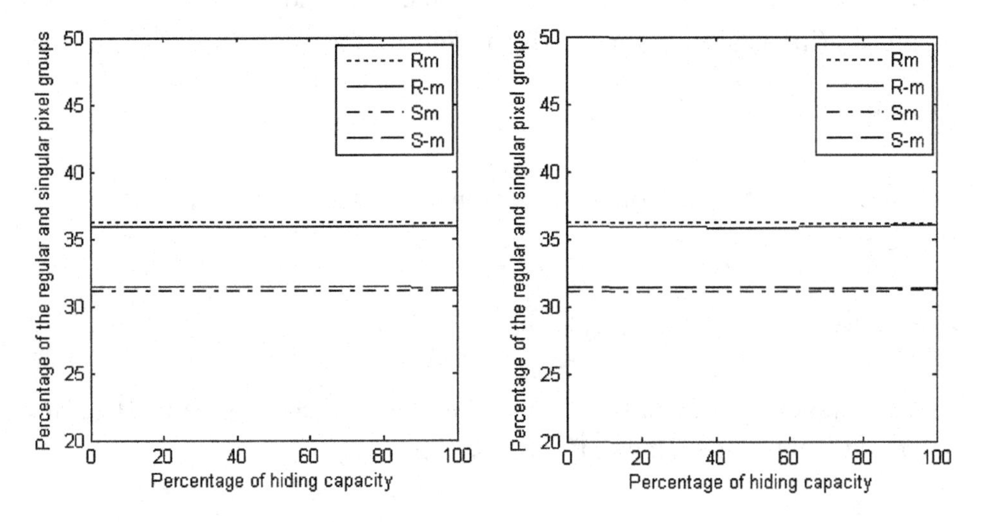

(a) Adaptive PVD with 2×2 pixel block (b) Adaptive PVD with 3×3 pixel block

Step 1

For i=1, 2, 3, 4, eight difference values, $d_{iu} = (g_i - g_u)$ and $d_{ib} = (g_i - g_b)$ are calculated.

Step 2

For i=1, 2, 3, 4, for target pixel g_i the lower and upper bounds of the range, l_i and u_i respectively are calculated based on the four cases narrated below.

Case 1: if $d_{iu} > 0$, & $d_{ib} > 0$, then $l_i = \max(g_u + 1,\ g_b + 1)$, and $u_i = 255$
Case 2: if $d_{iu} \leq 0$, & $d_{ib} \leq 0$, then $l_i = 0$, and $u_i = \min(g_u, g_b)$

The term min(a, b) is a function to find the minimum of two values a and b.

Case 3: if $d_{iu} > 0$, & $d_{ib} \leq 0$, then $l_i = g_u + 1$, and $u_i = g_b$
Case 4: if $d_{iu} \leq 0$, & $d_{ib} > 0$, then $l_i = g_b + 1$, and $u_i = g_u$

Thus, four sets of lower and upper bounds, (i) l_1 and u_1 for g_1, (ii) l_2 and u_2 for g_2, (iii) l_3 and u_3 for g_3, (iv) l_4 and u_4 for g_4 are calculated.

Step 3

For i=1, 2, 3, 4, the n_i, should be the embedding length in g_i. It is estimated by the Eq. (15).

$$n_i = \min(\text{floor}(\log_2 |u_i - l_i + 1|), 3) \tag{15}$$

In equation 1 floor is a function to find the lower integer of its floating-point argument. For example, floor (3.4) =3.

Step 4

For i=1, 2, 3, 4, the n_i, bits of secret data are taken and converted to decimal equivalents b_i. After hiding b_i in g_i, the new value g_i' is calculated as in Eq. (16).

$$g_i' = \underset{e}{\text{argmin}} \left\{ \left| e - g_i \right| \mid \left| e - g_u \right| \equiv b_i \left(\text{mod} 2^{n_i} \right), e \in \left[l_i, u_i \right] \right\} \tag{16}$$

It means, for the original pixel g_i, the stego pixel g_i' is a value e chosen from the range $[l_i, u_i]$ such that it satisfies the conditions, (i) $|e - g_u|$ mod 2^{n_i} $= b_i$, and (ii) $|e - g_i|$ is minimum. Thus, the stego-pixel block of size 2×3 is shown by Figure 14b.

The Data Extraction

The data extraction can be performed by traversing the stego image in raster scan fashion and partitioning it into blocks of sizes 2×3. Figure 14 (b) is an example of a 2×3 stego-pixel block. Data is to be extracted from the pixels g_1', g_2', g_3' and g_4' using the following steps.

Figure 14. (a) The original block, (b) The stego block

g_1	g_u	g_2
g_3	g_b	g_4

(a)

g_1'	g_u	g_2'
g_3'	g_b	g_4'

(b)

Step 1

For i=1, 2, 3, 4, the eight difference values $d_{iu} = (g_i' - g_u)$ and $d_{ib} = (g_i' - g_b)$ are calculated.

Step 2

For i=1, 2, 3, 4, assume that lower bounds and upper bounds of the ranges for the four corner pixels are l_i and u_i. These are calculated using the step 2 of embedding procedure.

Step 3

The embedding length, n_i is calculated using the equation in step 3 of embedding procedure.

Step 4

For i=1, 2, 3, 4, the decimal equivalent of the binary data to be extracted from g_i' is b_i. This is calculated using Eq. (17). Finally, each b_i is converted to n_i, binary bits.

$$b_i \equiv \left|g_i' - g_u\right| \left(\bmod 2^{n_i}\right). \tag{17}$$

Eq. (17) means that b_i is a smallest satisfying the condition $(b_i \bmod 2^{n_i}) = \left|g_i' - g_u\right|$.

Adaptive PVD Technique With 3×2 Pixel Blocks

The data embedding is performed by traversing the image in raster scan order and splitting the image into blocks of size 3×2 pixels. A sample block is given in Figure 15 (a). The four corner pixels, g_1, g_2, g_3 and g_4 are used to hide confidential message bits, based on the two center pixels g_L and g_r. The embedding scheme is narrated in the steps below.

Step 1

For i=1, 2, 3, 4, eight difference values, $d_{iL} = (g_i - g_L)$ and $d_{ir} = (g_i - g_r)$ are calculated.

Step 2

For i=1, 2, 3, 4, for target pixel g_i the lower and upper bounds of the range, l_i and u_i respectively are calculated based on the four cases narrated below.

Case 1: if $d_{iL} > 0$, & $d_{ir} > 0$, then $l_i = \max(g_L + 1,\ g_r + 1)$, and $u_i = 255$
Case 2: if $d_{iL} \leq 0$, & $d_{ir} \leq 0$, then $l_i = 0$, and $u_i = \min(g_L,\ g_r)$
Case 3: if $d_{iL} > 0$, & $d_{ir} \leq 0$, then $l_i = g_L + 1$, and $u_i = g_r$
Case 4: if $d_{iL} \leq 0$, & $d_{ir} > 0$, then $l_i = g_r + 1$, and $u_i = g_L$

Thus, four sets of lower and upper bounds, (i) l_1 and u_1 for g_1, (ii) l_2 and u_2 for g_2, (iii) l_3 and u_3 for g_3, (iv) l_4 and u_4 for g_4 are calculated.

Step 3

For i=1, 2, 3, 4, the the embedding length in g_i is n_i,. It is estimated by the Eq. (18). The term min(a, b) is a function to find the minimum of two values a and b

$$n_i = \min(\text{floor}(\log_2 |u_i - l_i + 1|), 3) \tag{18}$$

Step 4

For i=1, 2, 3, 4, the n_i, bits of secret data are taken and converted to decimal equivalents b_i. After hiding b_i in g_i, the new value $g_i^{'}$ is calculated by Eq. (19).

$$g_i^{'} = \underset{e}{\operatorname{argmin}} \left\{ \left| e - g_i \right| \mid \left| e - g_L \right| \equiv b_i \left(\bmod 2^{n_i} \right), e \in \left[l_i, u_i \right] \right\} \tag{19}$$

Thus, the stego-pixel block of size 3×2 is as given in Figure 15 (b).

The Data Extraction

The data extraction can be performed by traversing the stego image in raster scan fashion and partitioning into blocks of sizes 3×2. Figure 15(b) is an example of a 3×2 stego-pixel block. Data is to be extracted from the pixels $g_1^{'}$, $g_2^{'}$, $g_3^{'}$ and $g_4^{'}$ using the following steps.

Step 1

For i=1, 2, 3, 4, the eight difference values $d_{iL} = (g_i^{'} - g_L)$ and $d_{ir} = (g_i^{'} - g_r)$ are calculated.

Step 2

For i=1, 2, 3, 4, assume that lower bounds and upper bounds of the ranges for the four corner pixels are l_i and u_i. These are calculated using the step 2 of embedding procedure

Step 3

The embedding length, n_i is calculated using the equation in step 3 of the embedding procedure

Step 4

For i=1, 2, 3, 4, the decimal equivalent of the binary data to be extracted from $g_i^{'}$ is b_i. This is calculated using Eq. (20). Finally, each b_i is converted to n_i binary bits.

Figure 15. (a) The original block, (b) The stego block

g_1	g_2
g_L	g_r
g_3	g_4

(a)

g_1'	g_2'
g_L	g_r
g_3'	g_4'

(b)

$$b_i \equiv \left|g_i' - g_L\right| \left(\bmod 2^{n_i}\right) \tag{20}$$

Experimental Results and Discussion

Figure 16 and Figure 17 are the stego-images. The embedding length in each of these stego-images is 140000 (one lakh and forty thousand) bits.

Look at the last rows in Table 4 and Table 5, the average over the results of seven sample images is given. It can be noticed that both the capacity and PSNR of the optimizes adaptive PVD techniques are improved over the Swain's 2×2 and Luo et al.'s 1×3 pixel block adaptive PVD techniques.

The security of these techniques is evaluated by tools like, (i) RS steganalysis, and (ii) PDH steganalysis (Pradhan et al., 2016). The RS steganalysis graphs of Lena, Baboon, Peppers, and Jet images are represented in Figure 18 and Figure 19 for 2×3 pixel block adaptive PVD and 3×2 pixel block adaptive PVD respectively. In all the cases, graphs for R_m and R_{-m} are linear and very near to each other. Similarly, the graphs for S_m and S_{-m} are linear and

Figure 16. The stego images for adaptive PVD technique in 2×3 pixel blocks (variant 1)

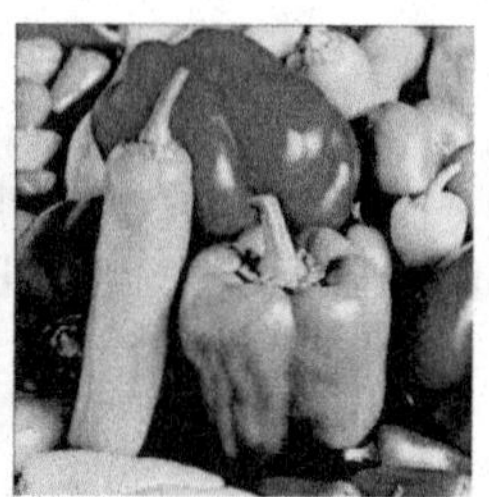

Figure 17. The stego images for adaptive PVD technique in 3×2 pixel blocks (variant 2)

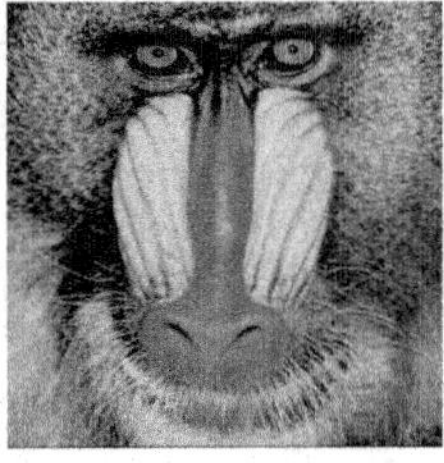
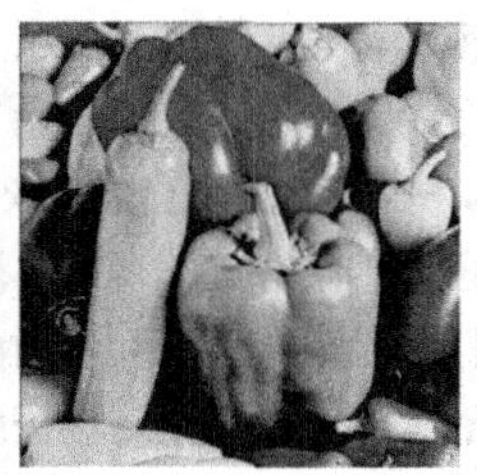

Table 4. Results of 2×2 and 1×3 pixel block adaptive PVD techniques

Images 512× 512	Swain's (2016) 2×2 Pixel Block Adaptive PVD				Luo et al.'s (2011) 1×3 Pixel Block Adaptive PVD			
	PSNR	**Capacity**	**Q**	**BPB**	**PSNR**	**Capacity**	**Q**	**BPB**
Lena	45.04	1341191	0.999	1.70	48.79	229037	0.999	0.29
Baboon	47.13	1489945	0.999	1.89	48.03	611197	0.999	0.77
Peppers	45.73	1350251	0.999	1.71	48.32	264058	0.999	0.33
Jet	44.86	1267690	0.999	1.61	48.76	145755	0.999	0.18
Boat	46.08	1424967	0.999	1.81	48.20	389588	0.999	0.49
House	43.58	1339985	0.999	1.70	48.41	259413	0.999	0.32
Tiffany	45.23	1341498	0.999	1.70	48.70	165873	0.999	0.21
Average	45.37	1365075	0.999	1.61	48.45	294988	0.999	0.37

Table 5. Results of 2×3 and 3×2 pixel block adaptive PVD technique

Images 512× 512	Pradhan et al.'s (2017) 2×3 Pixel Block Adaptive PVD				Pradhan et al.'s (2017) 3×2 Pixel Block Adaptive PVD			
	PSNR	**Capacity**	**Q**	**BPB**	**PSNR**	**Capacity**	**Q**	**BPB**
Lena	50.89	1445784	0.999	1.83	50.61	1425521	0.999	1.81
Baboon	52.29	1532417	0.999	1.94	52.36	1527208	0.999	1.94
Peppers	51.29	1418101	0.999	1.80	51.22	1409621	0.999	1.79
Jet	50.65	1381432	0.999	1.75	50.77	1362765	0.999	1.73
Boat	51.42	1479835	0.999	1.88	51.43	1474106	0.999	1.88
House	49.09	1431346	0.999	1.82	49.18	1429845	0.999	1.82
Tiffany	50.88	1430606	0.999	1.81	50.95	1420300	0.999	1.81
Average	**50.93**	**1445645**	0.999	1.83	**50.93**	**1435623**	0.999	1.82

close to each other. Hence the relation $R_m \cong R_{-m} > S_m \cong S_{-m}$ is valid. So, we can conclude that these techniques can't be detected by RS analysis.

Figure 20 and Figure 21 represents the PDH analysis for Lena, Baboon, Peppers, and Jet images for the 2×3 pixel block adaptive PVD and 3×2 pixel block adaptive PVD respectively. In all these eight graphs the solid line curve is for original image and the dotted line curve is for stego-image. We can verify that there are no step effects in the curves of the stego-images. This proves that these techniques could not be detected by pixel difference histogram analysis.

Figure 18. RS analysis of 2×3 pixel block adaptive PVD, for four Images

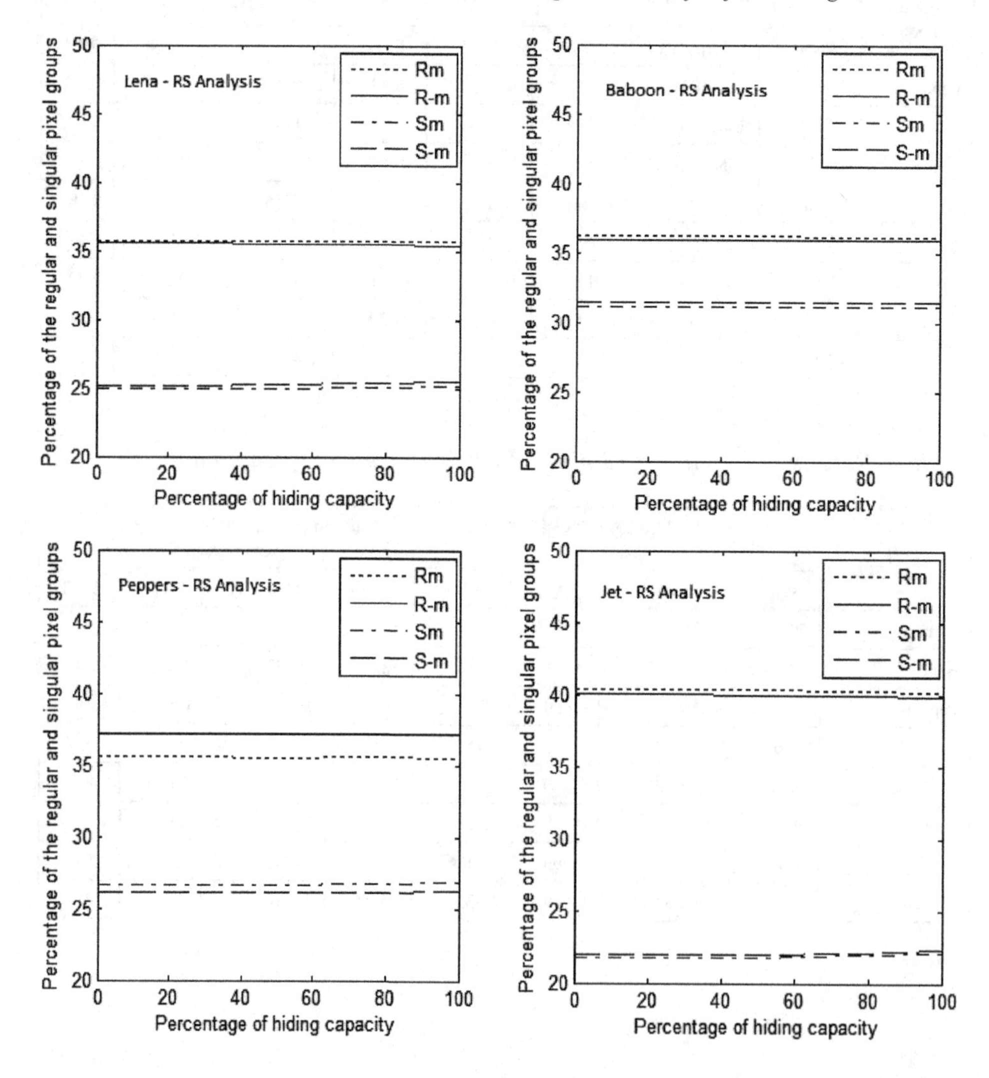

Figure 19. RS analysis of 3×2 pixel block adaptive PVD, for four Images

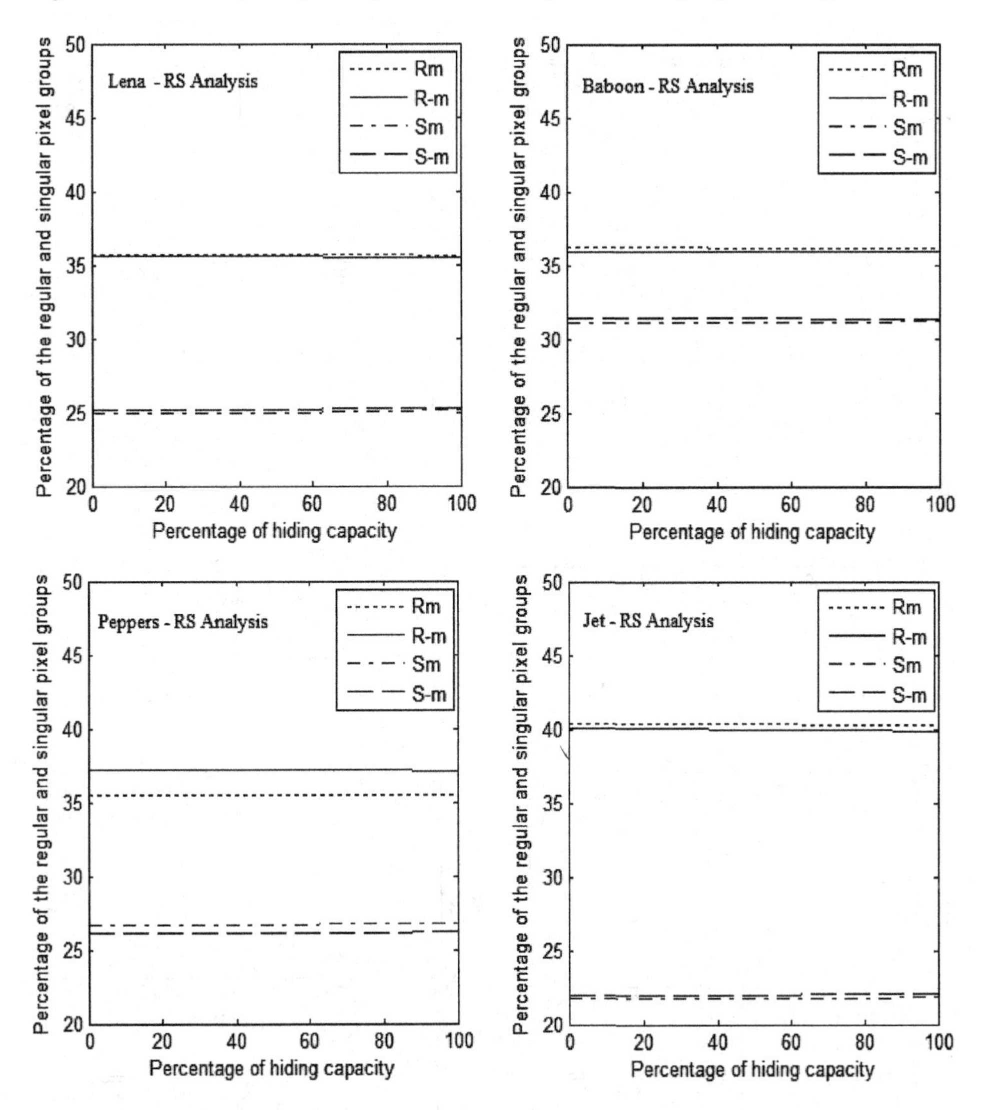

CONCLUSION

The one-way PVD technique is vulnerable to PDH analysis. The seven-way PVD increases the hiding capacity and is resistant to PDH analysis, but it reduces the PSNR slightly. The adaptive PVD techniques are state of art

Figure 20. PDH analysis of 2×3 pixel block adaptive PVD for four images

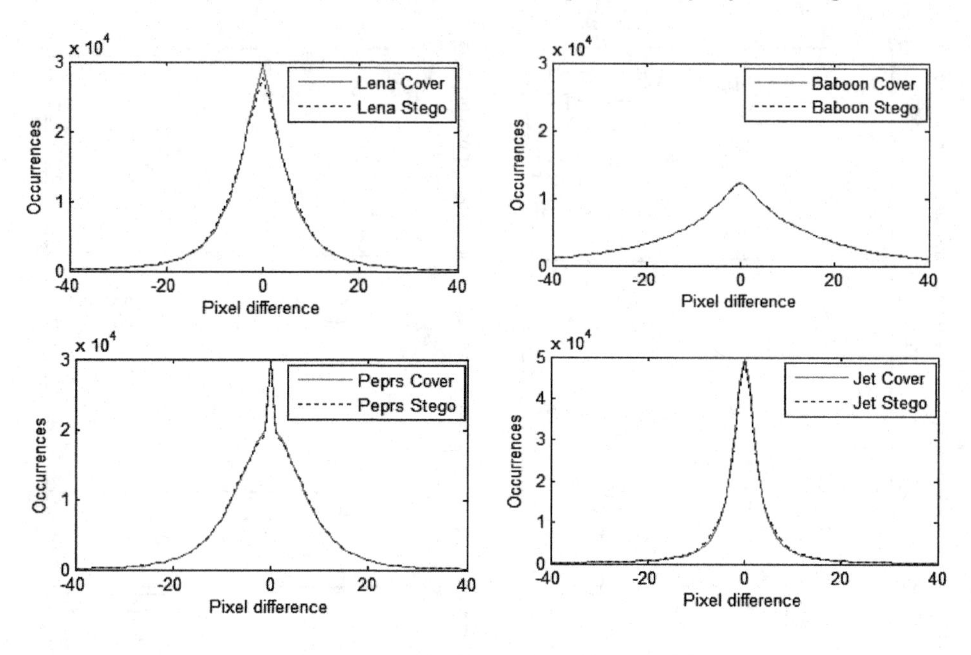

Figure 21. PDH analysis of 3×2 pixel block adaptive PVD for four images

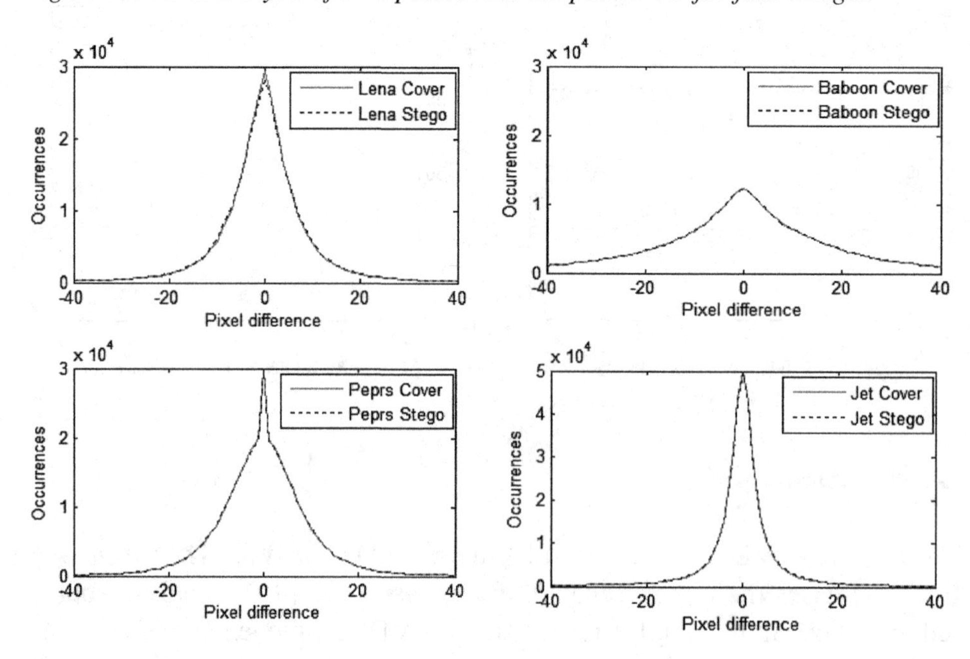

modern PVD techniques with tolerance to PDH analysis. The optimized adaptive technique achieves higher embedding length and lesser distortion as compared that of Luo et al.'s and Swain's adaptive PVD techniques. Furthermore, it has been experimentally proved that the RS analysis and PDH analysis can't detect the optimized adaptive PVD technique.

REFERENCES

Balasubramanian, C., Selvakumar, S., & Geetha, S. (2014). High payload image steganography with reduced distortion using octonary pairing scheme. *Multimedia Tools and Applications*, *73*(3), 2223–2245. doi:10.100711042-013-1640-4

Chang, K. C., Chang, C. P., Huang, P. S., & Tu, T. M. (2008). A novel image steganography method using tri-way pixel value differencing. *Journal of Multimedia*, *3*(2), 37–44. doi:10.4304/jmm.3.2.37-44

Lee, Y. P., Lee, J. C., Chen, W. K., Chang, K. C., Su, I. J., & Chang, C. P. (2012). High-payload image hiding with quality recovery using tri-way pixel-value differencing. *Information Sciences*, *191*, 214–225. doi:10.1016/j.ins.2012.01.002

Luo, W., Huang, F., & Huang, J. (2011). A more secure steganography based on adaptive pixel-value differencing scheme. *Multimedia Tools and Applications*, *52*(2-3), 407–430. doi:10.100711042-009-0440-3

Pradhan, A., Sahu, A. K., Swain, G., & Sekhar, K. R. (2016). Performance evaluation parameters of image steganography techniques. *Proceedings of IEEE International Conference on Research Advances in Integrated Navigation Systems*, 1-8. 10.1109/RAINS.2016.7764399

Pradhan, A., Sekhar, K. R., & Swain, G. (2016). Digital image steganography based on seven way pixel value differencing. *Indian Journal of Science and Technology*, *9*(37), 1–11. doi:10.17485/ijst/2016/v9i37/88557

Pradhan, A., Sekhar, K. R., & Swain, G. (2017). Adaptive PVD steganography using horizontal, vertical, and diagonal edges in six-pixel blocks. *Security and Communication Networks*, *2017*, 1–13. doi:10.1155/2017/1924618

Swain, G. (2016). Adaptive pixel value differencing steganography using both vertical and horizontal edges. *Multimedia Tools and Applications*, *75*(21), 13541–13556. doi:10.100711042-015-2937-2

Wu, D. C., & Tsai, W. H. (2003). A steganograhic method for images by pixel value differencing. *Pattern Recognition Letters*, *24*(9-10), 1613–1626. doi:10.1016/S0167-8655(02)00402-6

Zhang, X., & Wang, S. (2004). Vulnerability of pixel-value differencing steganography to histogram analysis and modification for enhanced security. *Pattern Recognition Letters*, *25*(3), 331–339. doi:10.1016/j.patrec.2003.10.014

Chapter 4
PVD Steganography Based on Correlation and Maximum Pixel Value Difference

ABSTRACT

In this chapter, the author describes the pixel value correlation-based steganography techniques and maximum pixel value difference-based steganography techniques. The pixel value-based correlation steganography techniques utilize the relationship among the pixel values of a block, whereas the maximum pixel value difference steganography techniques utilize the largest pixel value difference among different pairs of pixels in the block. Although the PSNR values of these techniques are better as compared to the traditional PVD schemes, the hiding capacity is not improved.

INTRODUCTION

The traditional pixel value differencing (PVD) techniques finds the difference value between two pixels and decides the embedding capacity accordingly (Wu & Tsai, 2003; Chang, Chang, Huang & Tu, 2008; Lee, Lee, Chen, Chang, Su & Chang, 2012). This chapter describes two new tracks of PVD, (i) PVD based on correlation, and (ii) PVD based on maximum difference. PVD steganography based on the correlation of target pixel with its neighboring pixels has seven variants, namely (i) two neighbor correlation, (ii) three neighbor correlation, (iii) four neighbor correlation, (iv) five neighbor

DOI: 10.4018/978-1-5225-7516-0.ch004

correlation, (v) six neighbor correlation, (vi) seven neighbor correlation, and (vii) eight neighbor correlation. These schemes exploit the correlation of target pixel with 2, 3, 4, 5, 6, 7, and 8 neighboring pixels respectively (Swain & Lenka, 2013; Swain & Lenka, 2015). PVD steganography techniques based on maximum pixel value difference has seven variants, namely (i) two neighbor maximum differencing, (ii) three neighbor maximum differencing, (iii) four neighbor maximum differencing, (iv) five neighbor maximum differencing, (v) six neighbor maximum differencing, (vi) seven neighbor maximum differencing, and (vii) eight neighbor maximum differencing. These schemes use 2, 3, 4, 5, 6, 7, and 8 neighboring pixels respectively (Pradhan, Sharma & Swain, 2012; Swain, 2014).

PVD STEGANOGRAPHY BASED ON CORRELATION

The PVD technique proposed by Chang & Tseng (2012) exploits the correlation of a target pixel with its neighboring pixels. Although they addressed the fall off boundary problem, but another problem, known as fall in error problem has occurred, which was explained in (Swain & Lenka, 2013). This section describes all the seven variants of PVD based on correlation of target pixel with neighboring pixels (Swain & Lenka, 2013; Swain & Lenka, 2015).

Two Neighbor Correlation

This scheme was proposed by Swain & Lenka (2013). The image is raster scanned and pixels are classified into three categories, Figure 1. The gray colored pixels can be used as targets and neighbors. The light gray colored pixels are not at all used. But the white colored pixels are treated as neighbors only.

The two neighbor correlation scheme uses two neighbors, upper-right and upper for calculating the embedding capacity of the target pixel. As shown in Figure 1, let P_X is a target pixel, P_U and P_{UR} are the two neighbors. Let g_x, g_u and g_{ur} are the respective pixel values. Then the difference d is calculated as in Eq. (1).

$$d = (g_u + g_{ur}) / 2 - g_x \quad (1)$$

The d value will be smaller for smoother regions and larger for edge regions. If d value is one in the list {-1, 0, 1} then the target pixel will not be used to hide data. Otherwise if d ≥2, n bits can be hidden in the target pixel. This n value is calculated using Eq. (2).

$$n = \log_2 |d|, \text{if } |d| > 1 \tag{2}$$

Now n data bits will be represented by a decimal value b. A new difference d' is calculated using Eq. (3).

$$d' = \begin{cases} 2^n + b, \ if\ d > 1 \\ -(2^n + b), \ if\ d < 1 \end{cases} \tag{3}$$

After embedding the new value for the target pixel is g_x'. It is calculated as in Eq. (4).

$$g_x' = (g_u + g_{ur}) / 2 - d' \tag{4}$$

For retrieving the data, the stego image is also raster scanned. Suppose P_X^* is the target with upper-right and upper neighbors being P_{UR}^* and P_U^* respectively. The respective pixel values are g_x^*, g_{ur}^* and g_u^*. Then the d^*, a difference value is calculated as in Eq. (5).

Figure 1. Sampling in 2 neighbor correlation scheme

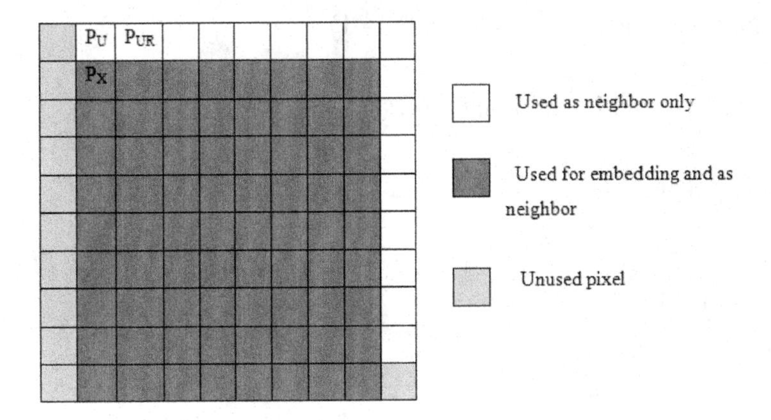

$$d^* = (g^*_{ur} + g^*_u)/2 - g^*_x \qquad (5)$$

If d^* lies in list {-1, 0, 1}, then g^*_x is ignored. Otherwise, n the length of embedded bit stream is estimated using Eq. (6).

$$n = \log_2 |d^*|, \text{if } |d^*| \rangle 1 \qquad (6)$$

Now a decimal value b which is equivalent to the hidden bit stream is calculated as in Eq. (7).

$$b = \begin{cases} d^* - 2^n, \textit{if } d^* > 1 \\ -d^* - 2^n, \textit{if } d^* < 1 \end{cases} \qquad (7)$$

Then the value b is converted to n binary bits.

In exceptional cases the stego gray value of P_X may not lie in the range {0, 255}, if the conditions in the following two cases are satisfied.

Case 1: $(g_u + g_{ur})/2 < 2^{n+1} - 1$ and $d > 1$

Proof:

From above Eq.4,

$$g'_x = (g_u + g_{ur})/2 - d' = (g_u + g_{ur})/2 - (2^n + b).$$

Suppose b value is

$2^n - 1$, then $g'_x = (g_u + g_{ur})/2 - (2^{n+1} - 1)$

Therefore, g'_x will be a negative if $(g_u + g_{ur})/2 < (2^{n+1} - 1)$.

Case 2: $(g_u + g_{ur})/2 + 2^{n+1} > 256$ and $d < 1$

Proof:

From above Eq.4,

$g_x' = (g_u + g_{ur})/2 - d' = (g_u + g_{ur})/2 + (2^n + b).$

Suppose b value is

$2^n - 1$, then $g_x' = (g_u + g_{ur})/2 + 2^{n+1} - 1$

Therefore, $g_x' > 255$ means $(g_u + g_{ur})/2 + 2^{n+1} > 256$.

For d = -1, 0 or 1 the embedding is not done because the extraction does not work at the receiver. This is called as fall in error problem (FOBP)

Case 3: when d value lies in list {-1, 0, 1}, embedding is not done

The FOBP and FIEP checking is applied at the sender during embedding and at receiver during extraction. Thus a target pixel which falls in conditions given in cases 1-3, or in FOBP, are neither used for embedding nor for extraction, simply ignored.

Three Neighbor Correlation

This scheme was proposed by Swain & Lenka (2013). The image is raster scanned and pixels are classified into 3 categories, Figure 2. The gray colored pixels can be used as targets and neighbors. The light gray colored pixels are not at all used. But the white colored pixels are treated as neighbors only.

The three-neighbor correlation scheme uses three neighbors, upper-right, upper-left and upper for calculating embedding capacity of a target pixel. As shown in Figure 2, let P_X is a target pixel, P_U, P_{UR}, and P_{UL} are the three neighbors. Let g_x, g_u, g_{ur}, and g_{ul} are the respective pixel values. Then a difference, d is calculated as in Eq. (8).

$$d = (g_{ur} + g_{ul} + g_u)/3 - g_x \quad (8)$$

The value of d will be smaller for smoother regions and larger for edge regions. But if d value is one in the list {-1, 0, 1} then the target pixel will not be used to hide data. Otherwise if d ≥2, n bits can be hidden. This n value is calculated as in Eq. (9).

$$n = \log_2 |d|, \text{if } |d| > 1 \quad (9)$$

Figure 2. Sampling in 3 neighbor correlation scheme

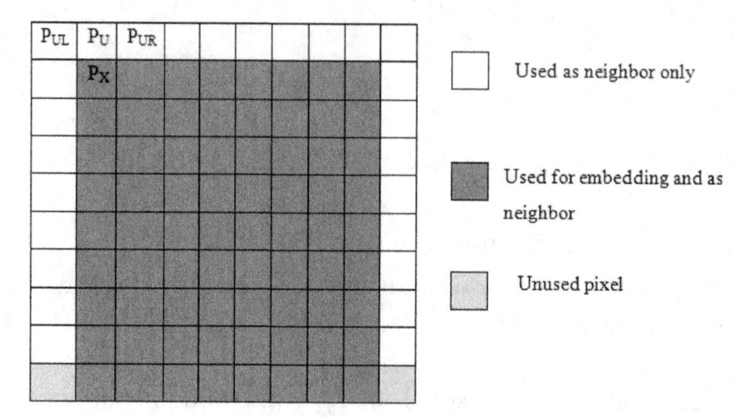

Now n data bits will be represented by a decimal value b. A new difference d' is calculated using Eq. (10).

$$d' = \begin{cases} 2^n + b, & if\, d > 1 \\ -\left(2^n + b\right), & if\, d < 1 \end{cases} \tag{10}$$

Not after embedding the new value for the target pixel is g_x'. This is done using Eq. (11).

$$g_x' = (g_u + g_{ur} + g_{ul}) / 3 - d' \tag{11}$$

The retrieval of data from the stego image is done in similar way as that of two neighbor correlation scheme. The two conditions, FOBP and FIEP are also suitably addressed as in two neighbor correlation scheme.

Four Neighbor Correlation

This scheme was proposed by Swain & Lenka (2013). The image is raster scanned and pixels are classified into 3 categories, Figure 3. The gray colored pixels can be used as targets and neighbors. The light gray colored pixels are not at all used. But the white colored pixels are used as neighbors only.

The four-neighbor correlation scheme uses four neighbors, upper-right, upper, left and upper-left for calculating embedding capacity of a target pixel. As shown in Figure 3, let P_X is a target pixel, P_{UR}, P_U, P_L, and P_{UL} are the

Figure 3. Sampling in 4 neighbor correlation scheme

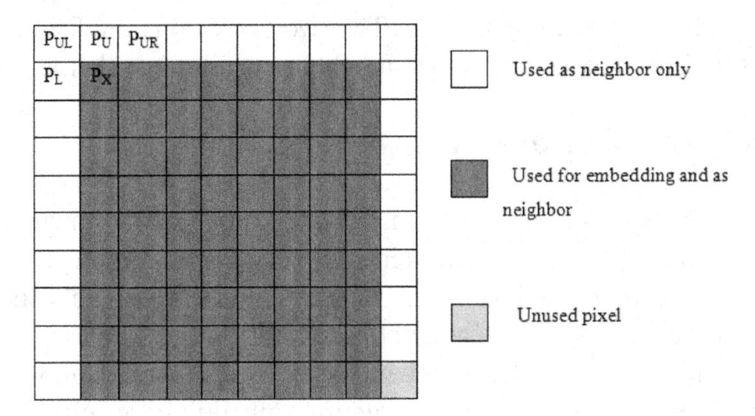

four neighbors. Let g_x, g_{ur}, g_u, g_l and g_{ul} are the respective pixel values. Then a difference, d is calculated as in Eq. (12).

$$d = (g_{ur} + g_u + g_l + g_{ul}) / 4 - g_x \tag{12}$$

The value of d will be smaller for smoother regions and larger for edge regions. But if d value is one in the list {-1, 0, 1} then the target pixel will not be used to hide data. Otherwise if d ≥2, n bits can be hidden. This n value is calculated using Eq. (13).

$$n = \log_2 |d|, \text{if } |d| > 1 \tag{13}$$

Now n data bits will be represented by a decimal value b. A new difference d' is calculated as in Eq. (14).

$$d' = \begin{cases} 2^n + b, & if\, d > 1 \\ -(2^n + b), & if\, d < 1 \end{cases} \tag{14}$$

Not after embedding the new value for the target pixel is g_x'. This is calculated using Eq. (15).

$$g_x' = (g_{ur} + g_u + g_l + g_{ul}) / 4 - d' \tag{15}$$

The retrieval of data from the stego image is done in similar way as that of two neighbor correlation scheme. The two conditions, FOBP and FIEP are also suitably addressed as in two neighbor correlation scheme.

Five Neighbor Correlation

This scheme was proposed by Swain & Lenka (2015). The image is raster scanned and the pixels are classified into two categories, Figure 4. The gray colored pixels can be used as targets and neighbors. The pixels shown by white color are only treated as neighbors.

The five-neighbor correlation scheme uses five neighbors, upper, upper-right, upper-left, left and right for calculating embedding capacity of a target pixel. As shown in Figure 4, let P_X is a target pixel, P_U, P_{UR}, P_{UL}, P_L and P_R are the five neighbors. Let g_x, g_u, g_{ur}, g_{ul}, g_l, and g_r are the respective pixel values. Then a difference, d is calculated as in Eq. (16).

$$d = (g_u + g_{ur} + g_{ul} + g_l + g_r) / 5 - g_x \tag{16}$$

The value of d will be smaller for smoother regions and larger for edge regions. But if d value is one in the list {-1, 0, 1} then the target pixel will not be used to hide data. Otherwise if d $\geq$2, n bits can be hidden. This n value is calculated using Eq. (17).

$$n = \log_2 |d|, \text{if } |d| > 1 \tag{17}$$

Now n data bits will be represented by a decimal value b. A new difference d' is calculated as in Eq. (18).

$$d' = \begin{cases} 2^n + b, \ if\, d > 1 \\ -(2^n + b), \ if\, d < 1 \end{cases} \tag{18}$$

Not after embedding the new value for the target pixel is g_x'. This is done using Eq. (19).

$$g_x' = (g_u + g_{ur} + g_{ul} + g_l + g_r) / 5 - d' \tag{19}$$

Figure 4. Sampling in 5 neighbor correlation scheme

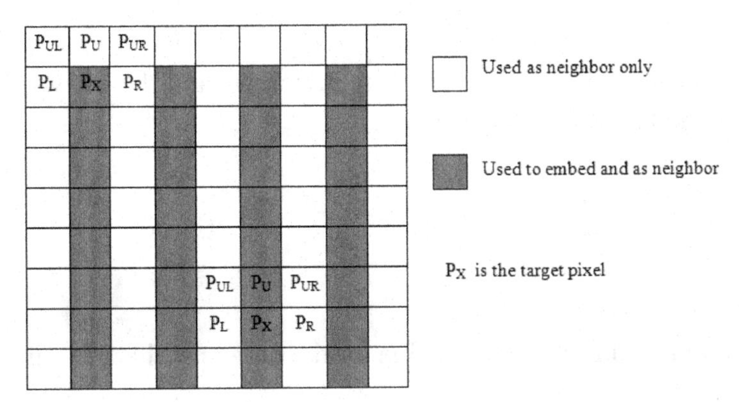

The retrieval of data from the stego image is done in similar way as that of two neighbor correlation scheme. The two conditions, FOBP and FIEP are also suitably addressed as in two neighbor correlation scheme.

Six Neighbor Correlation

This scheme was proposed by Swain & Lenka (2015). The image is raster scanned and the pixels are classified into three categories, Figure 5. The dark gray colored pixels can be used as targets and neighbors. The light gray colored pixels are not at all used. But the white colored pixels are treated as neighbors.

The six neighbor correlation scheme uses six neighbors, upper, upper-right, upper-left, left, right and bottom-left for calculating embedding capacity of a target pixel. As shown in Figure 5, let P_X is a target pixel, P_U, P_{UR}, P_{UL}, P_L, P_R and P_{BL} are the six neighbors. Let g_x, g_u, g_{ur}, g_{ul}, g_l, g_r and g_{bl} are the respective pixel values. Then a difference d, is calculated using Eq. (20).

$$d = (g_u + g_l + g_r + g_{ur} + g_{ul} + g_{bl}) / 6 - g_x \tag{20}$$

The value of d will be smaller for smoother regions and larger for edge regions. But if d value is one in the list {-1, 0, 1} then the target pixel will not be used to hide data. Otherwise if d ≥2, n bits can be hidden. This is done using Eq. (21).

$$n = \log_2 |d|, \text{if } |d| > 1 \quad (21)$$

Now n data bits will be represented by a decimal value b. A new difference d' is calculated as in Eq. (22).

$$d' = \begin{cases} 2^n + b, & if\, d > 1 \\ -\left(2^n + b\right), & if\, d < 1 \end{cases} \quad (22)$$

Not after embedding the new value for the target pixel is g_x'. This is done using Eq. (23).

$$g_x' = (g_u + g_l + g_r + g_{ur} + g_{ul} + g_{bl}) / 6 - d' \quad (23)$$

The retrieval of data from the stego image is done in similar way as that of two neighbor correlation scheme. The two conditions, FOBP and FIEP are also suitably addressed as in two neighbor correlation scheme.

Seven Neighbor Correlation

This scheme was proposed by Swain & Lenka (2015). The image is raster scanned and the pixels are classified into three categories, Figure 6. The dark gray colored pixels can be used as targets. The light gray colored pixel is not at all used. But the white colored pixels are treated only as neighbors.

Figure 5. Sampling in 6 neighbor correlation scheme

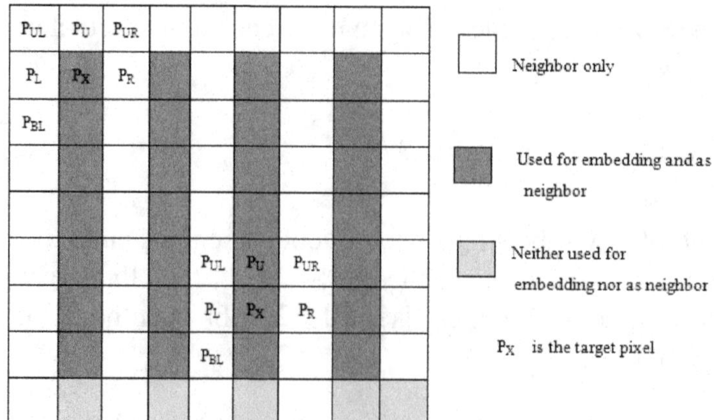

Figure 6. Sampling in 7 neighbor correlation scheme

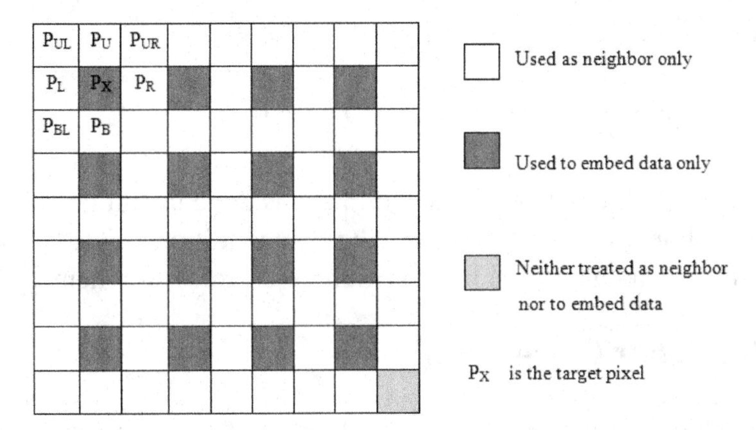

The seven neighbor correlation scheme uses seven neighbors, upper, upper-right, upper-left, left, right, bottom-left and bottom for calculating embedding capacity of a target pixel. As shown in Figure 6, let P_X is a target pixel, P_U, P_{UR}, P_{UL}, P_L, P_R, P_{BL} and P_B are the seven neighbors. Let g_x, g_u, g_{ur}, g_{ul}, g_l, g_r, g_{bl}, g_b are the respective pixel values. Then a difference, d is calculated as in Eq. (24).

$$d = (g_u + g_l + g_r + g_{ur} + g_{ul} + g_{bl} + g_b) / 7 - g_x \tag{24}$$

The value of d will be smaller for smoother regions and larger for edge regions. But if d value is one in the list {-1, 0, 1} then the target pixel will not be used to hide data. Otherwise if d ≥2, n bits can be hidden. This n value is calculated using Eq. (25).

$$n = \log_2 |d|, \text{if } |d| > 1 \tag{25}$$

Now n data bits will be represented by a decimal value b. A new difference d' is calculated as in Eq. (26).

$$d' = \begin{cases} 2^n + b, \ if\, d > 1 \\ -\left(2^n + b\right), \ if\, d < 1 \end{cases} \tag{26}$$

Not after embedding the new value for the target pixel is g_x'. This is done using Eq. (27).

$$g_x' = (g_u + g_l + g_r + g_{ur} + g_{ul} + g_{bl} + g_b) / 7 - d' \quad (27)$$

The retrieval of data from the stego image is done in similar way as that of two neighbor correlation scheme. The two conditions, FOBP and FIEP are also suitably addressed as in two neighbor correlation scheme.

Eight Neighbor Correlation

This scheme was proposed by Swain & Lenka (2015). The image is raster scanned and the pixels are classified into three categories, Figure 7. The dark gray colored pixels can be used as targets. The white colored pixels are treated only as neighbors.

The eight neighbor correlation scheme uses eight neighbors, upper, upper-right, upper-left, left, right, bottom-left, bottom and bottom-right for calculating embedding capacity of a target pixel. As shown in Figure 7, let P_X is a target pixel, P_U, P_{UR}, P_{UL}, P_L, P_R, P_{BL}, P_B and P_{BR} are the eight neighbors. Let g_x, g_u, g_{ur}, g_{ul}, g_l, g_r, g_{bl}, g_b, g_{br} are the respective pixel values. Then a difference, d is calculated using Eq. (28).

$$d = (g_u + g_{ur} + g_{ul} + g_l + g_r + g_{bl} + g_b + g_{br}) / 8 - g_x \quad (28)$$

The value of d will be smaller for smoother regions and larger for edge regions. But if d value is one in the list {-1, 0, 1} then the target pixel will not be used to hide data. Otherwise if d $\geq$2, n bits can be hidden. This n value is calculated using Eq. (29).

$$n = \log_2 |d|, \text{if } |d| > 1 \quad (29)$$

Now n data bits will be represented by a decimal value b. A new difference d' is calculated as in Eq. (30).

Figure 7. Sampling in 8 neighbor correlation scheme

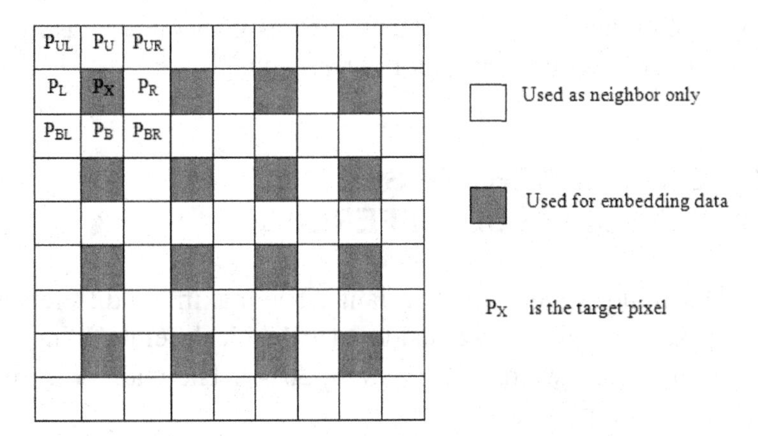

$$d' = \begin{cases} 2^n + b, \ if\, d > 1 \\ -(2^n + b), \ if\, d < 1 \end{cases} \tag{30}$$

Not after embedding the new value for the target pixel is g_x'. This is done using Eq. (31).

$$g_x' = (g_u + g_{ur} + g_{ul} + g_l + g_r + g_{bl} + g_b + g_{br}) / 8 - d' \tag{31}$$

The retrieval of data from the stego image is done in similar way as that of two neighbor correlation scheme. The two conditions, FOBP and FIEP are also suitably addressed as in two neighbor correlation scheme.

EXPERIMENTAL RESULTS AND DISCUSSION

Table 1 represents the PSNR comparison of schemes from 2 neighbor correlation to 8 neighbor correlation. The results are averages over a sample of 4 images, shown in Figure 8. It can be observed that the PSNR values goes on increasing from 2 neighbor correlation to seven neighbor correlation. The 8 neighbor correlation does not show any improvement in PSNR over 7 neighbor correlation. Thus, when we take more number of neighbor pixels to decide the embedding capacity of a target pixel the distortion reduces. Table 2 represents the hiding capacity comparison of 5, 6, 7, and 8 neighbor correlation schemes. The results are averaged over a sample of 4 images. It can be observed that the hiding capacity values goes on increasing from 8 neighbor correlation to four neighbor correlation.

PVD STEGANOGRAPHY BASED ON MAXIMUM PIXEL VALUE DIFFERENCE

In this PVD technique there are 7 variants. The maximum difference value from target pixel to neighbors is considered to decide the embedding decision (Pradhan, Sharma, & Swain, 2012; Swain, 2014). The main objective is to hider higher amount of data.

Figure 8. Test images, 256×256 (gray)

(a) Airplane (b) Lena (c) Pepper (d) baboon

Table 1. PSNR value of 2-7 neighbor correlation schemes

Image Name	Image Size (KB)	Amount of Hidden Data (Bytes)	PSNR Values						
			8 Neighbor Scheme	7 Neighbor Scheme	6 Neighbor Scheme	5 Neighbor Scheme	4 Neighbor Scheme	3 Neighbor Scheme	2 Neighbor Scheme
Airplane	192	5120	45.97	46.06	46.12	44.35	45.74	47.34	47.35
Lena	535	10240	50.40	50.59	50.07	49.00	49.40	49.03	49.33
Pepper	768	20480	49.88	49.65	49.37	48.24	47.11	46.60	46.74
Baboon	525	10240	45.04	45.30	45.13	44.18	42.90	41.61	41.64
Average			47.84	47.90	47.67	46.44	46.28	46.14	46.26

Table 2. Hiding capacities of 5-7 neighbor correlation schemes

Image Name	Image Size	Hiding Capacity 5-8 Neighbor Schemes			
		8 Neighbor Scheme	7 Neighbor Scheme	6 Neighbor Scheme	5 Neighbor Scheme
Airplane	192	93184	93553	191309	194537
Lena	535	212934	215609	448818	458103
Pepper	768	343958	348224	701477	718663
Baboon	525	365454	364949	749563	765733

Two Neighbor Maximum Difference

This scheme was proposed by Pradhan, Sharma & Swain (2012). The image is raster scanned. The blue colored pixels are the targets for hiding data. The pixels shown with white color are treated as neighbors. The pixels with cross mark are not used. See Figure 9.

In this scheme the two neighbor pixels from left and upper of a target are utilized. Suppose P_X is the target and its neighbors are P_L and P_U. Assume that the respective gray values are g_x, g_l and g_u. Then the following difference, d is calculated using Eq. (32).

$$d = g_{max} - g_{minx} \tag{32}$$

Where,

$$g_{max} = \max(g_l, g_u) \text{ and } g_{min} = \min(g_l, g_u).$$

In P_X, n number of bits can be hidden. This n value is calculated using Eq. (33).

$$n = \begin{cases} 1, & \text{if } 0 \le d \le 1 \\ \log_2 d, & \text{if } d > 1 \end{cases} \tag{33}$$

To minimize the distortion, for higher values of n i.e. if n lies in list {5, 6, 7, 8} then it is reset to 4. Now n bits of secret data is converted to a decimal value b, using it the stego value of the target pixel, $g_x^{'}$ is computed. This is done as in Eq. (34).

$$g_x^{'} = g_x - g_x \bmod 2^n + b \tag{34}$$

Furthermore, to reduce the distortion in $g_x^{'}$ it is further optimized as below. This is done using Eq. (35).

$$g_x^{'} = \begin{cases} g_x^{'} - 2^n, & if\ 2^{n-1} < \left(g_x^{'} - g_x\right) < 2^n\ and\ g_x^{'} \geq 2^n \\ g_x^{'} + 2^n, & if - 2^n < \left(g_x^{'} - g_x\right) < -2^{n-1}\ and\ g_x^{'} < 256 - 2^n \end{cases} \tag{35}$$

For retrieval of secret data also the stego image is raster scanned. Assume that for the target P_X^*, its neighbors are P_L^*, P_U^* and the respective gray values are g_x^*, g_l^* and g_u^*. Now a difference value d^* is calculated as in Eq. (36).

$$d^* = g_{max}^* - g_{min}^* \tag{36}$$

Where,

Figure 9. The sampling in 2 neighbor maximum differencing

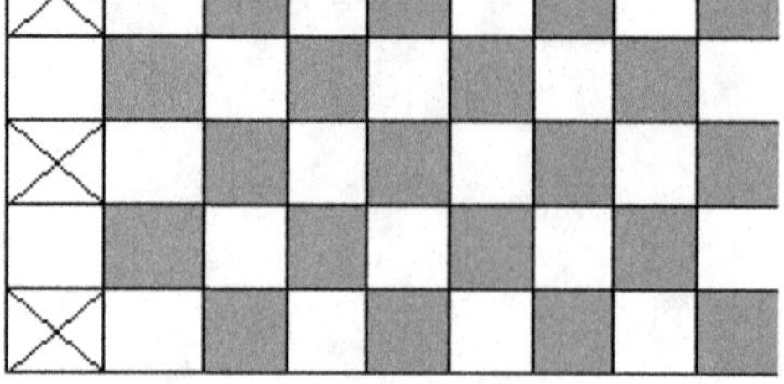

☒	P_U	☒		☒		☒		☒
P_L	P_X							

$g^*_{max} = \max(g^*_l, g^*_u)$ and $g^*_{min} = \min(g^*_l, g^*_u)$

We have to retrieve n^* bits of data from P^*_X. This n^* value is calculated using Eq. (37).

$$n^* = \begin{cases} 1, & \text{if } 0 \le d^* \le 1 \\ \log_2 d^*, & \text{if } d^* > 1 \end{cases} \tag{37}$$

If n^* lies in the list {5, 6, 7, 8} then it is reset to 4 and the decimal value b which was hidden in target pixel is calculated. This is done using Eq. (38).

$$b = g^*_x \bmod 2^{n^*} \tag{38}$$

This b is converted to n^* bits of binary data.

Three Neighbor Maximum Difference

This scheme was proposed by Pradhan, Sharma & Swain (2012). The image is raster scanned. The blue colored pixels are the targets for hiding data. The pixels shown with white color are treated as neighbors. The pixels with cross mark are not used. See Figure 10.

In this scheme the three neighboring pixels from left, right and upper of target are utilized. Suppose P_X is the target and its neighbors are P_L, P_R and P_U. Assume that the respective gray values are g_x, g_l, g_r and g_u. Then the following difference, d is calculated as in Eq. (39).

$$d = g_{max} - g_{minx} \tag{39}$$

Where

$g_{max} = \max(g_l, g_r, g_u)$ and $g_{min} = \min(g_l, g_r, g_u)$.

In P_X, n number of bits can be hidden. This n value is calculated using Eq. (40).

$$n = \begin{cases} 1, & \text{if } 0 \le d \le 1 \\ \log_2 d, & \text{if } d > 1 \end{cases} \quad (40)$$

To minimize the distortion, for higher values of n i.e. if n lies in list {5, 6, 7, 8} then it is reset to 4. Now n bits of secret data is converted to a decimal value b, using b the stego value of the target pixel, $g_x^{'}$ is computed. This is done using Eq. (41).

$$g_x^{'} = g_x - g_x \bmod 2^n + b \quad (41)$$

Furthermore, to reduce the distortion in $g_x^{'}$ it is further optimized as in Eq. (42).

$$g_x^{'} = \begin{cases} g_x^{'} - 2^n, & \text{if } 2^{n-1} < \left(g_x^{'} - g_x\right) < 2^n \text{ and } g_x^{'} \ge 2^n \\ g_x^{'} + 2^n, & \text{if } -2^n < \left(g_x^{'} - g_x\right) < -2^{n-1} \text{ and } g_x^{'} < 256 - 2^n \end{cases} \quad (42)$$

For retrieval of secret data also the stego image is raster scanned. Assume that for the target P_X^*, its neighbors are P_L^*, P_R^*, P_U^* and the respective gray values are g_x^*, g_l^*, g_r^* and g_u^*. Now a difference value d^* is calculated as in Eq. (43).

$$d^* = g_{max}^* - g_{min}^* \quad (43)$$

Where,

$$g_{max}^* = \max(g_l^*, g_r^*, g_u^*) \text{ and } g_{min}^* = \min(g_l^*, g_r^*, g_u^*)$$

We have to retrieve n^* bits of data from P_X^*. This n^* value is calculated using Eq. (44).

$$n^* = \begin{cases} 1, & \text{if } 0 \le d^* \le 1 \\ \log_2 d^*, & \text{if } d^* > 1 \end{cases} \quad (44)$$

If n^* lies in the list {5, 6, 7, 8} then it is reset to 4 and the decimal value b which was hidden in target pixel is calculated. This is done using Eq. (45).

$$b = g_x^* \bmod 2^{n^*} \tag{45}$$

This b is converted to n^* bits of binary data.

Four Neighbor Maximum Difference

This scheme was proposed by Pradhan, Sharma & Swain (2012). The image is raster scanned. The blue colored pixels are the targets for hiding data. The pixels shown with white color are treated as neighbors. The pixels with cross mark are not used. See Figure 11.

In this scheme the four neighboring pixels from left, right, bottom and upper of target are utilized. Suppose P_X is the target and its neighbors are P_L, P_R, P_B and P_U. Assume that the respective gray values are g_x, g_l, g_r, g_b and g_u. Then a difference, d is calculated as in Eq. (46).

$$d = g_{max} - g_{minx} \tag{46}$$

Figure 10. The sampling in 3 neighbor maximum differencing

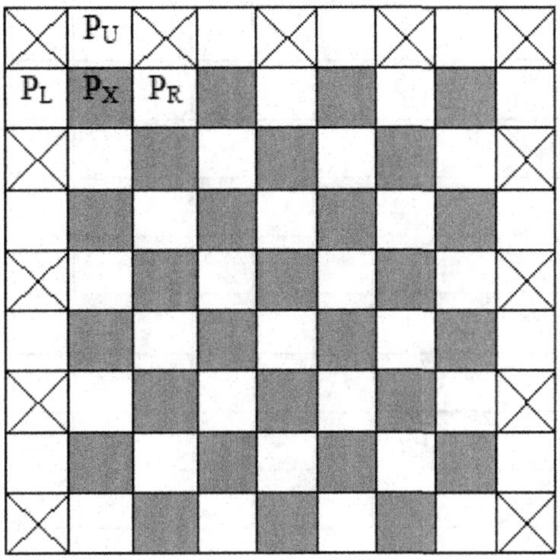

Where,

$g_{max} = \max(g_l, g_r, g_b, g_u)$ and $g_{min} = \min(g_l, g_r, g_b, g_u)$.

In P_X, n number of bits can be hidden. This n value is calculated using Eq. (47).

$$n = \begin{cases} 1, & \text{if } 0 \le d \le 1 \\ \log_2 d, & \text{if } d > 1 \end{cases} \tag{47}$$

To minimize the distortion, for higher values of n i.e. if n lies in list {5, 6, 7, 8} then it is reset to 4. Now n bits of secret data is converted to a decimal value b, using b the stego value of the target pixel, $g_x^{'}$ is computed. This is done as in Eq. (48).

$$g_x^{'} = g_x - g_x \bmod 2^n + b \tag{48}$$

Furthermore, to reduce the distortion in $g_x^{'}$ it is further optimized as in Eq. (49).

Figure 11. The sampling in 4 neighbor maximum differencing

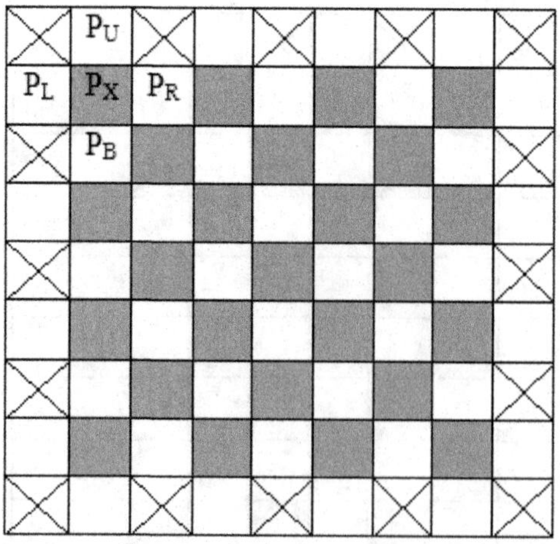

$$g_x' = \begin{cases} g_x' - 2^n, & if\, 2^{n-1} < \left(g_x' - g_x\right) < 2^n \; and\; g_x' \geq 2^n \\ g_x' + 2^n, & if - 2^n < \left(g_x' - g_x\right) < -2^{n-1} \; and\; g_x' < 256 - 2^n \end{cases} \tag{49}$$

For retrieval of secret data also the stego image is raster scanned. Assume that for the target P_X^*, its neighbors are $P_L^*, P_R^*, P_B^*, P_U^*$ and the respective gray values are g_x^*, g_l^*, g_r^*, g_b^*, g_u^*.

Now a difference value d^* is calculated as in Eq. (50).

$$d^* = g_{max}^* - g_{min}^* \tag{50}$$

Where,

$g_{max}^* = \max\,(g_l^*, g_r^*, g_b^*, g_u^*)$ and $g_{min}^* = \min(g_l^*, g_r^*, g_b^*, g_u^*)$

We have to retrieve n^* bits of data from P_X^*. This n^* value is calculated as in Eq. (51).

$$n^* = \begin{cases} 1, & \text{if}\; 0 \leq d^* \leq 1 \\ \log_2 d^*, & \text{if}\; d^* > 1 \end{cases} \tag{51}$$

If n^* lies in the list {5, 6, 7, 8} then it is reset to 4 and the decimal value b which was hidden in target pixel is calculated. This is done using Eq. (52).

$$b = g_x^* \bmod 2^{n^*} \tag{52}$$

This b is converted to n^* bits of binary data.

Five Neighbor Maximum Difference

This scheme was proposed by Swain (2014). The image is raster scanned. The blue colored pixels are the targets for hiding data. The pixels shown with white color are treated as neighbors. The pixels with gray color are not used. See Figure 12.

In this scheme the five neighboring pixels from left, right, upper, upper-right and bottom of target are utilized. Suppose P_X is the target and its neighbors are P_L, P_R, P_U, P_{UR} and P_B. Assume that the respective gray values are g_x, g_l, g_r, g_u, g_{ur} and g_b. Then a difference, d is calculated as in Eq. (53).

$$d = g_{max} - g_{minx} \tag{53}$$

Where

$g_{max} = \max(g_l, g_r, g_u, g_{ur}, g_b)$ and $g_{min} = \min(g_l, g_r, g_u, g_{ur}, g_b)$.

In P_X, n number of bits can be hidden. This n value is calculated using Eq. (54).

$$n = \begin{cases} 1, & \text{if } 0 \le d \le 1 \\ \log_2 d, & \text{if } d > 1 \end{cases} \tag{54}$$

To minimize the distortion, for higher values of n i.e. if n lies in list {5, 6, 7, 8} then it is reset to 4. Now n bits of secret data is converted to a decimal value b, using b the stego value of the target pixel, g'_x is computed. This is done using Eq. (55).

$$g'_x = g_x - g_x \bmod 2^n + b \tag{55}$$

Furthermore, to reduce the distortion in g'_x it is further optimized as in Eq. (55).

$$g'_x = \begin{cases} g'_x - 2^n, & \text{if } 2^{n-1} < \left(g'_x - g_x\right) < 2^n \text{ and } g'_x \ge 2^n \\ g'_x + 2^n, & \text{if } -2^n < \left(g'_x - g_x\right) < -2^{n-1} \text{ and } g'_x < 256 - 2^n \end{cases} \tag{55}$$

For retrieval of secret data also the stego image is raster scanned. Assume that for the target P^*_X, its neighbors are $P^*_L, P^*_R, P^*_U, P^*_{UR}, P^*_B$ and the respective gray values are g_x^*, g_l^*, g_r^*, g_u^*, g_{ur}^*, g_b^*. Now a difference value d^* is calculated as in Eq. (56).

$$d^* = g_{max}^* - g_{min}^* \tag{56}$$

Where,

$$g_{max}^* = \max(g_l^*, g_r^*, g_u^*, g_{ur}^*, g_b^*) \text{ and } g_{min}^* = \min(g_l^*, g_r^*, g_u^*, g_{ur}^*, g_b^*)$$

We have to retrieve n^* bits of data from P_X^*. This n^* is calculated using Eq. (57).

$$n^* = \begin{cases} 1, & \text{if } 0 \le d^* \le 1 \\ \log_2 d^*, & \text{if } d^* > 1 \end{cases} \tag{57}$$

If n^* lies in the list {5, 6, 7, 8} then it is reset to 4 and the decimal value b which was hidden in target pixel is calculated. This is done using Eq. (58).

$$b = g_x^* \bmod 2^{n^*} \tag{58}$$

This b is converted to n^* bits of binary data.

Figure 12. The sampling in 5 neighbor maximum differencing

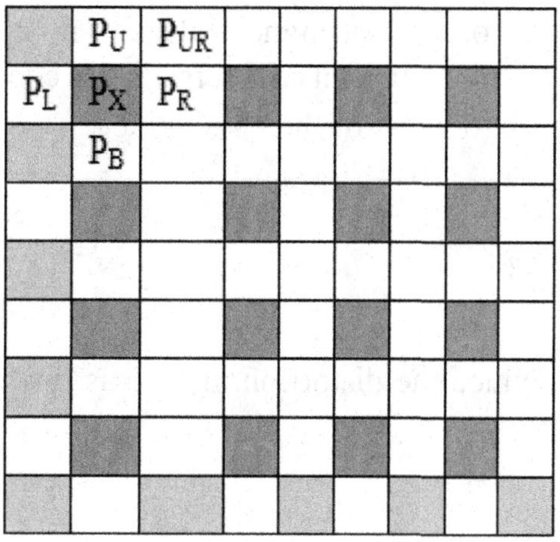

	P_U	P_{UR}						
P_L	P_X	P_R						
	P_B							

Six Neighbor Maximum Difference

This scheme was proposed by Swain (2014). The image is raster scanned. The blue colored pixels are the targets for hiding data. The pixels shown with white color are treated as neighbors. The pixels with gray color are not used. See Figure 13.

In this scheme the six neighboring pixels from left, right, upper, upper-right, upper-left and bottom of target are utilized. Suppose P_X is the target and its neighbors are P_L, P_R, P_U, P_{UR}, P_{UL}, P_B. Assume that the respective gray values are g_x, g_l, g_r, g_u, g_{ur}, g_{ul} and g_b. Then the difference, d is calculated as in Eq. (59).

$$d = g_{max} - g_{minx} \tag{59}$$

Where,

$g_{max} = \max(g_l, g_r, g_u, g_{ur}, g_{ul}, g_b)$ and $g_{min} = \min(g_l, g_r, g_u, g_{ur}, g_{ul}, g_b)$.

In P_X, n number of bits can be hidden. This n value is calculated using Eq. (60).

$$n = \begin{cases} 1, & \text{if } 0 \le d \le 1 \\ \log_2 d, & \text{if } d > 1 \end{cases} \tag{60}$$

To minimize the distortion, for higher values of n i.e. if n lies in list {5, 6, 7, 8} then it is reset to 4. Now n bits of secret data is converted to a decimal value b, using b the stego value of the target pixel, g_x' is computed. This is done using Eq. (61).

$$g_x' = g_x - g_x \bmod 2^n + b \tag{61}$$

Furthermore, to reduce the distortion in g_x' it is further optimized as in Eq. (62).

$$g_x' = \begin{cases} g_x' - 2^n, & \text{if } 2^{n-1} < \left(g_x' - g_x\right) < 2^n \text{ and } g_x' \geq 2^n \\ g_x' + 2^n, & \text{if } -2^n < \left(g_x' - g_x\right) < -2^{n-1} \text{ and } g_x' < 256 - 2^n \end{cases} \quad (62)$$

For retrieval of secret data also the stego image is raster scanned. Assume that for the target P_X^*, its neighbors are $P_L^*, P_R^*, P_U^*, P_{UR}^*, P_{UL}^*, P_B^*$ and the respective gray values are g_x^*, g_l^*, g_r^*, g_u^*, g_{ur}^*, g_{ul}^*, g_b^*. Now a difference value d^* is calculated as in Eq. (63).

$$d^* = g_{max}^* - g_{min}^* \quad (63)$$

Where,

$$g_{max}^* = \max\left(g_l^*, g_r^*, g_u^*, g_{ur}^*, g_{ul}^*, g_b^*\right)$$

and

$$g_{min}^* = \min\left(g_l^*, g_r^*, g_u^*, g_{ur}^*, g_{ul}^*, g_b^*\right)$$

We have to retrieve n^* bits of data from P_X^*. This value n^* is computed using Eq. (64).

$$n^* = \begin{cases} 1, & \text{if } 0 \leq d^* \leq 1 \\ \log_2 d^*, & \text{if } d^* > 1 \end{cases} \quad (64)$$

If n^* lies in the list {5, 6, 7, 8} then it is reset to 4 and the decimal value b which was hidden in target pixel is calculated as in Eq. (65). This b is converted to n^* bits of binary data.

$$b = g_x^* \bmod 2^{n^*} \quad (65)$$

Figure 13. The sampling in 6 neighbor maximum differencing

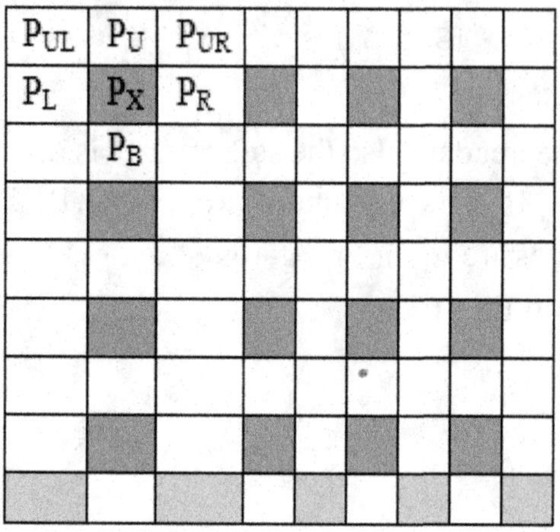

P_{UL}	P_U	P_{UR}						
P_L	P_X	P_R						
	P_B							

Seven Neighbor Maximum Difference

This scheme was proposed by Swain (2014). The image is raster scanned. The blue colored pixels are the targets for hiding data. The pixels shown with white color are treated as neighbors. The pixels with gray color are not used. See Figure 14.

In this scheme the seven neighboring pixels from left, right, upper, upper-right, upper-left bottom and bottom-left of target are utilized. Suppose P_X is the target and its neighbors are P_L, P_R, P_U, P_{UR}, P_{UL}, P_B, P_{BL}. Assume that the respective gray values are g_x, g_l, g_r, g_u, g_{ur}, g_{ul}, g_b, g_{bl}. Then the following difference, d is calculated as in Eq. (66).

$$d = g_{max} - g_{minx} \tag{66}$$

Where,

$$g_{max} = \max(g_l, g_r, g_u, g_{ur}, g_{ul}, g_b, g_{bl})$$

and

$$g_{min} = \min(g_l, g_r, g_u, g_{ur}, g_{ul}, g_b, g_{bl}).$$

In P_X, n number of bits can be hidden. This n value is calculated using Eq. (67).

$$n = \begin{cases} 1, & \text{if } 0 \le d \le 1 \\ \log_2 d, & \text{if } d > 1 \end{cases} \tag{67}$$

To minimize the distortion, for higher values of n i.e. if n lies in list {5, 6, 7, 8} then it is reset to 4. Now n bits of secret data is converted to a decimal value b, using b the stego value of the target pixel, $g_x^{'}$ is computed. This is done using Eq. (68).

$$g_x^{'} = g_x - g_x \bmod 2^n + b \tag{68}$$

Furthermore, to reduce the distortion in $g_x^{'}$ it is further optimized as in Eq. (69).

$$g_x^{'} = \begin{cases} g_x^{'} - 2^n, & if\, 2^{n-1} < \left(g_x^{'} - g_x\right) < 2^n \, and\, g_x^{'} \ge 2^n \\ g_x^{'} + 2^n, & if - 2^n < \left(g_x^{'} - g_x\right) < -2^{n-1} \, and\, g_x^{'} < 256 - 2^n \end{cases} \tag{69}$$

For retrieval of secret data also the stego image is raster scanned. Assume that for the target P_X^*, its neighbors are $P_L^*, P_R^*, P_U^*, P_{UR}^*, P_{UL}^*, P_B^*, P_{BL}^*$ and the

Figure 14. The sampling in 7 neighbor maximum differencing

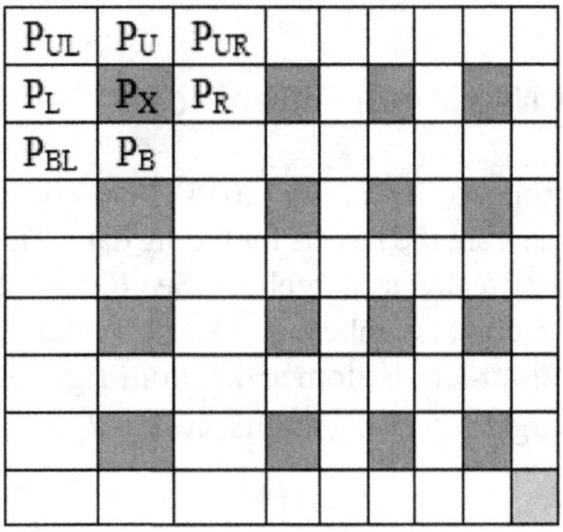

P_{UL}	P_U	P_{UR}						
P_L	P_X	P_R						
P_{BL}	P_B							

respective gray values are g^*_x, g^*_l, g^*_r, g^*_u, g^*_{ur}, g^*_{ul}, g^*_b, g^*_{bl}. Now a difference value d^* is calculated using Eq. (70).

$$d^* = g^*_{max} - g^*_{min} \tag{70}$$

Where,

$$g^*_{max} = \max(g^*_l, g^*_r, g^*_u, g^*_{ur}, g^*_{ul}, g^*_b, g^*_{bl})$$

and

$$g^*_{min} = \min(g^*_l, g^*_r, g^*_u, g^*_{ur}, g^*_{ul}, g^*_b, g^*_{bl})$$

We have to retrieve n^* bits of data from P^*_X. This n^* value is calculated using Eq. (71).

$$n^* = \begin{cases} 1, & \text{if } 0 \le d^* \le 1 \\ \log_2 d^*, & \text{if } d^* > 1 \end{cases} \tag{71}$$

If n^* lies in the list {5, 6, 7, 8} then it is reset to 4 and the decimal value b which was hidden in target pixel is calculated. This is done using Eq. (72). This b is converted to n^* bits of binary data.

$$b = g^*_x \bmod 2^{n^*} \tag{72}$$

Eight Neighbor Maximum Difference

This scheme was proposed by Swain (2014). The image is raster scanned. The blue colored pixels are the targets for hiding data. The pixels shown with white color pixels are treated as neighbors. See Figure 15.

In this scheme the eight neighboring pixels from left, right, upper, upper-right, upper-left, bottom-left, bottom and bottom-right of target are utilized. Suppose P_X is the target and its neighbors are P_L, P_R, P_U, P_{UR}, P_{UL}, P_{BL}, P_B,

P_{BR}. Assume that the respective gray values are g_x, g_u, g_l, g_r, g_b, g_{ur}, g_{ul}, g_{bl}, g_{br}. Then a difference, d is calculated is calculated as in Eq. (73).

$$d = g_{max} - g_{minx} \tag{73}$$

Where

$$g_{max} = \max(g_l, g_r, g_u, g_{ur}, g_{ul}, g_{bl}, g_b, g_{br})$$

and

$$g_{min} = \min(g_l, g_r, g_u, g_{ur}, g_{ul}, g_{bl}, g_b, g_{br}).$$

In P_X, n number of bits can be hidden. This n value is calculated using Eq. (74).

$$n = \begin{cases} 1, & \text{if } 0 \le d \le 1 \\ \log_2 d, & \text{if } d > 1 \end{cases} \tag{74}$$

To minimize the distortion, for higher values of n i.e. if n lies in list {5, 6, 7, 8} then it is reset to 4. Now n bits of secret data is converted to a decimal value b, using b the stego value of the target pixel, g_x' is computed. This is done using Eq. (75).

$$g_x' = g_x - g_x \bmod 2^n + b \tag{75}$$

Furthermore, to reduce the distortion in g_x' it is further optimized as in Eq. (76).

$$g_x' = \begin{cases} g_x' - 2^n, & \text{if } 2^{n-1} < (g_x' - g_x) < 2^n \text{ and } g_x' \ge 2^n \\ g_x' + 2^n, & \text{if } -2^n < (g_x' - g_x) < -2^{n-1} \text{ and } g_x' < 256 - 2^n \end{cases} \tag{76}$$

For retrieval of secret data also the stego image is raster scanned. Assume that for the target P_X^*, its neighbors are $P_L^*, P_R^*, P_U^*, P_{UR}^*, P_{UL}^*, P_{BL}^*, P_B^*, P_{BR}^*$ and the respective gray values are g_x^*, g_l^*, g_r^*, g_u^*, g_{ur}^*, g_{ul}^*, g_{bl}^*, g_b^*, g_{br}^*. Now a difference value d^* is calculated as in Eq. (77).

$$d^* = g_{max}^* - g_{min}^* \tag{77}$$

Where,

$$g_{max}^* = \max\left(g_l^*, g_r^*, g_u^*, g_{ur}^*, g_{ul}^*, g_{bl}^*, g_b^*, g_{br}^*\right)$$

and

$$g_{min}^* = \min\left(g_l^*, g_r^*, g_u^*, g_{ur}^*, g_{ul}^*, g_{bl}^*, g_b^*, g_{br}^*\right)$$

We have to retrieve n^* bits of data from P_X^*. This n^* value is calculated using Eq. (78).

$$n^* = \begin{cases} 1, & \text{if } 0 \le d^* \le 1 \\ \log_2 d^*, & \text{if } d^* > 1 \end{cases} \tag{78}$$

Figure 15. The sampling in 8 neighbor maximum differencing

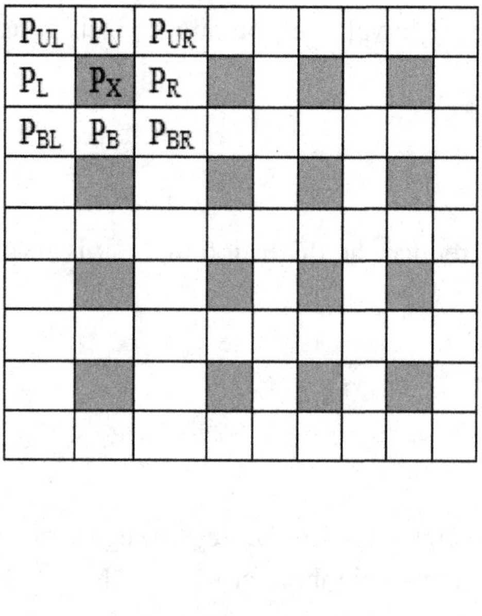

P_{UL}	P_U	P_{UR}						
P_L	P_X	P_R						
P_{BL}	P_B	P_{BR}						

If n^* lies in the list {5, 6, 7, 8} then it is reset to 4 and the decimal value b which was hidden in target pixel is calculated. This is done using Eq. (79). This b is converted to n^* bits of binary data.

$$b = g_x^* \bmod 2^{n^*} \tag{79}$$

Results and Discussion

While using eight neighbor maximum differencing we can get a higher value of difference compared to lesser number of neighbors. Obviously, the hiding capacity of eight neighbor maximum differencing will be higher as compared to others. In reverse the PSNR of two neighbor maximum differencing is higher as compared to all the remaining schemes. Figure 16 represents three test images used for evaluation of PSNR. The results can be observed in Table 3.

Figure 16. Test images

(a) Airplane (b) Boat (c) House

Table 3. The comparison of PSNR values

Image Name	Image Size (in kb)	Hidden Data Size (in Bytes)	The Different Methods						
			8 Neighbor	7 Neighbor	6 Neighbor	5 Neighbor	4 Neighbor	3 Neighbor	2 Neighbor
Airplane	192	2048	49.41	49.13	49.51	49.91	49.93	52.33	52.31
Boat	768	1024	50.58	50.89	50.70	50.90	50.94	51.38	51.83
House	768	1024	53.79	54.22	53.82	54.30	54.83	55.04	55.88

CONCLUSION

The PVD schemes based on correlation of target pixel with neighboring pixels are quite good. Although the PSNR values are better as compared to traditional PVD schemes, but the hiding capacity is not improved. The PVD schemes based on maximum differencing among the neighboring pixels are also equally good. Although the PSNR value are better as compared to traditional PVD schemes, but the hiding capacity is not improved. These techniques do not use LSB substitution, so RS analysis (is not necessary. But as the PVD is used so PDH analysis was required. But there is no evidence that these techniques qualify through PDH analysis.

REFERENCES

Chang, C. C., & Tseng, H. W. (2004). A steganographic method for digital images using side match. *Pattern Recognition Letters*, *25*(12), 1431–1437. doi:10.1016/j.patrec.2004.05.006

Chang, K. C., Chang, C. P., Huang, P. S., & Tu, T. M. (2008). A novel image steganography method using tri-way pixel value differencing. *Journal of Multimedia*, *3*(2), 37–44. doi:10.4304/jmm.3.2.37-44

Fridrich, J., Goljian, M., & Du, R. (2001). Detecting LSB steganography in color and gray-scale images. *Magazine of IEEE Multimedia Special Issue on Security*, *8*(4), 22–28. doi:10.1109/93.959097

Lee, Y. P., Lee, J. C., Chen, W. K., Chang, K. C., Su, I. J., & Chang, C. P. (2012). High-payload image hiding with quality recovery using tri-way pixel-value differencing. *Information Sciences*, *191*, 214–225. doi:10.1016/j.ins.2012.01.002

Pradhan, A., Sahu, A. K., Swain, G., & Sekhar, K. R. (2016). Performance evaluation parameters of image steganography techniques. *Proceedings of IEEE International Conference on Research Advances in Integrated Navigation Systems*, 1-8. 10.1109/RAINS.2016.7764399

Pradhan, A., Sharma, D. S., & Swain, G. (2012). Variable rate steganography in digital images using two, three and four neighbor pixels. *Indian Journal of Computer Science and Engineering*, *3*(3), 457–463.

Swain, G. (2014). Digital image steganography using nine-pixel differencing and modified LSB substitution. *Indian Journal of Science and Technology*, *7*(9), 1444–1450.

Swain, G., & Lenka, S. K. (2013). Steganography using two sided, three sided, and four sided side match methods. *CSI Transactions on ICT*, *1*(2), 127–133. doi:10.100740012-013-0015-3

Swain, G., & Lenka, S. K. (2015). Pixel value differencing steganography using correlation of target pixel with neighboring pixels. *Proceedings of IEEE International Conference on Electrical, Computer and Communication Technologies*, 599-604. 10.1109/ICECCT.2015.7226029

Wu, D. C., & Tsai, W. H. (2003). A steganograhic method for images by pixel value differencing. *Pattern Recognition Letters*, *24*(9-10), 1613–1626. doi:10.1016/S0167-8655(02)00402-6

Chapter 5
Steganography Using LSB Substitution and Pixel Value Differencing

ABSTRACT

This chapter describes four techniques that use both the principles of LSB substitution and pixel value differencing (PVD). These techniques use 1×3, 2×2, 2×3, and 3×3 size pixel blocks. In a block, LSB substitution is applied on one of the pixels, which is designated as the central pixel. Using the new value of this central pixel, pixel differences are computed with all its neighboring pixels. Based on these pixel value differences, embedding capacity is decided, and embedding is performed by addition and subtraction operations. The experimental results reveal that when the block size increases, the tolerance to RS analysis and pixel difference histogram (PDH) analysis also increases.

INTRODUCTION

This chapter describes four techniques those use both the principles of LSB substitution and pixel value differencing (PVD). The first technique proposed by Khodaei & Faez (2012) applies a combination of LSB substitution and PVD in 1×3 pixel blocks. The second technique proposed by Swain (2016), applies a combination of LSB substitution and PVD in 2×2 pixel blocks. Similarly, the third technique proposed by Pradhan, Sekhar & Swain (2016a) applies a combination of LSB substitution and PVD in 2×3 pixel blocks. The

DOI: 10.4018/978-1-5225-7516-0.ch005

fourth technique proposed by Swain (2018) applies a combination of LSB substitution and PVD in 3×3 pixel blocks. As these techniques use both the LSB substitution and PVD principle, so both RS analysis (Fridrich, Goljian, & Du, 2001; Swain & Lenka, 2015) and pixel difference histogram analysis (Zhang & Wang, 2004; Pradhan, Sahu, Swain & Sekhar, 2016) should be used to check their security strength.

STEGANOGRAPHY USING LSB SUBSTITUTION AND PVD IN A BLOCK

Khodaei and Faez's LSB+PVD Technique

This technique was proposed by Khodaei & Faez (2012). The embedding procedure is mentioned in the following steps.

Step 1: The image is raster scanned and divided into 1×3 size non-overlapping blocks, Figure 1. The pixels are designated as g_x, g_l, and g_r.

Step 2: In g_x k-bit LSB substitution is applied, where k is chosen from the list {5, 6, 7, 8}. The new value of g_x is $g_x^{'}$. Let L be the decimal value of the k LSBs of g_x and S be the decimal value of k-data bits hidden in $g_x^{'}$. The $g_x^{'}$ value can be further optimized using Eq. (1), where d=L-S.

$$g_x^{'} = \begin{cases} g_x^{'} + 2^k & if\, d > 2^{k-1}\, and\, 0 \leq g_x^{'} + 2^k \leq 255 \\ g_x^{'} - 2^k & if\, d < -2^{k-1}\, and\, 0 \leq g_x^{'} - 2^k \leq 255 \\ g_x^{'} & otherwise \end{cases} \tag{1}$$

Step 3: Using $g_x^{'}$ .the following two differences are calculated as in Eq. (2).

Figure 1. A pixel block

g_l	g_x	g_r

$$d_1 = |g_x' - g_l|,\ d_2 = |g_x' - g_r| \tag{2}$$

Step 4: The Table 1 is range table for variant-1 and Table 2 is range table for variant 2.

Step 5: The value d_1 falls into a range whose embedding length is t_1 and lower bound is l_1. Similarly, the value d_2 falls into a range whose embedding length is t_2 and lower bound is l_2.

Step 6: From the secret binary data stream t_1 bits of data is taken and converted to a decimal value s_1. Similarly, from the secret binary data stream t_2 bits of data is taken and converted to a decimal value s_2. Two new difference values d_1' and d_2' are computed as in Eq. (3).

$$d_1' = l_1 + s_1,\ d_2' = l_2 + s_2 \tag{3}$$

Step 7: Using g_x' and d_1' two new values for g_l namely, g_l'' and g_l'''.are calculated. Similarly, using g_x' and d_2' two new values for g_r namely, g_r'' and g_r''' are calculated using Eq. (4).

$$g_l'' = g_x' - d_1',\ g_l''' = g_x' + d_1',\ g_r'' = g_x' - d_2',\ g_r''' = g_x' + d_2' \tag{4}$$

Table 1. Range table of variant 1

Range	R_1 =[0,7]	R_2 =[8,15]	R_3 =[16,31]	R_4 =[32,63]	R_5 =[64,255]
Embedding length	3	3	3	4	4

Table 2. Range table of variant 2

Range	R_1 =[0,7]	R_2 =[8,15]	R_3 =[16,31]	R_4 =[32,63]	R_5 =[64, 255]
Embedding length	3	3	4	5	6

Step 8: Now the stego value of g_l, say g_l' is calculated using g_l'' and g_l'''. Similarly, the stego value of g_r, say g_r' is calculated using g_r'' and g_r'''. This is done using Eq. (5) and Eq. (6).

$$g_l' = \begin{cases} g_l'' & if \left|g_l - g_l''\right| < \left|g_l - g_l'''\right| and\, 0 \leq g_l'' \leq 255 \\ g_l''' & otherwise \end{cases} \quad (5)$$

$$g_r' = \begin{cases} g_r'' & if \left|g_r - g_r''\right| < \left|g_r - g_r'''\right| and\, 0 \leq g_r'' \leq 255 \\ g_r''' & otherwise \end{cases} \quad (6)$$

Hence the stego block is represented in Figure 2.

The extraction of secret embedded data can be done in the following manner. Suppose the stego-block is as shown in Figure 2 from which we have to extract the hidden data. The following steps are used.

Step 1: From the center pixel g_x', k-LSBs are extracted. The value k is one of the values in the list $\{5, 6, 7, 8\}$ which was chosen during embedding.

Step 2: Using g_x' and g_l', the difference value d_1' is computed. Similarly, using g_x' and g_r', the difference value d_2' is computed as in Eq. (7).

$$d_1' = \left|g_l' - g_x'\right|,\ d_2' = \left|g_r' - g_x'\right| \quad (7)$$

Step 3: The difference d_1' belongs to a range whose lower bound is l_1 and embedding length is t_1. Similarly, the difference d_2' belongs to a range whose lower bound is l_2 and embedding length is t_2. Refer the range table.

Figure 2. The stego-block

g_l'	g_x'	g_r'

Step 4: As in Eq. (8), using $d_1^{'}$ and l_1, calculate the decimal value s_1 and convert s_1 to t_1 binary bits. Similarly using $d_2^{'}$ and l_2, calculate the decimal value s_2 and convert s_2 to t_2 binary bits.

$$s_1 = d_1^{'} - l_1 ,\ s_2 = d_2^{'} - l_2 \tag{8}$$

Swain's LSB+PVD Technique

This technique was proposed by Swain (2016). The embedding procedure is mentioned in the following steps.

Step 1: The image is raster scanned and divided into 2×2 size non-overlapping blocks, Figure 3. The pixels are designated as g_x, g_r, g_b, and g_d.

Step 2: In g_x k-bit LSB substitution is applied, where k is chosen from tht list {5, 6, 7, 8}. The new value of g_x is $g_x^{'}$. Let L be the decimal value of the k LSBs of g_x and S be the decimal value of k-data bits hidden in $g_x^{'}$. The $g_x^{'}$ value can be further optimized by using Eq. (9), where d=L-S.

$$g_x^{'} = \begin{cases} g_x^{'} + 2^k & if\, d > 2^{k-1}\, and\, 0 \le g_x^{'} + 2^k \le 255 \\ g_x^{'} - 2^k & if\, d < -2^{k-1}\, and\, 0 \le g_x^{'} - 2^k \le 255 \\ g_x^{'} & otherwise \end{cases} \tag{9}$$

Step 3: As in Eq. (10), using $g_x^{'}$ the three differences are calculated.

Figure 3. A pixel block

g_x	g_r
g_b	g_d

$$d_1 = |g_x^{'} - g_r|,\ d_2 = |g_x^{'} - g_b|,\ d_3 = |g_x^{'} - g_d| \tag{10}$$

Step 4: The Table 1 is range table for variant-1 and Table 2 is range table for variant 2.

Step 5: The value d_1 falls into a range whose embedding length is t_1 and lower bound is l_1. The value d_2 falls into a range whose embedding length is t_2 and lower bound is l_2. Similarly, the value d_3 falls into a range whose embedding length is t_3 and lower bound is l_3.

Step 6: From the secret binary data stream t_1 bits of data is taken and converted to a decimal value s_1. Similarly, from the secret binary data stream t_2 bits of data is taken and converted to a decimal value s_2. From the secret binary data stream t_3 bits of data is taken and converted to a decimal value s_3. Three new difference values $d_1^{'}$, $d_2^{'}$ and $d_3^{'}$ are computed as in Eq. (11).

$$d_1^{'} = l_1 + s_1,\ d_2^{'} = l_2 + s_2,\ d_3^{'} = l_3 + s_3 \tag{11}$$

Step 7: Using $g_x^{'}$ and $d_1^{'}$ two new values for g_r namely, $g_r^{''}$ and $g_r^{'''}$ are calculated. Similarly, using $g_x^{'}$ and $d_2^{'}$ two new values for g_b namely, $g_b^{''}$ and $g_b^{'''}$ are calculated. Using $g_x^{'}$ and $d_3^{'}$ two new values for g_d namely, $g_d^{''}$ and $g_d^{'''}$ are calculated. This is shown in Eq. (12).

$$g_r^{''} = g_x^{'} - d_1^{'},\ g_r^{'''} = g_x^{'} + d_1^{'},\ g_b^{''} = g_x^{'} - d_2^{'},\ g_b^{'''} = g_x^{'} + d_2^{'},\ g_d^{''} = g_x^{'} - d_3^{'},\ g_d^{'''} = g_x^{'} + d_3^{'} \tag{12}$$

Step 8: Now the stego value of g_r, say $g_r^{'}$ is calculated using $g_r^{''}$ and $g_r^{'''}$. Similarly, the stego value of g_b, say $g_b^{'}$ is calculated using $g_b^{''}$ and $g_b^{'''}$. The stego value of g_d, say $g_d^{'}$ is calculated using $g_d^{''}$ and $g_d^{'''}$. This is shown in Eqs. (13)

$$
\begin{aligned}
g_r' &= \begin{cases} g_r'' & if \left|g_r - g_r''\right| < \left|g_r - g_r'''\right| and\, 0 \le g_r'' \le 255 \\ g_r''' & otherwise \end{cases} \\
g_b' &= \begin{cases} g_b'' & if \left|g_b - g_b''\right| < \left|g_b - g_b'''\right| and\, 0 \le g_b'' \le 255 \\ g_b''' & otherwise \end{cases} \\
g_d' &= \begin{cases} g_d'' & if \left|g_d - g_d''\right| < \left|g_d - g_d'''\right| and\, 0 \le g_d'' \le 255 \\ g_d''' & otherwise \end{cases}
\end{aligned} \tag{13}
$$

Thus, the stego block is as in Figure 4.

The extraction of secret embedded data can be done in the following manner. Suppose the stego block is as shown in Figure 4 from which we have to extract the hidden data. The following steps are used.

Step 1: From the centre pixel g_x', k-LSBs are extracted. The value k is one of the values in the list $\{5, 6, 7, 8\}$ which was chosen during embedding.

Step 2: Using g_x' and g_r', the difference value d_1' is computed. Similarly, using g_x' and g_b', the difference value d_2' is computed. Using g_x' and g_d', the difference value d_3' is computed. These calculations are as shown in Eq. (14).

$$d_1' = \left|g_r' - g_x'\right|,\ d_2' = \left|g_b' - g_x'\right|,\ d_3' = \left|g_d' - g_x'\right| \tag{14}$$

Step 3: The difference d_1' belongs to a range whose lower bound is l_1 and embedding length is t_1. Similarly, the difference d_2' belongs to a range whose lower bound is l_2 and embedding length is t_2. Refer the range

Figure 4. The Stego pixel block

g_x'	g_r'
g_b'	g_d'

table. The difference d_3' belongs to a range whose lower bound is l_3 and embedding length is t_3.

Step 4: Using d_1' and l_1, calculate the decimal value s_1 and convert s_1 to t_1 binary bits. Similarly using d_2' and l_2, calculate the decimal value s_2 and convert s_2 to t_2 binary bits. Using d_3' and l_3, calculate the decimal value s_3 and convert s_3 to t_3 binary bits. These calculations are as shown in Eq. (15).

$$s_1 = d_1' - l_1,\ s_2 = d_2' - l_2,\ s_3 = d_3' - l_3 \tag{15}$$

Pradhan et al.'s LSB+PVD Technique

This technique was proposed by Pradhan, Sekhar & Swain (2016a). The embedding procedure is mentioned in the following steps.

Step 1: The image is raster scanned and divided into 2×3 size non-overlapping blocks, Figure 5. The pixels are designated as g_{ul}, g_x, g_{ur}, g_{bl}, g_b, and g_{br}.

Step 2: In g_x k-bit LSB substitution is applied, where k is chosen from the list {5, 6, 7, 8}. The new value of g_x is g_x'. Let L be the decimal value of the k LSBs of g_x and S be the decimal value of k-data bits hidden in g_x'. The g_x' value can be further optimized using Eq. (16), where d=L-S.

$$g_x' = \begin{cases} g_x' + 2^k & if\ d > 2^{k-1}\ and\ 0 \le g_x' + 2^k \le 255 \\ g_x' - 2^k & if\ d < -2^{k-1}\ and\ 0 \le g_x' - 2^k \le 255 \\ g_x' & otherwise \end{cases} \tag{16}$$

Step 3: As shown in Eqs. (17), using g_x' the following five differences are calculated.

$$d_1 = \left| g_x' - g_{ul} \right|$$

Figure 5. Original block

g_{ul}	g_x	g_{ur}
g_{bl}	g_b	g_{br}

$$d_2 = \left|g_x^{'} - g_{ur}\right|$$

$$d_3 = \left|g_x^{'} - g_{bl}\right| \quad (17)$$

$$d_4 = \left|g_x^{'} - g_b\right|$$

$$d_5 = \left|g_x^{'} - g_{br}\right|$$

Step 4: The Table 1 is range table for variant-1 and Table 2 is range table for variant 2.

Step 5: The value d_1 falls into a range whose embedding length is t_1 and lower bound is l_1. The value d_2 falls into a range whose embedding length is t_2 and lower bound is l_2. The value d_3 falls into a range whose embedding length is t_3 and lower bound is l_3. The value d_4 falls into a range whose embedding length is t_4 and lower bound is l_4. Similarly, the value d_5 falls into a range whose embedding length is t_5 and lower bound is l_5.

Step 6: From the secret binary data stream t_1 bits of data is taken and converted to a decimal value s_1. Similarly, convert t_2 bits of data to a decimal value s_2, convert t_3 bits of data to a decimal value s_3, convert t_4 bits of data to a decimal value s_4 and convert t_5 bits of data to a decimal value s_5. Five new difference values $d_1^{'}$, $d_2^{'}$, $d_3^{'}$, $d_4^{'}$ and $d_5^{'}$ are computed as in Eq. (18).

$$d'_1 = l_1 + s_1,\ d'_2 = l_2 + s_2,\ d'_3 = l_3 + s_3,\ d'_4 = l_4 + s_4,\ d'_5 = l_5 + s_5 \quad (18)$$

Step 7: Using g'_x and d'_1 two new values for g_{ul} namely, g''_{ul} and g'''_{ul} are calculated. Similarly, g''_{ur}, g'''_{ur}, g''_{bl}, g'''_{bl}, g''_b, g'''_b, g''_{br}, g'''_{br} are calculated. These are done using Eq. (19) and Eq. (20).

$$g''_{ul} = g'_x - d'_1,\ g'''_{ul} = g'_x + d'_1,\ g''_{ur} = g'_x - d'_2,\ g'''_{ur} = g'_x + d'_2,\ g''_{bl} = g'_x - d'_3 \quad (19)$$

$$g'''_{bl} = g'_x + d'_3,\ g''_b = g'_x - d'_4,\ g'''_b = g'_x + d'_4,\ g''_{br} = g'_x - d'_5,\ g'''_{br} = g'_x + d'_5 \quad (20)$$

Step 8: Now the stego value of g_{ul}, say g'_{ul} is calculated using g''_{ul} and g'''_{ul}. Similarly, the stego values g'_{ur}, g'_{bl}, g'_b, and g'_{br} are calculated. These are done using Eqs. (21).

$$g'_{ul} = \begin{cases} g''_{ul} & if \left|g_{ul} - g''_{ul}\right| < \left|g_{ul} - g'''_{ul}\right| \, and\, 0 \le g''_{ul} \le 255 \\ g'''_{ul} & otherwise \end{cases}$$
$$g'_{ur} = \begin{cases} g''_{ur} & if \left|g_{ur} - g''_{ur}\right| < \left|g_{ur} - g'''_{ur}\right| \, and\, 0 \le g''_{ur} \le 255 \\ g'''_{ur} & otherwise \end{cases}$$
$$g'_{bl} = \begin{cases} g''_{bl} & if \left|g_{bl} - g''_{bl}\right| < \left|g_{bl} - g'''_{bl}\right| \, and\, 0 \le g''_{bl} \le 255 \\ g'''_{bl} & otherwise \end{cases} \quad (21)$$
$$g'_{b} = \begin{cases} g''_{b} & if \left|g_{b} - g''_{b}\right| < \left|g_{b} - g'''_{b}\right| \, and\, 0 \le g''_{b} \le 255 \\ g'''_{b} & otherwise \end{cases}$$
$$g'_{br} = \begin{cases} g''_{br} & if \left|g_{br} - g''_{br}\right| < \left|g_{br} - g'''_{br}\right| \, and\, 0 \le g''_{br} \le 255 \\ g'''_{br} & otherwise \end{cases}$$

Hence the stego block is as shown in Figure 6.

The extraction of secret embedded data can be done in the following manner. Suppose the stego block is as shown in Figure 6 from which we have to extract the hidden data. The following steps are used.

Figure 6. The stego block

g'_{ul}	g'_{x}	g'_{ur}
g'_{bl}	g'_{b}	g'_{br}

Step 1: From the centre pixel g'_x, k-LSBs are extracted. The value k is one of the values in the list {5, 6, 7, 8} which was chosen during embedding.

Step 2: The five difference values are calculated using Eqs. (22).

$$d'_1 = |g'_{ul} - g'_x|$$

$$d'_2 = |g'_{ur} - g'_x|$$

$$d'_3 = |g'_{bl} - g'_x| \quad (22)$$

$$d'_4 = |g'_{b} - g'_x|$$

$$d'_5 = |g'_{br} - g'_x|$$

Step 3: The differences d'_1, d'_2, d'_3, d'_4 and d'_5 belongs to some ranges in the range table. Corresponding to these ranges the lower bounds and embedding lengths are l_1, l_2, l_3, l_4, l_5 and t_1, t_2, t_3, t_4, t_5.

Step 4: Using l_1, l_2, l_3, l_4, l_5 and d_1, d_2, d_3, d_4, d_5 the decimal equivalents of the embedded secret bit streams are calculated as in Eqs (23).

$$s_1 = d'_1 - l_1,\ s_2 = d'_2 - l_2,\ s_3 = d'_3 - l_3,\ s_4 = d'_4 - l_4,\ s_5 = d'_5 - l_5 \quad (23)$$

Then the decimal values s_1, s_2, s_3, s_4, and s_5 are converted into t_1, t_2, t_3, t_4, and t_5 binary bits respectively.

Results of LSB+PVD Techniques

The experimental results for the above LSB+PVD techniques are given in Tables 3-5. The test images are shown in Figure 7. In Khodaei & Faez's (2012) technique, the Type 1 provides higher PSNR compared to Type2, but Type 2 provides higher capacity compared to Type 1. In Swain's (2016) technique, the Type 1 provides higher PSNR compared to Type2, but Type 2 provides higher capacity compared to Type 1. Similarly, in Pradhan et al.'s (2016a) technique, the Type 1 provides higher PSNR compared to Type2, but Type 2 provides higher capacity compared to Type 1. When we compare the Type 1 of all the three techniques, the Swain's is the higher PSNR as compared to the other two techniques. Similarly, when we compare the Type 2 of all the three techniques, the Pradhan et al.'s is the higher PSNR as compared to the other two techniques.

Figure 7. (a)-(h) Test Images

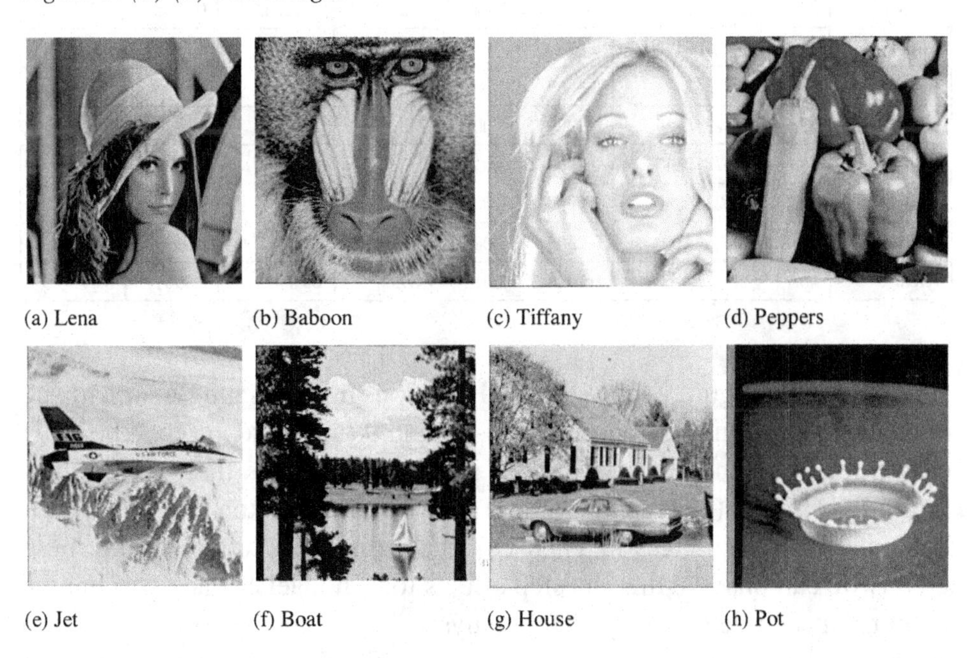

(a) Lena (b) Baboon (c) Tiffany (d) Peppers

(e) Jet (f) Boat (g) House (h) Pot

Table 3. Results for Khodaei and Faez's (2012) Technique

Images 512×512 (Color)	Khodaei and Faez's Type1				Khodaei and Faez's Type2			
	PSNR	Capacity	Q	Bit Rate	PSNR	Capacity	Q	Bit Rate
Lena	42.79	2375248	0.9991	3.02	41.36	2434603	0.9988	3.09
Baboon	37.75	2443361	0.9981	3.10	34.65	2662080	0.9963	3.38
Tiffany	39.71	2372396	0.9965	3.01	40.29	2416944	0.9968	3.07
Peppers	39.33	2372858	0.9989	3.01	38.15	2435223	0.9985	3.09
Jet	40.91	2374048	0.9987	3.01	40.96	2418419	0.9987	3.07
Boat	40.08	2391994	0.9992	3.04	37.66	2504613	0.9988	3.18
House	39.16	2387183	0.9986	3.03	38.88	2470824	0.9985	3.14
Pot	41.32	2366001	0.9993	3.00	38.18	2387494	0.9985	3.03
Average	40.13	2385386	0.9985	3.03	38.76	**2466275**	0.9981	3.13

Table 4. Results for Swain's (2016) Technique

Images 512×512 (Color)	Swain's Type1				Swain's Type2			
	PSNR	Capacity	Q	Bit Rate	PSNR	Capacity	Q	Bit Rate
Lena	43.17	2361875	0.9991	3.00	41.91	2437700	0.9989	3.09
Baboon	35.17	2393475	0.9966	3.04	32.99	2772545	0.9945	3.52
Tiffany	42.82	2363192	0.9980	3.00	42.36	2425193	0.9978	3.08
Peppers	39.82	2364428	0.9989	3.00	38.78	2447737	0.9985	3.11
Jet	42.63	2365839	0.9990	3.00	42.82	2443492	0.9990	3.10
Boat	38.68	2370147	0.9990	3.01	36.97	2539530	0.9985	3.22
House	40.45	2366686	0.9989	3.00	39.67	2510373	0.9987	3.19
Pot	43.17	2364360	0.9995	3.00	42.01	2394782	0.9993	3.04
Average	40.73	2368750	0.9986	3.01	39.68	**2496419**	0.9981	3.17

Figure 8 and Figure 9 shows the PDH analysis for Lena and Baboon image in these three techniques. Figure 8 (a)-(c) and 9 (a)–(c) represents the PDH curves for Lena and Baboon images in Type 1 of these three techniques. Similarly, Figure 8(d)-(f) and Figure 9 (d)–(f) represents the PDH curves for Lena and Baboon images in Type 2 of these three techniques. From these graphs we can observe that the step effects for Khodaei & Faez's technique is more, means detected by PDH analysis. In Swain's technique the step effects are lesser as compared to Khodaei & Faez's technique. In Pradhan

Table 5. Results for Pradhan et al.'s (2016a) Technique

Images 512×512 (Color)	Pradhan et al.'s Type1				Pradhan et al.'s Type2			
	PSNR	**Capacity**	**Q**	**Bit Rate**	**PSNR**	**Capacity**	**Q**	**Bit Rate**
Lena	42.79	2362944	0.9991	3.00	41.23	2451046	0.9987	3.11
Baboon	34.84	2396696	0.9963	3.04	32.50	2816768	0.9939	3.58
Tiffany	41.55	2363455	0.9975	3.00	41.51	2432745	0.9974	3.09
Peppers	38.58	2365366	0.9986	3.00	36.90	2459762	0.9980	3.12
Jet	42.09	2366486	0.9989	3.00	41.30	2454060	0.9987	3.12
Boat	37.69	2372127	0.9988	3.01	35.54	2565007	0.9980	3.26
House	39.45	2368303	0.9986	3.01	38.40	2533362	0.9983	3.22
Pot	40.98	2364549	0.9992	3.00	37.50	2399556	0.9983	3.05
Average	39.74	2369990	0.9983	3.01	38.11	**2514038**	0.9976	3.19

et al.'s technique the step effects are further reduced. Thus Pradhan et al.'s technique is better than the other two as far as PDH analysis is concerned.

Figure 10 represents the RS analysis of Swain's technique on Lena and Baboon images for both Type 1 and Type 2. We can notice that the relation $R_m \approx R_{-m} > S_m \approx S_{-m}$ is satisfied. It implies that Swain's technique is undetected by RS analysis. Khodaei & Faez and Pradhan et al. did not prove that their techniques are undetected by RS analysis.

EXPLOITING MAXIMUM NUMBER OF DIRECTIONS

Eight Directional PVD Technique

This technique was proposed by Swain (2018). The embedding algorithm operates on 3×3 pixel blocks. The blocks are formed in a non-overlapping manner. Let us denote a typical block as in Figure 11 (a). The central pixel is P_c and its surrounding pixels are P_1, P_2, P_3, P_4, P_5, P_6, P_7 and P_8. In central pixel t bit LSB substitution is performed. For type 1, the t value is 3 and range table is Table 6. For type 2, the t value is 4 and the range table is Table 7.

After performing t bit LSB substitution in P_c, the stego-value is $P_c^{'}$. Suppose the integer (decimal) value of t LSB bits in P_c is dec_{old} and the integer (decimal) value of t LSB bits in $P_c^{'}$ is dec_{new}. Now find the deviation,

$dev = dec_{old}$ - dec_{new}. Furthermore, calculate a modified value of P_c' as in Eq. (24)

$$P_c' = \begin{cases} P_c' + 2^t & \textit{if } dev > 2^{t-1} \textit{ and } 0 \le P_c' + 2^t \le 255 \\ P_c' - 2^t & \textit{if } dev < -2^{t-1} \textit{ and } 0 \le P_c' - 2^t \le 255 \\ P_c' & \textit{otherwise} \end{cases} \quad (24)$$

Using this modified value P_c', calculate eight difference values d_i, for i= 1 to 8 as in Eq. (25)

$$d_i = |P_c' - P_i| \quad (25)$$

The difference value d_1 belongs to one of the six ranges. Suppose the lower bound is denoted as L_1 and hiding capacity as t_1 for the range of d_1. Similarly L_2, L_3, L_4, L_5, L_6, L_7, L_8 are the lower bounds and t_2, t_3, t_4., t_5, t_6, t_7, t_8 are the hiding capacities of the ranges of d_2, d_3, d_4, d_5, d_6, d_7 and d_8 respectively.

Now take t_1, t_2, t_3, t_4, t_5, t_6, t_7 and t_8 bits of data separately and convert to their decimal values S_1, S_2, S_3, S_4, S_5, S_6, S_7 and S_8 respectively.

Now for i=1 to 8, calculate new difference values d_i' using Eq. (26).

$$d_i' = L_i + S_i \quad (26)$$

For i = 1 to 8 a pair of new values for each P_i is calculated as in Eq. (27).

$$P_i'' = P_c' - d_i',\ P_i''' = P_c' + d_i' \quad (27)$$

Now out of two new values P_i'' and P_i''', one value is chosen for P_i' ing Eq. (28).

$$P_i' = \begin{cases} P_i'' & \textit{if } |P_i - P_i''| < |P_i - P_i'''| \textit{ and } 0 \le P_i'' \le 255 \\ P_i''' & \textit{otherwise} \end{cases} \quad (28)$$

Figure 8. PDH analysis for Lena image

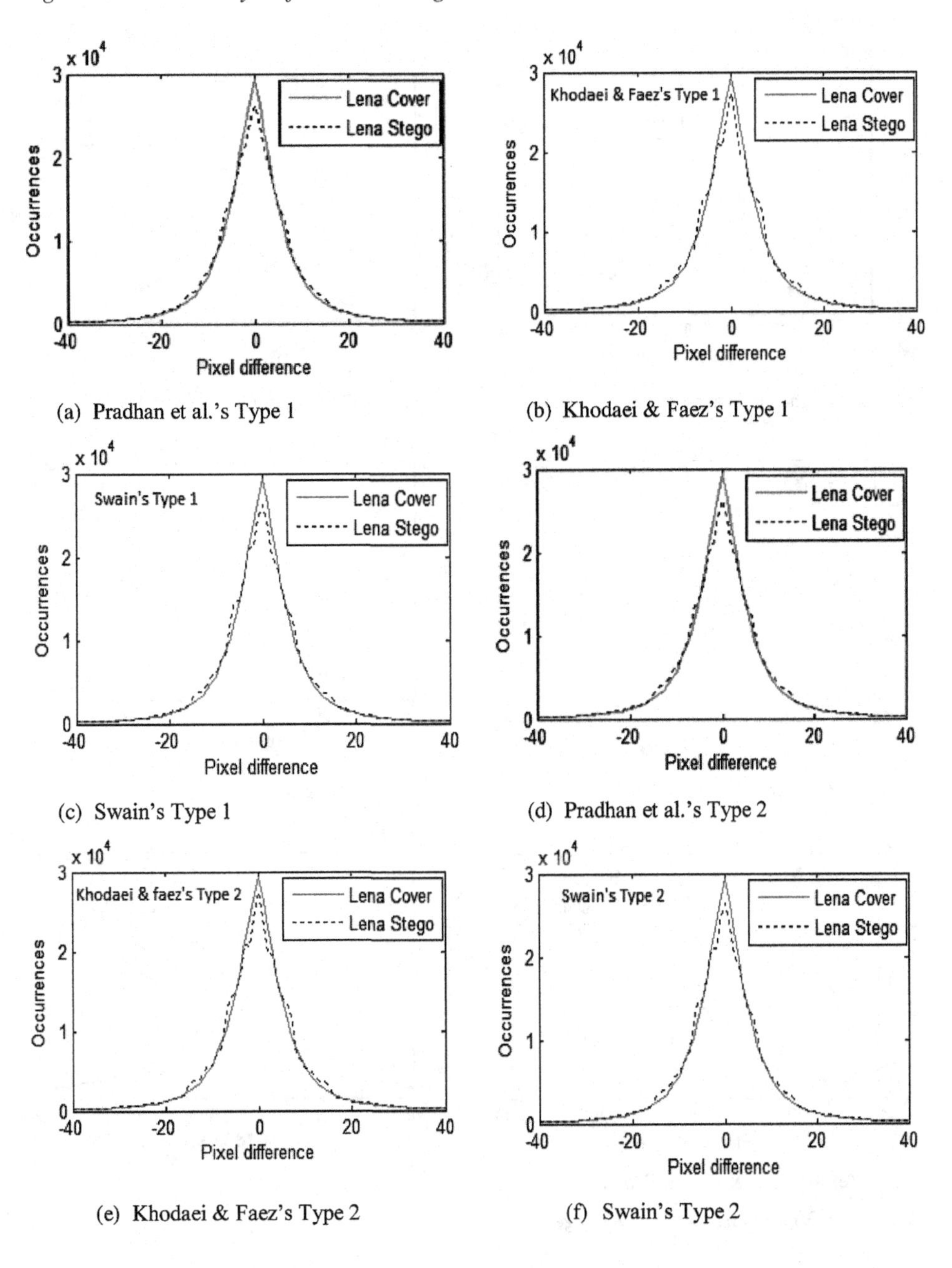

(a) Pradhan et al.'s Type 1

(b) Khodaei & Faez's Type 1

(c) Swain's Type 1

(d) Pradhan et al.'s Type 2

(e) Khodaei & Faez's Type 2

(f) Swain's Type 2

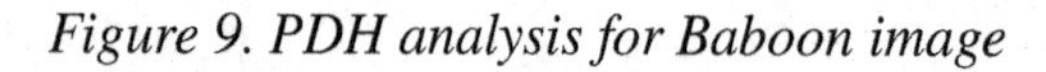

Figure 9. PDH analysis for Baboon image

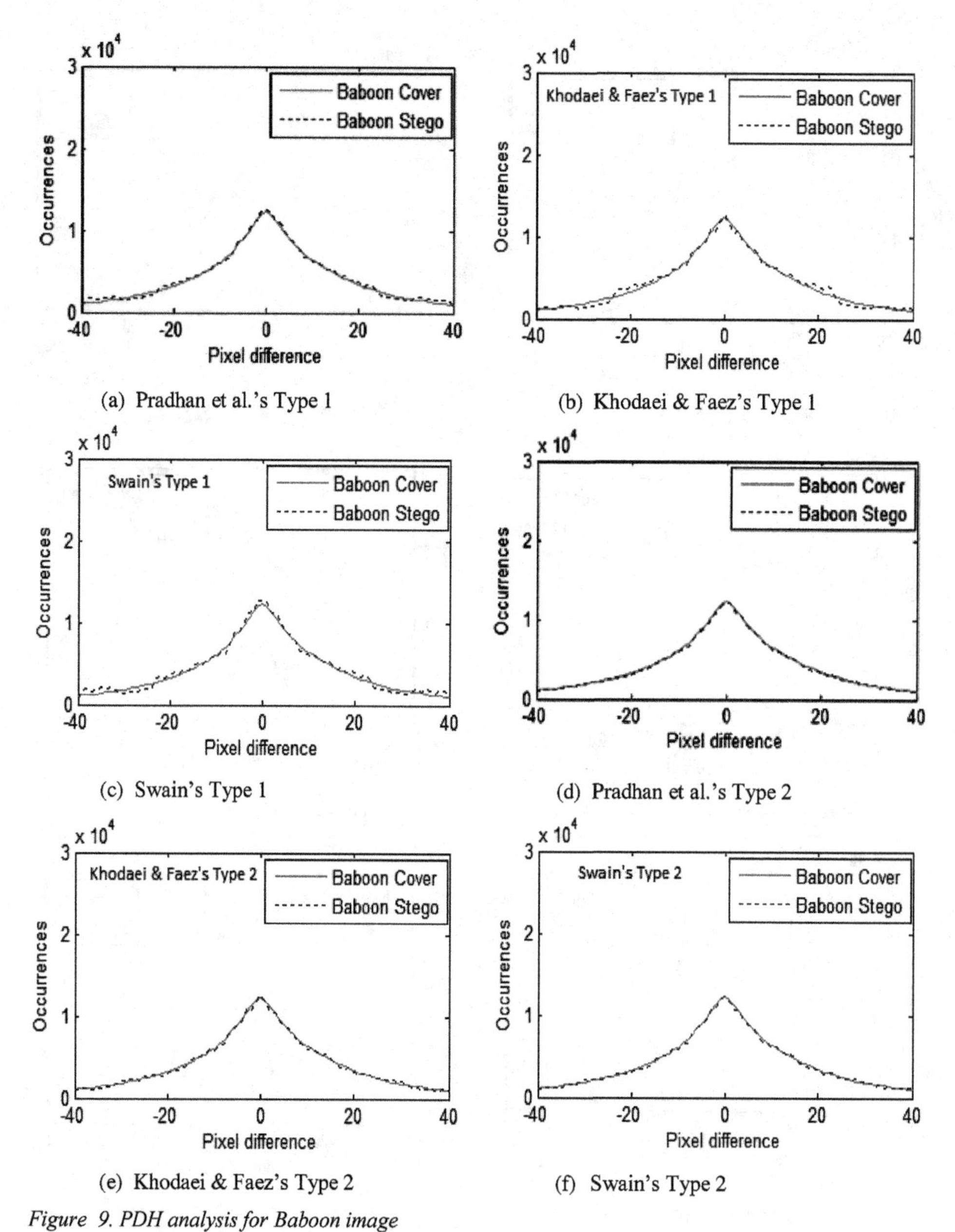

Figure 9. PDH analysis for Baboon image

Figure 10. The RS Analysis curves for Lena and Baboon images of Swain's Technique

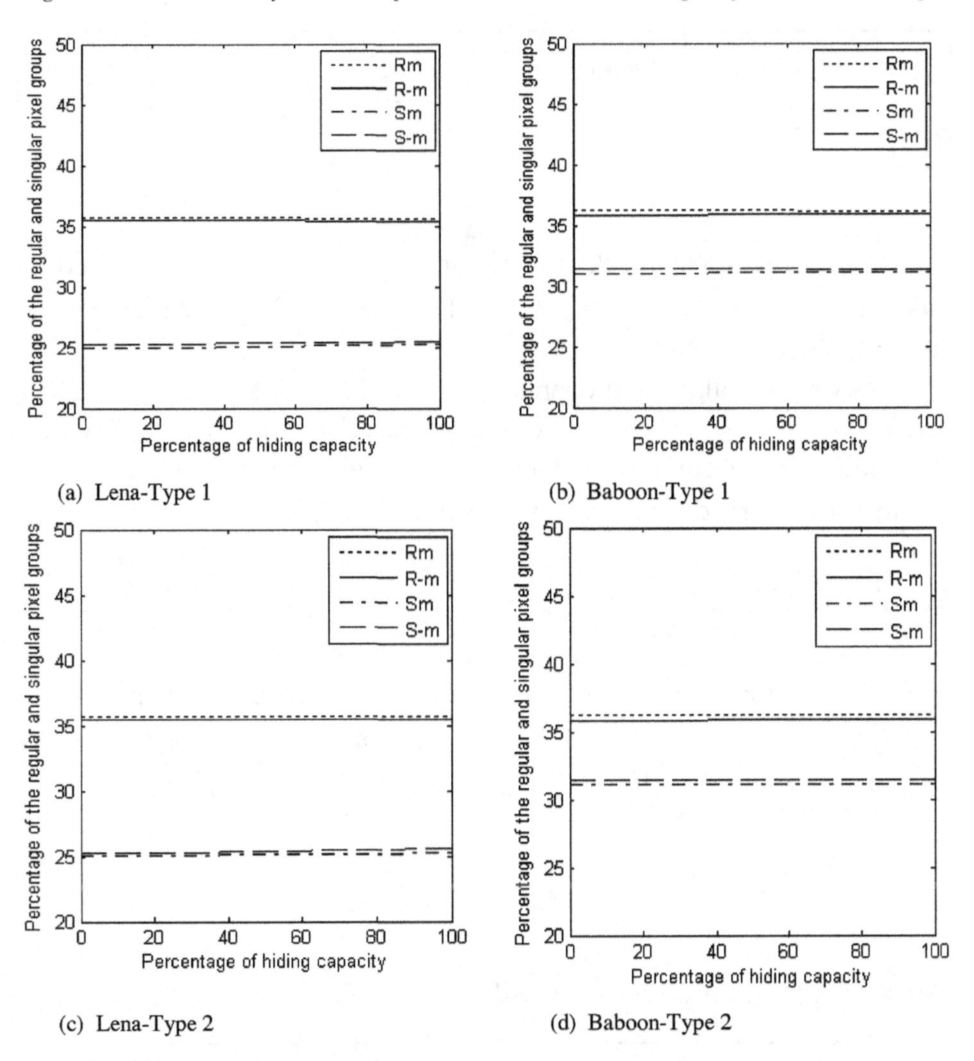

(a) Lena-Type 1
(b) Baboon-Type 1
(c) Lena-Type 2
(d) Baboon-Type 2

Table 6. Range table 1 (for type 1)

Range	R_1 =[0,7]	R_2 =[8,15]	R_3 =[16,31]	R_4 =[32,63]	R_5 =[64,127]	R_6 =[128,255]
capacity	3	3	3	3	4	4

Table 7. Range Table 2 (for type 2)

Range	R_1 =[0,7]	R_2 =[8,15]	R_3 =[16,31]	R_4 =[32,63]	R_5 =[64,127]	R_6 =[128,255]
capacity	3	3	4	5	6	6

Thus the stego-pixel block after hiding t, t_1, t_2, t_3, t_4, t_5, t_6, t_7 and t_8 bits of data in pixels P_c, P_1, P_2, P_3, P_4, P_5, P_6, P_7 and P_8 respectively is as shown in Figure 11 (b).

The extraction algorithm operates on 3×3 pixel blocks as in embedding algorithm. The blocks are formed in a non-overlapping manner. A typical stego-block is represented in Figure 11 (b). Retrieve the t LSBs from P_c'. For i=1 to 8, find eight difference values as in Eq. (29).

$$d_i' = \left|P_c' - P_i'\right| \tag{29}$$

Each d_i' belongs to a range whose embedding capacity is t_i and lower bound is L_i. For i=1 to 8, find the decimal values of the embedded secret bit streams using Eq. (30).

$$S_i = d_i' - L_i \tag{30}$$

Figure 11. (a) original block, (b) stego-block

P_1	P_2	P_3
P_4	P_c	P_5
P_6	P_7	P_8

(a)

P_1'	P_2'	P_3'
P_4'	P_c'	P_5'
P_6'	P_7'	P_8'

(b)

Now convert S_1, S_2, S_3, S_4, S_5, S_6, S_7 and S_8 into t_1, t_2, t_3, t_4, t_5, t_6, t_7, t_8 binary bits respectively.

Results of Eight Directional PVD Technique

The results are discussed with 8 standard RGB color images from SIPI image data base. The R, G and B components (each 8 bits) of a pixel are treated as a single unit. Figure 12 shows the original images, Figure 13 shows the stego-images of type 1 and Figure 14 shows the stego-images of type 2. In each of these stego-images seven lakhs (7,00,000) bits of data is hidden. The evaluation parameters are, (i) hiding capacity, (ii) bit rate (BPB) (Pradhan, Sahu, Swain & Sekhar, 2016), (iii) PSNR (Pradhan, Sahu, Swain & Sekhar, 2016), and (iv) quality index (Q) (Wang & Bovic, 2002).

Table 8 notes the results of seven-way PVD (Pradhan, Sekhar & Swain, 2016b) which is an extension of Wu & Tsai's technique (Wu & Tsai, 2003). Table 9 notes the results of Khodaei & Faez's technique (Khodaei & Faez, 2012) and Table 10 notes the results of the eight directional PVD technique (Swain, 2018). The PSNR and capacity of eight directional PVD technique (both type 1 and type 2) are better than seven-way PVD. The bit rate and Q are also better. Although as compared to Khodaei & Faez's technique the PSNR is not improved, but the hiding capacity is improved. The major advantage over Khodaei & Faez's technique is that the eight directional PVD

Figure 12. Original images

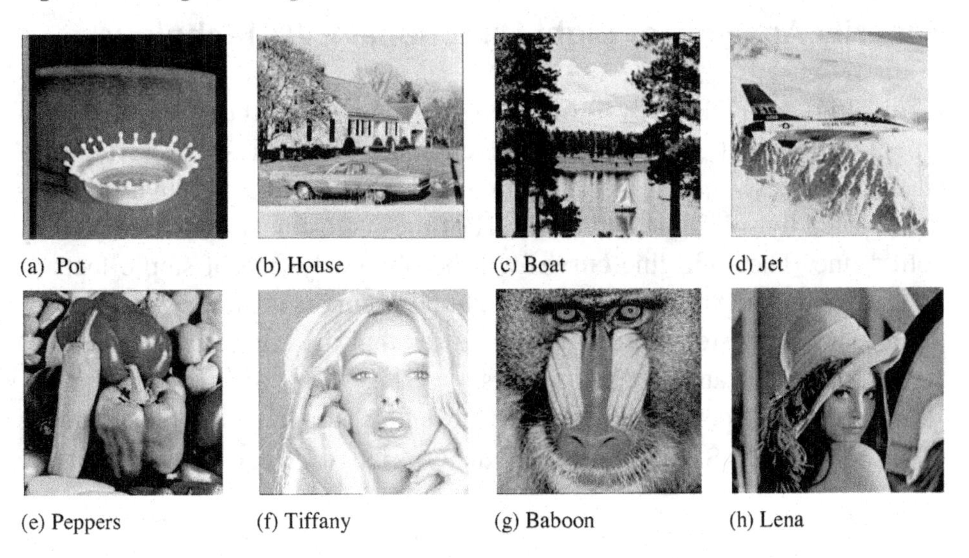

Figure 13. Stego-images of eight directional PVD- type 1 (t=3, range table 6)

technique is resistant to PDH analysis, but Khodaei & Faez's technique is detectable by PDH analysis. This is made possible by exploiting the edges in eight directions.

Now let us observe the results of eight directional PVD technique and compare the type 1 and type 2. We can observe that the capacity is higher in type 2 as compared to type 1. This is because of the 4 LSBs substitution in type 2 at the central pixel i.e. the t value is 4. On the other hand, the PSNR of the type 1 is better than that of type 2.

Security Analysis of Eight Directional PVD Technique

Figure 15 is the PDH analysis of type 1 and Figure 16 is the PDH analysis of type 2 of the eight directional PVD technique. The analysis is carried over all the eight test images. For each image the PDH of the original image is represented by solid line and the PDH of the stego-image is represented by dotted line. The solid line curves will be obviously free of step effects as they are of the original images. The dotted line curves in all the sixteen cases do not show any step effects. This justifies that the eight directional PVD technique is resistant to PDH analysis.

RS analysis is performed by using these four parameters. If the condition $R_m \approx R_{-m} > S_m \approx S_{-m}$ is true, then RS analysis fails to detect the steganography

Figure 14. Stego-images of eight directional PVD- type 2 (t=4, range table 7)

Table 8. Results of seven-way PVD technique (Pradhan, Sekhar & Swain, 2016b)

Images 512×512×3	Seven-Way PVD				Seven Way+ One Way PVD			
	PSNR	Capacity	Q	BPB	PSNR	Capacity	Q	BPB
Pot	42.37	1795551	0.9996	2.28	42.40	1803635	0.9996	2.29
House	38.97	1972223	0.9986	2.50	38.98	1977403	0.9986	2.51
Boat	37.89	1972086	0.9988	2.50	37.91	1991005	0.9988	2.53
Jet	42.09	1906254	0.9989	2.42	41.98	1909595	0.9989	2.42
Peppers	40.42	1778072	0.9993	2.26	40.20	1806166	0.9992	2.29
Tiffany	41.23	1400756	0.9986	1.78	41.30	1450799	0.9986	1.84
Baboon	33.79	2226806	0.9957	2.83	33.77	2243218	0.9957	2.85
Lena	41.73	1896662	0.9993	2.41	41.73	1901149	0.9993	2.41
Average	**39.81**	1868551	0.9986	2.37	39.78	**1885371**	0.9985	2.39

technique. But if the condition $R_{-m} - S_{-m} > R_m - S_m$ is true, then the RS analysis succeeds in detecting the steganography technique.

Figure 17 represents the RS analysis for the eight directional PVD technique. Figure 17(a) and (b) stands for RS analysis over Lena & baboon images respectively of type 1. Similarly, Figure 17(c) and (d) stands for RS analysis over Lena & Baboon images respectively of type 2. In all the four cases the condition $R_m \approx R_{-m} > S_m \approx S_{-m}$ is true, so we can conclude that RS analysis

Table 9. Results of Khodaei & Faez's technique

Images 512×512×3	Khodaei & Faez (2012) - type1				Khodaei & Faez (2012) - type2			
	PSNR	Capacity	Q	BPB	PSNR	Capacity	Q	BPB
Pot	41.21	2366001	0.9995	3.00	37.83	2387494	0.9990	3.03
House	39.16	2387183	0.9986	3.03	38.75	2470824	0.9985	3.14
Boat	40.05	2391994	0.9993	3.04	37.49	2504613	0.9987	3.18
Jet	40.89	2374048	0.9986	3.01	40.64	2418419	0.9985	3.07
Peppers	39.32	2372858	0.9991	3.01	37.91	2435223	0.9987	3.09
Tiffany	39.73	2372396	0.9980	3.01	40.25	2416944	0.9982	3.07
Baboon	37.77	2443361	0.9982	3.10	34.49	2662080	0.9963	3.38
Lena	42.78	2375248	0.9995	3.02	41.25	2434603	0.9993	3.09
Average	**40.11**	2385386	0.9988	3.03	38.57	**2466275**	0.9984	3.13

Table 10. Eight directional PVD (ED-PVD) technique (Swain, 2018)

Images 512×512×3	ED-PVD - type1 (t=3, Range Table 1)				ED-PVD - type2 (t=4, Range Table 2)			
	PSNR	Capacity	Q	BPB	PSNR	Capacity	Q	BPB
Pot	41.15	2354240	.9996	2.99	37.11	2475977	.9988	3.15
House	39.69	2358575	.9988	3.00	38.39	2625804	.9984	3.34
Boat	37.25	2364685	.9987	3.01	34.08	2659795	.9973	3.38
Jet	42.21	2356828	.9989	3.00	40.38	2538801	.9985	3.23
Peppers	37.81	2356645	.9988	3.00	34.69	2544392	.9975	3.24
Tiffany	41.46	2353505	.9987	2.99	40.53	2511139	.9984	3.19
Baboon	34.26	2392573	.9961	3.04	32.09	2939376	.9937	3.74
Lena	42.62	2353892	.9995	2.99	40.48	2533551	.9992	3.22
Average	**39.55**	2361368	.9986	3.00	37.22	**2603604**	.9977	**3.31**

could not detect the eight directional PVD technique. The Lena image has more smooth regions and Baboon image has more edge regions, all the remaining six images are in between these two in terms of smoothness. So, it is sufficient to draw a conclusion based on these two images.

CONCLUSION

These first three techniques discussed in this chapter use the principles of LSB substitution and pixel value differencing. So their security can be checked

Figure 15. PDH Analysis for type 1 of the eight directional PVD technique

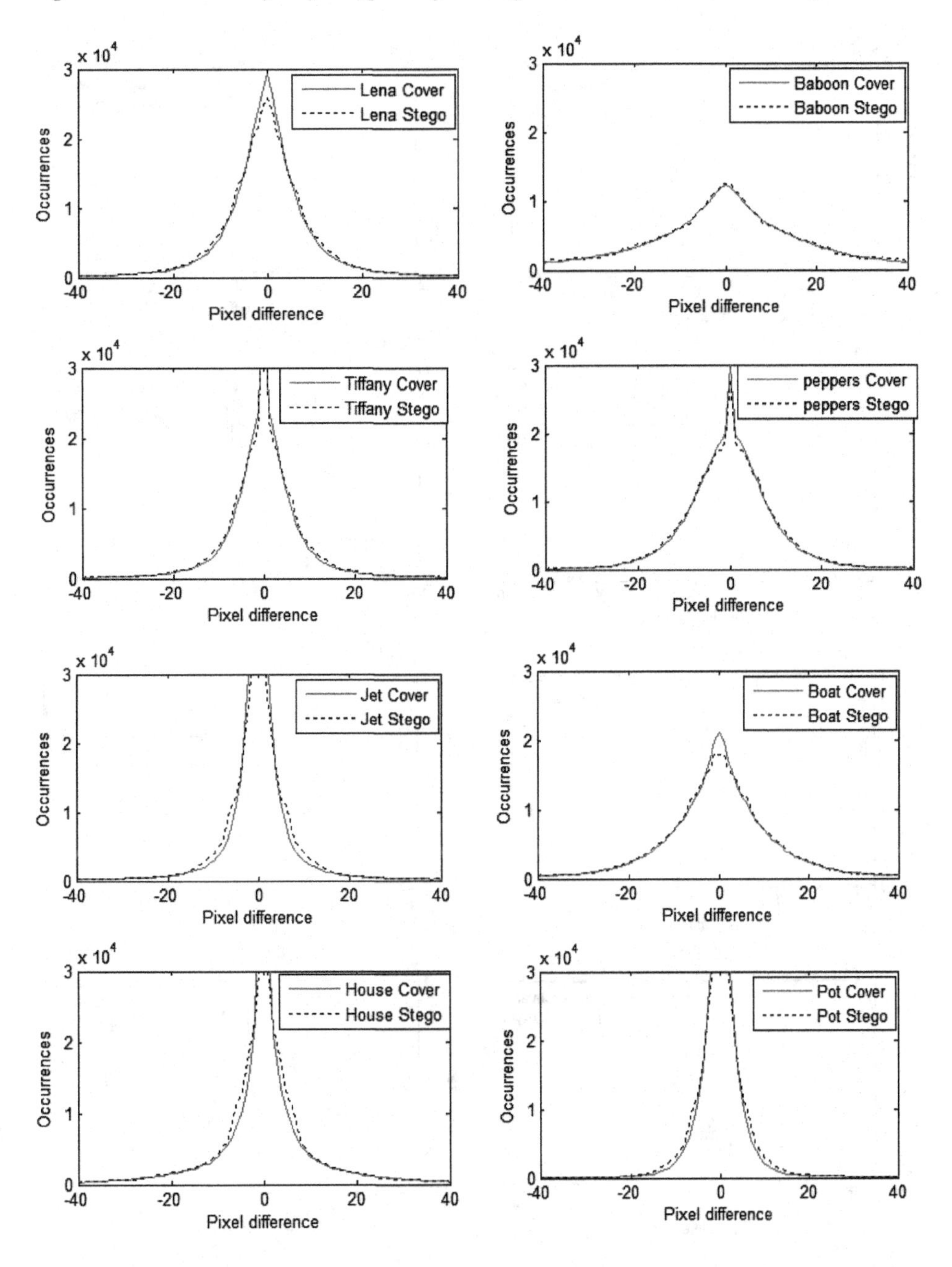

Figure 16. PDH Analysis for type 2 of the eight directional PVD technique

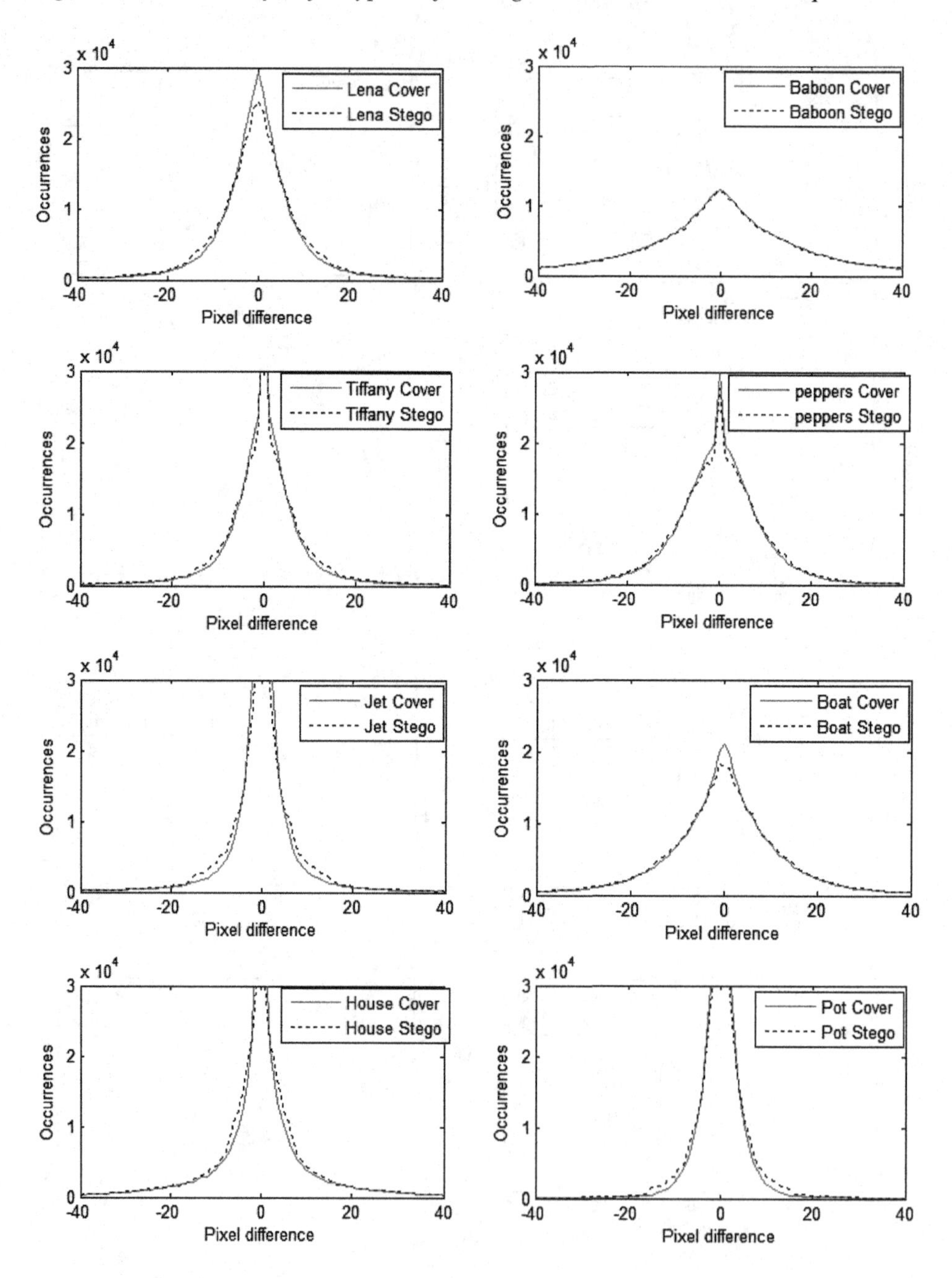

Figure 17. RS Analysis for type 1 and type 2 of eight directional PVD technique

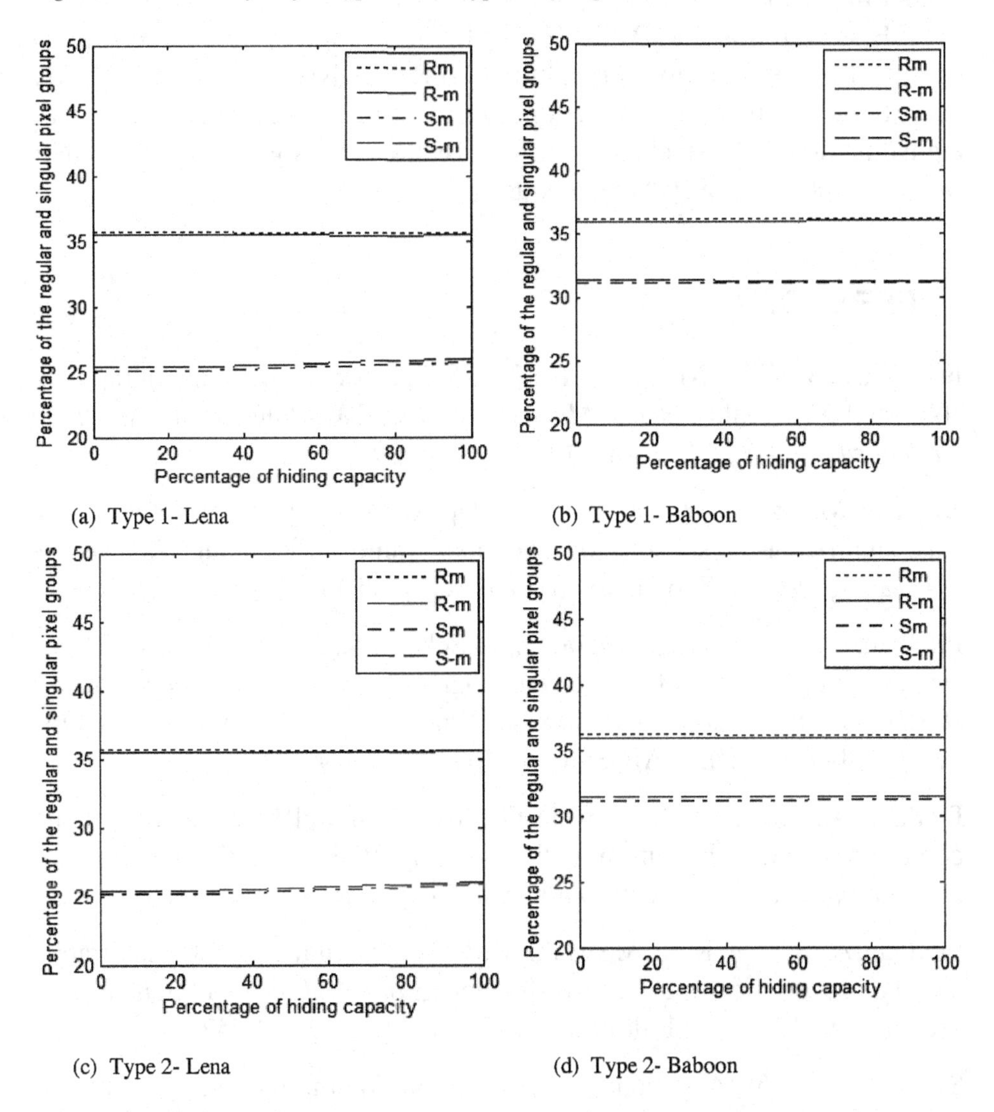

by analyzing through RS analysis and PDH analysis. All the three techniques are analyzed by PDH analysis. The Pradhan et al.'s (2016a) technique is less vulnerable as compared to the other two techniques. The RS analysis for Swain's technique shows that the relation $R_m \approx R_{-m} > S_m \approx S_{-m}$ is be satisfied. It implies that Swain's technique is undetected by RS analysis. But the authors of other two techniques did not justify that their technique is undetected by RS analysis. The fourth technique exploits multi-directional edges to avoid the step effects in PDH of stego-images. It judiciously combines of LSB substitution and PVD. The LSB substitution is performed only in one pixel out of nine pixels in a block, so RS analysis cannot detect it. By using the edges in multiple directions, the PDH analysis cannot detect it. This eight directional PVD technique performs better in hiding capacity and PSNR over other competing PVD techniques.

REFERENCES

Fridrich, J., Goljian, M., & Du, R. (2001). Detecting LSB steganography in color and gray-scale images. *Magazine of IEEE Multimedia Special Issue on Security*, *8*(4), 22–28. doi:10.1109/93.959097

Khodaei, M., & Faez, K. (2012). New adaptive steganographic method using least-significant-bit substitution and pixel-value differencing. *IET Image Processing*, *6*(6), 677–686. doi:10.1049/iet-ipr.2011.0059

Pradhan, A., Sahu, A. K., Swain, G., & Sekhar, K. R. (2016). Performance evaluation parameters of image steganography techniques. *Proceedings of IEEE International Conference on Research Advances in Integrated Navigation Systems*, 1-8. 10.1109/RAINS.2016.7764399

Pradhan, A., Sekhar, K. R., & Swain, G. (2016a). Digital image steganography combining LSB substitution with five way PVD in 2×3 pixel blocks. *International Journal of Pharmacy and Technology*, *8*(4), 22051–22061.

Pradhan, A., Sekhar, K. R., & Swain, G. (2016b). Digital image steganography based on seven way pixel value differencing. *Indian Journal of Science and Technology*, *9*(37), 1–11. doi:10.17485/ijst/2016/v9i37/88557

Swain, G. (2016). A steganographic method combining LSB substitution and PVD in a block. *Procedia Computer Science*, *85*, 39–44. doi:10.1016/j.procs.2016.05.174

Swain, G. (2018). Digital image steganography using eight directional PVD against RS analysis and PDH analysis. *Advances in Multimedia*, *2018*, 1–13. doi:10.1155/2018/4847098

Swain, G., & Lenka, S. K. (2015). A novel steganography technique by mapping words with LSB array. *International Journal of Signal and Imaging Systems Engineering*, *8*(1), 115–122. doi:10.1504/IJSISE.2015.067052

Wang, Z., & Bovic, A. C. (2002). A universal image quality index. *IEEE Signal Processing Letters*, *9*(3), 81–84. doi:10.1109/97.995823

Wu, D. C., & Tsai, W. H. (2003). A steganograhic method for images by pixel value differencing. *Pattern Recognition Letters*, *24*(9-10), 1613–1626. doi:10.1016/S0167-8655(02)00402-6

Zhang, X., & Wang, S. (2004). Vulnerability of pixel-value differencing steganography to histogram analysis and modification for enhanced security. *Pattern Recognition Letters*, *25*(3), 331–339. doi:10.1016/j.patrec.2003.10.014

Chapter 6
Adaptive LSB Substitution and Combination of LSB Substitution, PVD, and EMD

ABSTRACT

This chapter describes two types of steganography techniques: (1) adaptive LSB substitution and (2) combination of LSB substitution, PVD, and exploiting modification directions (EMD). The adaptive LSB substitution technique embeds a variable number of bits in different pixel blocks depending on the smoothness of the block. This improves the security and reduces the distortion. In the second technique, the LSB substitution, PVD, and exploiting modification directions (EMD) principles are judiciously combined in pixel blocks to get higher embedding capacity, lesser distortion, and improved security. These hybrid techniques survive from both RS analysis and pixel difference histogram (PDH) analysis.

INTRODUCTION

There are two categories of steganography techniques discussed in this chapter. The first category is called adaptive LSB substitution. The adaptive LSB substitution techniques calculates the average pixel value difference in a block. based on this difference the number of LSBs to be embedded is decided. There are two techniques of this category described in this chapter. The first technique uses 2×2 pixel blocks and divides the blocks into two

DOI: 10.4018/978-1-5225-7516-0.ch006

types such as lower and higher, based on the average pixel value difference (Liao, Wen, & Zhang, 2011). In lower block, a smaller number of bits can be hidden and in higher block, a greater number of bits can be hidden. Similarly, the second technique uses 3×3 pixel blocks and divides the blocks into four categories based on average pixel value difference (Swain, 2014).

The second category of techniques is a combination of LSB substitution, PVD and EMD (Pradhan, Sekhar & Swain, 2018). There are two techniques in this category. The first one uses 2×2 pixel blocks and the second one uses 3×3 pixel blocks.

Zhang and Wang (2006) proposed exploiting modification direction (EMD) steganography. The principal goal in it is that a group of secret bits be converted to a digit in (2n+1)-ary notational system, where n is the size of pixel block. This secret digit could be hidden in the pixel block by adding ±1 to only one pixel. In this technique the hiding capacity is not good. Shen and Huang (2015) made the hiding capacity of a block adaptive by using PVD with EMD. This PVD with EMD technique provides higher hiding capacity and better PSNR. To protect from pixel difference histogram (PDH) analysis and RS analysis, two hybrid image steganography techniques by appropriate combination of LSB substitution, pixel value differencing (PVD) and exploiting modification directions (EMD) has been proposed in (Pradhan, Sekhar & Swain, 2018).

As all the above techniques use both the LSB substitution and PVD principle, so both RS analysis (Fridrich, Goljian & Du, 2001; Swain & Lenka, 2015) and pixel difference histogram (PDH) analysis (Zhang & Wang, 2004; Pradhan, Sahu, Swain & Sekhar, 2016) could be used to check the security strength in them.

PIXEL DIFFERENCING AND MODIFIED LSB SUBSTITUTION

Four Pixel Differencing and Modified LSB Substitution

Liao, Wen, & Zhang (2011) proposed an adaptive LSB substitution technique based on PVD in 2×2 pixel blocks. This technique is as described below. The image is scanned in raster scan order and is partitioned into non-overlapping

Figure 1. A 2x2 sample block

x_0	x_1
x_2	x_3

blocks consisting 2×2 pixels as shown in Figure 1, where x_0, x_1, x_2, and x_3 are the different pixel values.

The average difference value, d of the block is calculated as in Eq. (1), where x_{min} is one of the four values x_0, x_1, x_2 and x_3, whose value is minimum.

$$d = \frac{1}{3}\sum_{i=0}^{8}\left|x_i - x_{min}\right| \tag{1}$$

For some chosen value T, if the $d \leq T$, then the block belongs to lower-level and k_l bits of data can be hidden using LSB substitution. If the $d > T$, then the block belongs to higher-level and k_h bits of data can be hidden using LSB substitution. The conditions $k_l \leq k_h$ and $1 \leq k_l, k_h \leq 5$ should be true. Thus, the number of bits that can be hidden in a pixel is n, where $n = k_l$ for lower block and $n = k_h$ for higher block.

If for a block $d \leq T$ and $\left(x_{max} x_{min}\right) > 2T+2$, ($x_{max}$ is one of the four-pixel values x_0, x_1, x_2 & x_3, whose value is maximum), then it is an error block, so embedding is not done in it. Otherwise for i=0, 1, 2, 3 embed k bits of secret data in x_i using LSB substitution and let the stego pixel be y_i. Now modify each y_i to optimize its value. Say the optimized value is z_i, as shown in Eq. (2).

$$z_i = \begin{cases} y_i - 2^n & \textit{if } y_i \geq \left(x_i + 2^{n-1} + 1\right) \\ y_i + 2^n & \textit{if } y_i \leq \left(x_i - 2^{n-1} + 1\right) \\ y_i + 2^n & \textit{otherwise} \end{cases} \tag{2}$$

For i=0, 1, 2, 3, the final stego values, x_i' can be calculated as $x_i' = z_i + l \times 2^k$, where $l \in \{0, 1, -1\}$. The x_i' values should be searched satisfying the following three conditions,

1. d and d′ belongs to the same level, where $d' = \frac{1}{3}\sum_{i=0}^{8}\left|x_i' - x_{min}'\right|$, and $x_{min}' = \min\left\{x_1', x_2', x_3', x_4'\right\}$
2. The final stego block is not an error block
3. The value $\sum_{i=0}^{3}\left(x_i' - x_i\right)^2$ is minimized

The final stego-block is as shown in Figure 2.

The extraction procedure is very simple. The stego-image is scanned in raster scan order and is partitioned into non-overlapping blocks consisting 2×2 pixels as in embedding. Suppose the block shown in Figure 2 is a stego block. Then calculate the difference $d' = \frac{1}{3}\sum_{i=0}^{8}\left|x_i' - x_{min}'\right|$ where, $x_{min}' = \min\left\{x_1', x_2', x_3', x_4'\right\}$. If $d' < T$, then set $n = k_l$ otherwise set $n = k_h$. Now verify whether the block is an error block or not. If it is an error block ignore it. If it is not an error block then extract the n LSB bits from each pixel, x_i', for $i = 0,1,2,$ and 3.

Nine-Pixel Differencing and Modified LSB Substitution

Swain (2014) proposed an adaptive LSB substitution technique using 3×3 pixel blocks. The embedding and extraction procedures are narrated below. The image is scanned in raster scan order and is partitioned into non-overlapping blocks consisting 3×3 pixels as shown in Figure 3, where x_0, x_1, x_2, x_3, x_4, x_5, x_6, x_7, and x_8 are the different pixel values.

Figure 2. The 3×3 stego-block

x_0'	x_1'
x_2'	x_3'

Figure 3. A 3x3 sample block

x_0	x_1	x_2
x_3	x_4	x_5
x_6	x_7	x_8

The average difference value, d of the block is calculated as in Eq. (3), where x_{min} is the minimum value of x_i, for i=0,1,2, …,8.

$$d = \frac{1}{8}\sum_{i=0}^{8}\left|x_i - x_{min}\right| \tag{3}$$

If the $d \le 7$, then the block belongs to lower-level and 2-bit LSB substitution is applied. If $8 \le d \le 15$, then the block belongs to lower-middle level and 3-bit LSB substitution is applied. If, $16 \le d \le 31$, then the block belongs to higher-middle level and 4-bit LSB substitution is applied. If $d \ge 32$, then the block belongs to higher level and 5-bit LSB substitution is applied.

Suppose n-bit substitution is applied in a block, where n value is 2, 3, 4, and 5 corresponding to lower, lower-middle, higher-middle, and higher level respectively. The two LSBs of x_8 i.e. 7th and 8th bit locations are reserved to behave as indicator during extraction, but the other bit locations like 4th, 5th, and 6th can be utilized for data embedding if granted as per the block-level. These two bits are set to 00 if the block belongs to lower level. Similarly, these two bits are set to 01, 10, and 11 if the block belongs to lower-middle, higher-middle, and higher level respectively. Thus, in total a block can hide a total of (9×n-2) number of bits. Let y_0, y_1, y_2, y_3, y_4, y_5, y_6, y_7, and y_8 are the new pixel values corresponding to x_0, x_1, x_2, x_3, x_4, x_5, x_6, x_7, and x_8 respectively.

After applying the n-bit LSB substitution, now the adjustments are applied to y_0, y_1, y_2, y_3, y_4, y_5, y_6, y_7, and y_8 to minimize the distortion. Let z_0, z_1, z_2, z_3, z_4, z_5, z_6, z_7, and z_8 are modified values. These are calculated using Eq. (4), for i= 0 to 8.

$$z_i = \begin{cases} y_i - 2^n & if\ y_i \geq \left(x_i + 2^{n-1} + 1\right) \\ y_i + 2^n & if\ y_i \leq \left(x_i - 2^{n-1} + 1\right) \\ y_i + 2^n & otherwise \end{cases} \tag{4}$$

After this adjustment if the z_i value falls off boundary {0, 255}, then the below Eq. is applied to make it fall within boundary {0, 255}. This is done using Eq. (5).

$$z_i = \begin{cases} z_i + 2^n & if\ z_i < 0 \\ z_i + 2^n & if\ z_i > 255 \end{cases} \tag{5}$$

Now, the final stego-block comprises of the pixel values $z_{0,}$ $z_{1,}$ $z_{2,}$ $z_{3,}$ $z_{4,}$ $z_{5,}$ $z_{6,}$ $z_{7,}$ and z_8 as in Figure 4 corresponding to the original pixel block given in Figure 3.

The extraction procedure is very simple. The stego-image is scanned in raster scan order and is partitioned into non-overlapping blocks consisting 3x3 pixels as in embedding procedure. Let $s_{0,}$ $s_{1,}$ $s_{2,}$ $s_{3,}$ $s_{4,}$ $s_{5,}$ $s_{6,}$ $s_{7,}$ and s_8 are the different stego-pixel values and the pixel s_8 is represented by the eight bits as below.

s_8=b_1 b_2b_3 b_4b_5 $b_6b_7b_8$, where each b_i for i=0, 1, 2... 8 is a bit.

If b_7b_8 is 00, then two LSBs from each of the pixels $s_{0,}$ $s_{1,}$ $s_{2,}$ $s_{3,}$ $s_{4,}$ $s_{5,}$ $s_{6,}$ and $s_{7,}$ are extracted and from s_8 nothing is extracted.

Figure 4. The 3×3 stego-block

Z_0	Z_1	Z_2
Z_3	Z_4	Z_5
Z_6	Z_7	Z_8

If b_7b_8 is 01, then three LSBs from each of the pixels $s_{0,}$ $s_{1,}$ $s_{2,}$ $s_{3,}$ $s_{4,}$ $s_{5,}$ $s_{6,}$ and $s_{7,}$ are extracted and from s_8 the bit from 6th location, i.e. b_6 is extracted.

If b_7b_8 is 10, then four LSBs from each of the pixels $s_{0,}$ $s_{1,}$ $s_{2,}$ $s_{3,}$ $s_{4,}$ $s_{5,}$ $s_{6,}$ and $s_{7,}$ are extracted and from s_8 the bits from 5th and 6th locations, i.e. b_5b_6 are also extracted.

If b_7b_8 is 11, then five LSBs from each of the pixels $s_{0,}$ $s_{1,}$ $s_{2,}$ $s_{3,}$ $s_{4,}$ $s_{5,}$ $s_{6,}$ and $s_{7,}$ are extracted and from s_8 the bits from 4th, 5th and 6th locations, i.e. $b_4b_5b_6$ are also extracted.

Results of Adaptive LSB Substitution Techniques

The performance of second technique (9-pixel differencing with modified LSB substitution) is obviously better as compared to the first technique (4-pixel differencing with modified LSB substitution) because the number of levels is greater in second technique as compared to the first technique. The experimental results for second technique over 10 sample images (shown Figure 5 and Figure 6) are discussed below.

Table 1 shows the results of second technique. The PSNR is estimated by hiding 1,40,000 bits of data in these sample images. From Table 1 we can see that the recorded PSNR, hiding capacity and other parameters are very good. Table 2 records the number of blocks falling into different levels for each of these sample images. It can be observed that, 74.74% of the blocks are using 3-bit LSB substitution. The rest 25.26% of the blocks uses 2-bit, 4-bit and 5-bit LSB substitution. By scattering the distribution of the blocks to these four levels and embedding variable number of bits in the different pixels, the security aspect has been addressed.

Figure 5. Original images (256 × 256 color)

(a) Girl1 (b) Couple (c) House1 (d) Tree (e) Jelly beans2

Figure 6. Original images (512 × 512 color)

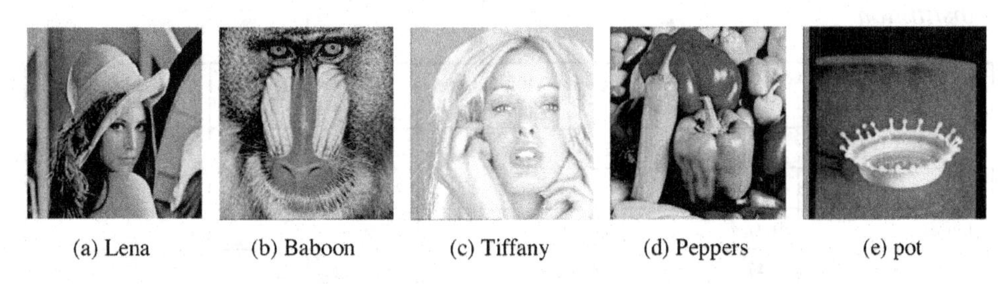

(a) Lena (b) Baboon (c) Tiffany (d) Peppers (e) pot

Table 1. Results of 9-pixel differencing with modified LSB substitution

Images	MSE	PSNR	r	Capacity
Girl1	2.9854	43.38	0.9991	569929
Couple	3.9785	42.13	0.9980	553882
House1	3.2775	42.97	0.9992	571801
Tree	4.4748	41.62	0.9994	626638
Jelly beans2	2.1138	44.88	0.9994	520483
Lena	5.6115	40.64	0.9984	2297680
Baboon	19.5127	35.22	0.9966	2877658
Tiffany	6.2199	40.19	0.9965	2159377
Peppers	7.2495	39.52	0.9986	2286574
Pot	4.8308	41.29	0.9991	2167504
Average	6.0254	41.18	0.9984	1463152

THE LSB+PVD+EMD TECHNIQUE

The LSB+PVD+EMD Technique in 2×2 Pixel Blocks

Pradhan, Sekhar & Swain, (2018) proposed a combination of LSB substitution, PVD and EMD with 2×2 size pixel blocks. The embedding procedure is as discussed below.

Step 1: The image is traversed in raster scan order and partitioned into non-overlapping blocks of size 2×2. A sample block is shown in Figure 7 (a).

Table 2. The distribution of blocks in 9-pixel differencing with modified LSB substitution

Images	Lower-Level Count	Lower-Middle Level Count	Higher-Middle Level Count	Higher-Level Count
Girl1	761	18102	2152	745
Couple	2339	16690	2025	706
House1	1097	17807	1526	1330
Tree	1147	13762	3373	3478
Jelly beans2	6498	12683	1273	1306
Lena	353	75857	7787	3043
Baboon	12	34124	27834	25070
Tiffany	12428	66191	6261	2160
Peppers	2146	74204	6948	3742
Pot	6229	77129	2079	1603
Average	3301	40654	6125	4318
	6.07%	74.74%	11.26%	7.93%
	3301+40654+6125+4318 = 54398 (100%)			

Figure 7. (a) cover pixel block, (b) stego block, and (c) stego block used for extraction

P_c	P_1
P_2	P_3

(a)

p'_c	p'_1
p'_2	p'_3

(b)

p^*_c	p^*_1
p^*_2	p^*_3

(c)

Step 2: For every block the average pixel value difference, $d = \frac{1}{3}\sum_{i=1}^{3}\left|P_c - P_i\right|$ is computed. If d is greater than 15, then the block is said to be an edge area, otherwise it is a smooth area.

Step 3: In an edge area embedding is done using LSB substitution and PVD.

Step 4: In a smooth area embedding is done using LSB substitution and EMD.

The LSB+PVD Embedding Approach

The first LSB of pixel P_c is substituted by bit 1, to act as an indicator during extraction. The other 2 LSBs are substituted by 2 data bits. A new value of this pixel $p_c^{'}$ is obtained. Suppose, the decimal value of the three LSBs of $p_c^{'}$ is s_1 and the decimal value of the three LSBs of P_c is i_1. A difference value $df_1 = i_1 - s_1$ is calculated and $p_c^{'}$ is optimized by Eq. (6).

$$p_c^{'} = \begin{cases} p_c^{'} + 2^3 & \text{if } df_1 > 2^{3-1} \text{ and } 0 \le (p_c^{'} + 2^3) \le 255 \\ p_c^{'} - 2^3 & \text{if } df_1 < -2^{3-1} \text{ and } 0 \le (p_c^{'} - 2^3) \le 255 \\ p_c^{'} & \text{otherwise} \end{cases} \quad (6)$$

Now calculate three difference values, $d_i = \left|p_c^{'} - p_i\right|$ for i = 1, 2, 3. It falls into one of the ranges in range table. Based on the range of d_i, the number of bits to be hidden (n_i) can be decided. Table 3 can be referred as Type 1 and Table 4 can be referred as Type 2. Now convert each n_i bits of confidential data to its decimal value ds_i for i = 1, 2, 3. Then compute the new value for this difference as $d_i^{'} = l_i + ds_i$ for i = 1, 2, 3. Now for each p_i where i = 1, 2, 3, calculate two new values $p_i^{''} = p_c^{'} - d_i^{'}$ and $p_i^{'''} = p_c^{'} + d_i^{'}$. Select one of these two values as $p_i^{'}$ by applying Eq. (7).

$$p_i^{'} = \begin{cases} p_i^{''} & \text{if } \left|p_i - p_i^{''}\right| < \left|p_i - p_i^{'''}\right| \text{ and } 0 \le p_i^{''} \le 255 \\ p_i^{'''} & \text{otherwise} \end{cases} \quad (7)$$

The LSB+EMD Embedding Approach

The first LSB bit of pixel p_c is substituted by bit 0, which can act as an indicator during extraction. The other two LSBs of p_c are substituted by two

Table 3. Range table (Type 1)

Range, {l_i, u_i}	R_1 ={0, 7}	R_2 ={8, 15}	R_3 ={16, 31}	R_4 ={32, 63}	R_5 ={64,127}	R_6 ={128, 255}
No of bits to be hidden, n_i	3	3	3	3	4	4

Table 4. Range table (Type 2)

Range, $\{l_i, u_i\}$	$R_1 = \{0, 7\}$	$R_2 = \{8, 15\}$	$R_3 = \{16, 31\}$	$R_4 = \{32, 63\}$	$R_5 = \{64, 127\}$	$R_6 = \{128, 255\}$
No of bits to be hidden, n_i	3	3	4	5	6	6

data bits. Thus a new value p_c' of the pixel p_c is obtained. Suppose, the decimal value of the three LSBs of p_c' is s_1 and the decimal value of the three LSBs of P_c is i_1. A difference value $df_1 = i_1 - s_1$ is calculated and p_c' is optimized by Eq. (6).

Suppose we denote the remaining pixels (p_1, p_2, p_3) by a name p_k, where k = 1, 2, 3. Now apply EMD for each p_k as follows. Each p_k has to hide 2 bits of data. The decimal equivalent of the two data bits is m_k. Now select x from {-3, -2, -1, 0} and calculate $p_k'' = p_k + x$ such that the condition, (p_k'' mod 4 = m_k) satisfies. Similarly select x from {1, 2, 3} and calculate $p_k''' = p_k + x$ such that the condition (p_k''' mod 4 = m_k) satisfies. If for all the three values in list {1, 2, 3}, the condition (p_k''' mod 4 = m_k) does not satisfy then set $p_k''' = -10$. Now calculate the stego value p_k' for p_k by Eq. (8).

$$p_k' = \begin{cases} p_k'', & \text{if } \left\{\left(p_k''' \langle 0 \text{ or } p_k''' \rangle 255\right) \text{and } 0 \le p_k'' \le 255\right\} \textit{or} \\ & \left\{0 \le \left(p_k'', p_k'''\right) \le 255 \text{ and } \left|p_k - p_k''\right| \le \left|p_k - p_k'''\right|\right\} \\ p_k''', & \text{if } \left\{\left(p_k'' \langle 0 \text{ or } p_k'' \rangle 255\right) \text{and } 0 \le p_k''' \le 255\right\} \textit{or} \\ & \left\{0 \le \left(p_k'', p_k'''\right) \le 255 \text{ and } \left|p_k - p_k'''\right| \le \left|p_k - p_k''\right|\right\} \end{cases} \tag{8}$$

Thus Figure 7(b) represents the stego-pixel block.

The extraction procedure is as discussed below.

Step 1: The stego image is traversed in raster scan order and partitioned into non-overlapping blocks of size 2×2. Figure 7(c) represents a sample 2×2 stego-pixel block.

Step 2: The LSB bit of p_c^* is checked, if it is 1 then for this block the extraction procedure of LSB+PVD approach is used as follows. The next two LSBs of p_c^* are extracted. Furthermore, the $d_i^* = |p_c^* - p_i^*|$ and $s_i^* = d_i^* - l_i$ for i = 1, 2, 3 are calculated. Where, d_i^* belongs to the range R_i and l_i is the lower bound of this range. Now each of these s_i^* is converted to n_i binary bits. Where n_i is the value corresponding to the same range R_i of d_i^*. Note that the same range table (Table 3 or Table 4) which was used during embedding should be used during extraction.

Step 3: If the LSB bit of p_c^* is 0, then for this block the extraction procedure of LSB+EMD is applied as follows. The next two LSBs of p_c^* are extracted. For all the remaining pixels (p_1^*, p_2^*, p_3^*) the decimal equivalent of the embedded bits, m_k is calculated as $m_k = p_k^* \bmod 4$, for k= 1, 2, 3. Now each m_k is converted to 2 binary bits.

The LSB+PVD+EMD Technique in 3×3 Pixel Blocks

Pradhan, Sekhar & Swain, (2018) proposed a combination of LSB substitution, PVD and EMD with 3×3 size pixel blocks. The Embedding procedure is as described below.

Step 1: The image is traversed in raster scan order and partitioned into non-overlapping blocks of size 3×3. A sample block is shown in Figure 8(a).

Step 2: An average pixel value difference, $d = \frac{1}{8}\sum_{i=1}^{8}|P_c - P_i|$ is calculated.

Step 3: If d value is greater than 15 then a combination of LSB substitution and PVD is applied.

Step 4: If d value is less than or equal to 15 then a combination of LSB substitution and EMD is applied.

Figure 8. (a) Cover pixel block, (b) stego block, and (c) stego block used for extraction

P_4	P_3	P_2
P_5	P_c	P_1
P_6	P_7	P_8

(a)

p'_4	p'_3	p'_2
p'_5	p'_c	p'_1
p'_6	p'_7	p'_8

(b)

p^*_4	p^*_3	p^*_2
p^*_5	p^*_c	p^*_1
p^*_6	p^*_7	p^*_8

(c)

The LSB+PVD Embedding Approach

In the central pixel, P_c 3 LSBs are substituted by 3 data bits. A new value of the central pixel is found. Say it is p_c'. In pixel p_8 the first LSB is substituted by bit 1, which will be used as indicator during extraction procedure. The other two LSBs in it are substituted by two data bits. After substituting, three LSBs, suppose the new value of pixel p_8 is p_8'. The decimal value of the three LSBs of p_c' is s_1 and the decimal value of three LSBs of P_c is i_1. Similarly, the decimal value of three LSBs of p_8' is s_2 and the decimal value of three LSBs of p_8 is i_2. Now calculate the differences df_1 and df_2 as, $df_1 = i_1 - s_1$ and $df_2 = i_2 - s_2$. Now optimize the values of p_c' and p_8' using Eq. (6) and Eq. (9) respectively.

$$p_8' = \begin{cases} p_8' + 2^3 & \textit{if}\, df_2 > 2^{3-1}\, \textit{and}\, 0 \leq (p_8' + 2^3) \leq 255 \\ p_8' - 2^3 & \textit{if}\, df_2 < -2^{3-1}\, \textit{and}\, 0 \leq (p_8' - 2^3) \leq 255 \\ p_8' & \textit{otherwise} \end{cases} \tag{9}$$

Now calculate seven difference values, $d_i = \left| p_c' - p_i \right|$ for i = 1, 2, …,7. These difference values lie in one of the ranges of the range table. Table 3 can be chosen as Type 1 or Table 4 can be chosen as Type 2. Based on the range of d_i, the number of bits to be hidden (n_i) can be decided from the range table.

Now convert each n_i bits of confidential data to its decimal value ds_i for i = 1, 2, …, 7. Then compute the new values for the seven differences as d_i' = l_i + ds_i for i = 1, 2, …,7. Now for each p_i where i = 1, 2, …,7, calculate two new values $p_i'' = p_c' - d_i'$ and $p_i''' = p_c' + d_i'$. Select one of these two values as p_i' by applying Eq. (2). This p_i' is the stego value of p_i.

The LSB+EMD Embedding Approach

The first LSB of pixel p_8 is substituted by 0 and the next two LSBs are substituted by two data bits. After embedding, say it is p_8'. The decimal value of the three LSBs of p_8' is s_2 and the decimal value of three LSBs of p_8 is

i_2. Now calculate the difference df_2 as, $df_2 = i_2 - s_2$. Now optimize the value of $p_8^{'}$ using Eq. (9).

Suppose we denote the remaining pixels (p_1, p_2, p_3, p_4, p_5, p_6, p_7, p_c) by a name p_k, where k = 1, 2, 3, 4, 5, 6, 7, c. Now apply EMD for each p_k as follows. Each p_k has to hide 2 bits of data. The decimal equivalent of the two data bits is m_k. Now select x from {-3, -2, -1, 0} and calculate $p_k^{''} = p_k + x$ such that the condition, ($p_k^{''}$ mod 4 $= m_k$) satisfies. Similarly, select x from {1, 2, 3} and calculate $p_k^{'''} = p_k + x$ such that the condition ($p_k^{'''}$ mod 4 = m_k) satisfies. If for all the three values in list {1, 2, 3}, the condition ($p_k^{'''}$ mod 4 $= m_k$) does not satisfy then set $p_k^{'''} = -10$. Now calculate $p_k^{'}$ by Eq. 3. This $p_k^{'}$ is the stego value of p_k.

Thus Figure 8(b) represents the stego pixel block.

The extraction procedure is as described below.

Step 1: The stego image is traversed in raster scan order and partitioned into non-overlapping blocks of size 3×3. Figure 8 (c) represents a sample 3×3 stego-pixel block.

Step 2: The LSB bit of p_8^{*} is checked, if it is 1 then for this block the extraction procedure of LSB+PVD approach is used as follows. The three LSBs of p_c^{*} and next two LSBs of p_8^{*} are extracted. Furthermore, the $d_i^{*} = \left|p_c^{*} - p_i^{*}\right|$ and $s_i^{*} = d_i^{*} - l_i$ for i = 1, 2, 3,…,7 are calculated. Where, d_i^{*} belongs to the range R_i and l_i is the lower bound of this range. Now each of these s_i^{*} is converted to n_i binary bits. Where n_i is the value corresponding to the same range R_i of d_i^{*}. Note that the same range table (Table 3 or Table 4) which was used during embedding should be used during extraction.

Step 3: If the LSB bit of p_8^{*} is 0, then for this block the extraction procedure of LSB+EMD is applied as follows. The next two LSBs of p_8^{*} are extracted. For all the remaining pixels (p_1^{*}, p_2^{*}, p_3^{*}, p_4^{*}, p_5^{*}, p_6^{*}, p_7^{*}, p_c^{*}), the decimal equivalent of the embedded bits, m_k is calculated as $m_k = p_k^{*} \bmod 4$, for k=1, 2, 3, 4, 5, 6, 7, c. Now each m_k is converted to 2 binary bits.

Results and Discussion of LSB+PVD+EMD Techniques

The implementation work is done using MATLAB tool and with the RGB color images. The data hiding is performed in Red, Green, and Blue planes separately. It can also be applied on gray scale images. Experiments are done with many images. Few samples stego-images are shown in Figure 9. Each stego image has hidden 700000 (seven lakhs) bits of secret data. These stego-images look innocuous and no distortion is observable.

In Table 5 the results of Wu & Tsai's (2003) PVD technique and Shen & Huang's (2015) PVD+EMD technique are given. Table 6 shows the results of the 3PVD+ 3LSB + EMD (Pradhan, Sekhar & Swain, 2018) technique and Table 7 shows the results of the 7PVD+ 3LSB + EMD (Pradhan, Sekhar & Swain, 2018) technique. These results comprise of four parameters, (i) hiding capacity (Liao, Wen, & Zhang, 2011), (ii) bits per byte (BPB) (Zhang & Wang, 2004), (iii) PSNR (Liao, Wen, & Zhang, 2011), and (iv) quality index, Q (Pradhan, Sahu, Swain & Sekhar, 2016).

It can be found from Tables 5, 6 and 7, that the hiding capacity and BPB of 3PVD+ 3LSB + EMD technique (Type 1 and Type 2) and 7PVD+ 3LSB + EMD technique (Type 1 and Type 2) are significantly enhanced as compared to that of Wu & Tsai and Shen & Huang's techniques. Furthermore, the PSNR of the proposed 3PVD+ 3LSB + EMD technique (Type 1 and Type 2) and 7PVD+ 3LSB + EMD technique (Type 1 and Type 2) are nearly equal to that of Wu & Tsai and Shen & Huang's techniques.

Now let us come to security analysis. The PDH analysis diagrams clearly reveal the step effects in Shen & Huang's technique, Figure 10 (a)-(b). Wu & Tsai's technique is also detected by PDH analysis, proved in (Pradhan, Sekhar & Swain, 2016). But for the 3PVD+ 3LSB + EMD (Pradhan, Sekhar & Swain, 2018) technique and 7PVD+ 3LSB + EMD (Pradhan, Sekhar &

Figure 9. Stego-images with 700000 (seven lakhs) bits of secret data inside

Lena

Baboon

Boat

Pot

Table 5. Results of Existing Techniques

Images 512× 512×3	Wu & Tsai (2003)				Shen & Huang (2015)			
	PSNR	Capacity	Q	BPB	PSNR	Capacity	Q	BPB
Lena	43.67	1232606	0.999	1.56	38.01	1223062	0.998	1.55
Baboon	38.40	1403491	0.998	1.78	40.14	1343274	0.999	1.70
Peppers	43.13	1174751	0.999	1.49	41.57	1226139	0.999	1.55
Jet	43.97	1220544	0.999	1.55	43.35	1212350	0.999	1.54
Boat	41.33	1278971	0.999	1.62	41.35	1264742	0.999	1.60
House	41.27	1256404	0.999	1.59	41.75	1242081	0.999	1.57
Pot	44.01	1163700	0.999	1.47	43.38	1195641	0.999	1.52
Average	42.25	1247209	0.999	1.57	41.36	1243898	0.999	1.58

Table 6. Results of 3PVD+ 3LSB + EMD (Pradhan, Sekhar & Swain, 2018) technique

Images 512× 512×3	Proposed 3 PVD+ 3 LSB + EMD (Type 1)				Proposed 3 PVD+ 3 LSB + EMD (Type 2)			
	PSNR	Capacity	Q	BPB	PSNR	Capacity	Q	BPB
Lena	44.45	1631063	0.999	2.07	41.33	1687353	0.999	2.15
Baboon	34.85	1898778	0.997	2.41	32.54	2237194	0.994	2.84
Peppers	40.26	1635779	0.999	2.08	38.73	1693901	0.999	2.15
Jet	42.88	1637898	0.999	2.08	42.04	1702029	0.999	2.16
Boat	38.50	1708242	0.999	2.17	36.09	1840256	0.998	2.34
House	40.23	1691500	0.999	2.15	39.18	1808544	0.998	2.30
Pot	46.35	1599030	0.999	2.03	42.80	1622565	0.999	2.06
Average	**41.07**	1686041	0.999	2.14	38.95	**1798834**	0.998	**2.28**

Table 7. Results of 7PVD+ 3LSB + EMD (Pradhan, Sekhar & Swain, 2018) technique

Images 512× 512×3	Proposed 7 PVD+ 3 LSB + EMD (Type 1)				Proposed 7 PVD+ 3 LSB + EMD (Type 2)			
	PSNR	Capacity	Q	BPB	PSNR	Capacity	Q	BPB
Lena	44.98	1639022	0.999	2.09	41.26	1690031	0.999	2.15
Baboon	34.67	1987328	0.996	2.54	32.49	2338643	0.994	2.98
Peppers	38.14	1640887	0.998	2.09	34.70	1693278	0.997	2.16
Jet	43.00	1647786	0.999	2.10	40.46	1709098	0.998	2.18
Boat	37.76	1740611	0.998	2.22	34.36	1873870	0.997	2.39
House	40.12	1724458	0.998	2.20	38.79	1841047	0.998	2.35
Pot	43.28	1596123	0.999	2.04	38.80	1617011	0.999	2.06
Average	**40.28**	1710888	0.998	2.18	37.26	**1823282**	0.998	**2.32**

Figure 10. PDH analysis for Shen & Huang's technique

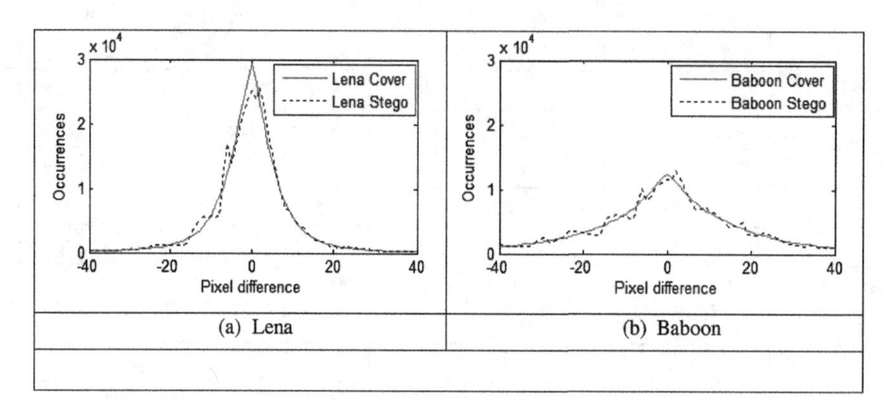

(a) Lena

(b) Baboon

Swain, 2018) technique, Figure 11 (a)-(d) and Figure 12 (a)-(d) the step effects are not observable.

We can observe the RS analysis curves of the 3PVD+ 3LSB + EMD technique in Figure 13. In Lena image there are more number of smooth blocks, but in Baboon image there are more number of edge blocks. For Baboon image curves for R_m and R_{-m} are linear and nearly parallel to each other. Similarly, curves for S_m and S_{-m} are linear and nearly parallel to each other. Hence the relation $R_m \cong R_{-m} > S_m \cong S_{-m}$ is strongly satisfied. For Lena image curve for R_m is linear and the curve for R_{-m} is slightly diverging from it. Similarly, curves for S_m is linear and the curve for S_{-m} is slightly diverging from it. Hence the relation $R_m \cong R_{-m} > S_m \cong S_{-m}$ is weakly satisfied for Lena image. Figure 14 represents the RS analysis for 7PVD+ 3LSB + EMD technique. In all the four cases, the graphs for R_m and R_{-m} are linear, nearly overlap with one another and the graphs for S_m and S_{-m} are linear and nearly overlap with one another. Hence the relation $R_m \cong R_{-m} > S_m \cong S_{-m}$ is strongly satisfied. Hence it can be concluded that RS analysis can't detect the proposed steganography techniques.

CONCLUSION

The adaptive LSB substitution techniques discussed in this chapter use the principles of modified LSB substitution based on pixel value differencing. So, their security must be checked by applying RS analysis and PDH analysis.

Figure 11. PDH analysis for 3 PVD + 3 LSB + EMD technique (Type 1 and Type 2)

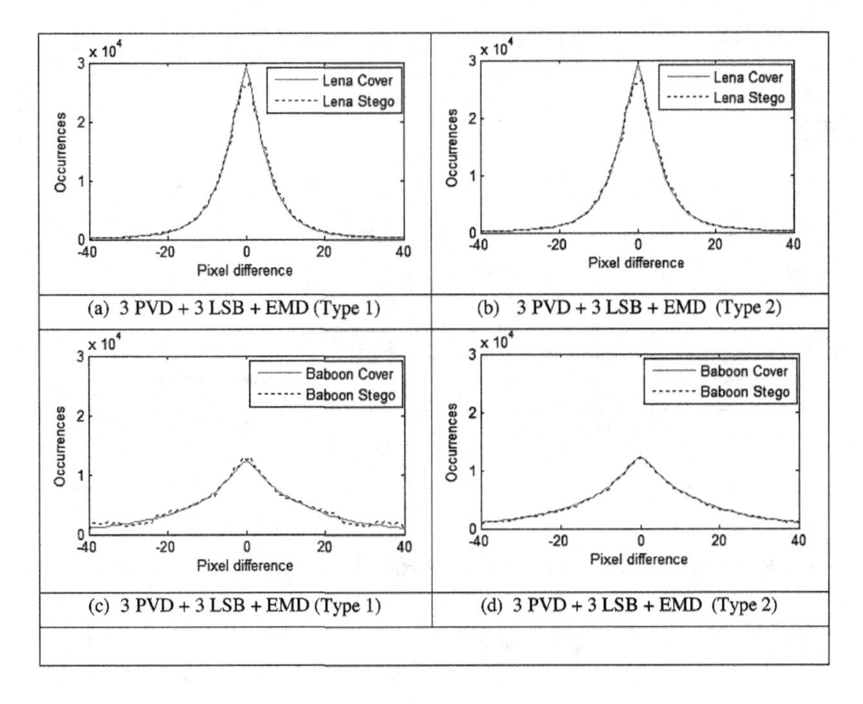

(a) 3 PVD + 3 LSB + EMD (Type 1)

(b) 3 PVD + 3 LSB + EMD (Type 2)

(c) 3 PVD + 3 LSB + EMD (Type 1)

(d) 3 PVD + 3 LSB + EMD (Type 2)

Figure 12. PDH analysis for 7 PVD+3 LSB +EMD technique (Type 1 and Type 2)

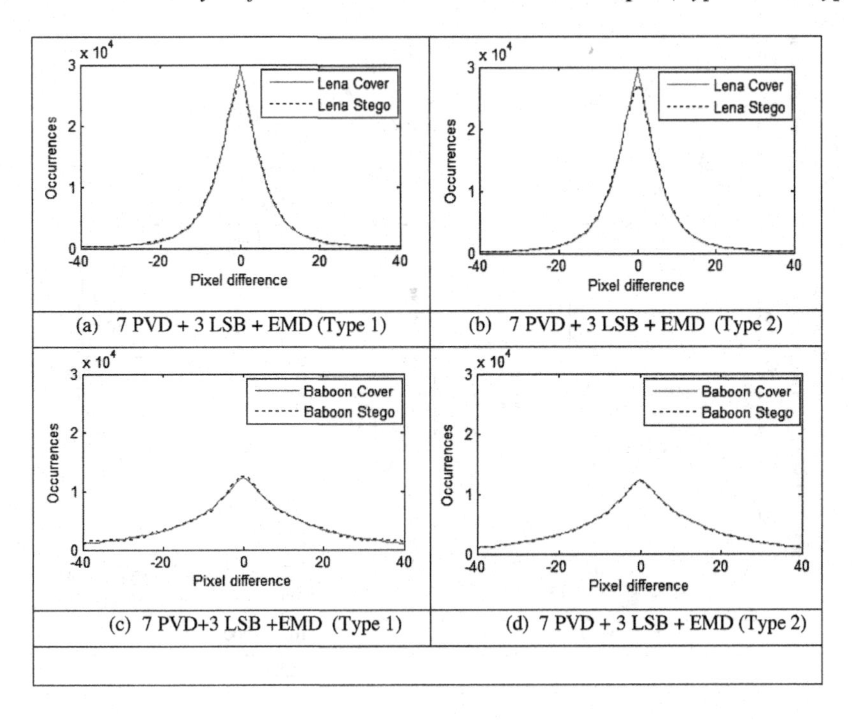

(a) 7 PVD + 3 LSB + EMD (Type 1)

(b) 7 PVD + 3 LSB + EMD (Type 2)

(c) 7 PVD+3 LSB +EMD (Type 1)

(d) 7 PVD + 3 LSB + EMD (Type 2)

Figure 13. RS analysis for 3 PVD + 3 LSB + EMD technique (Type 1 and Type 2)

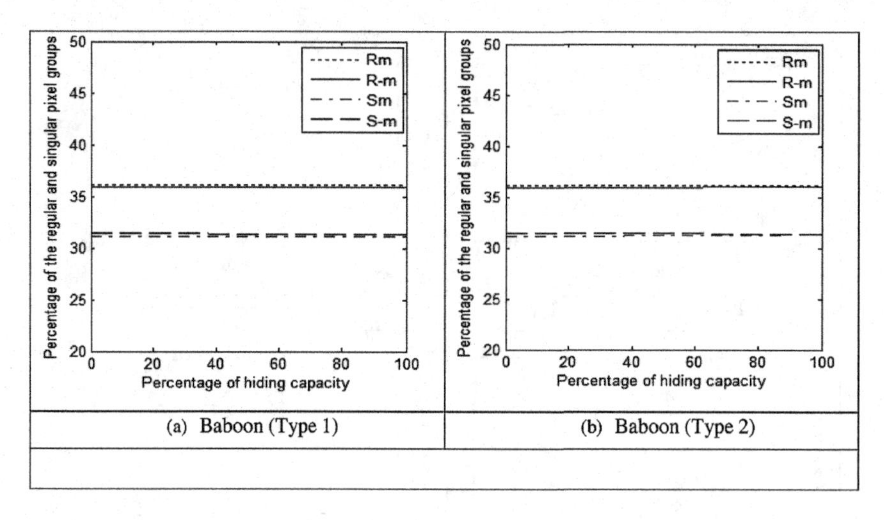

(a) Baboon (Type 1) | (b) Baboon (Type 2)

Figure 14. RS analysis of 7 PVD+3 LSB +EMD technique (Type 1 and Type 2)

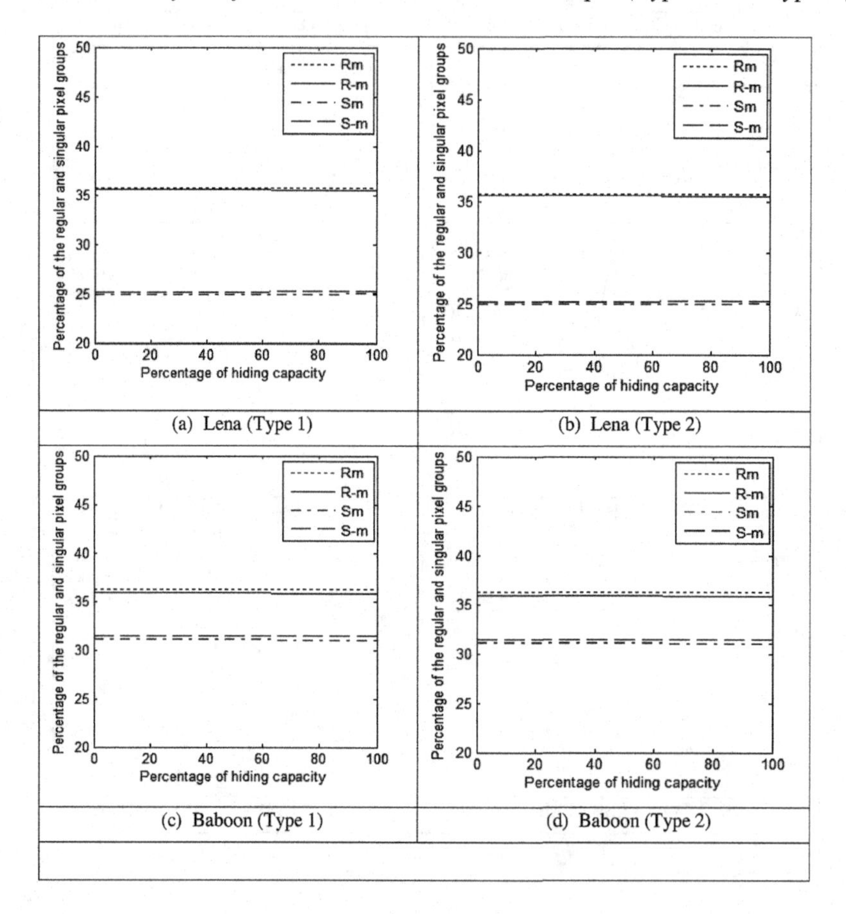

(a) Lena (Type 1) | (b) Lena (Type 2)

(c) Baboon (Type 1) | (d) Baboon (Type 2)

These techniques are neither analyzed through RS analysis nor through PDH analysis. So their security is not ensured. Shen & Huang proposed PVD in connection with EMD to achieve greater hiding capacity and higher PSNR. But it is found to be detectable by pixel difference histogram analysis. To fix this problem, a combination of LSB substitution, PVD, and EMD is proposed in 3PVD+ 3LSB + EMD technique and 7PVD+ 3LSB + EMD technique. These techniques operate on 2×2 and 3×3 pixel blocks respectively, by calculating the average of the pixel value differences. Based on this average value, either PVD or EMD is applied in combination with LSB. Both the techniques give higher hiding capacity compared to that of Shen & Huang's technique. The recorded PSNR values are also as good as that of Shen & Huang's technique. If we compare between 3PVD+ 3LSB + EMD technique and 7PVD+ 3LSB + EMD technique, then Type 1 of 3PVD+ 3LSB + EMD technique is good for PSNR and Type 2 of 7PVD+ 3LSB + EMD technique is good for hiding capacity. Furthermore, it has been proved that 3PVD+ 3LSB + EMD technique and 7PVD+ 3LSB + EMD technique are not detectable by RS analysis.

REFERENCES

Fridrich, J., Goljian, M., & Du, R. (2001). Detecting LSB steganography in color and gray-scale images. *Magazine of IEEE Multimedia Special Issue on Security*, *8*(4), 22–28. doi:10.1109/93.959097

Liao, X., Wen, Q. Y., & Zhang, J. (2011). A steganographic technique for digital images with four-pixel differencing and modified LSB Substitution. *Journal of Visual Communication and Image Representation*, *22*(1), 1–8. doi:10.1016/j.jvcir.2010.08.007

Pradhan, A., Sahu, A. K., Swain, G., & Sekhar, K. R. (2016). Performance evaluation parameters of image steganography techniques. *Proceedings of IEEE International Conference on Research Advances in Integrated Navigation Systems*, 1-8. 10.1109/RAINS.2016.7764399

Pradhan, A., Sekhar, K. R., & Swain, G. (2016). Digital image steganography based on seven way pixel value differencing. *Indian Journal of Science and Technology*, *9*(37), 1–11. doi:10.17485/ijst/2016/v9i37/88557

Pradhan, A., Sekhar, K. R., & Swain, G. (2018). Digital image steganography using LSB substitution, PVD, and EMD. *Mathematical Problems in Engineering*, *2018*, 1–13. doi:10.1155/2018/1804953

Shen, S. Y., & Huang, L. H. (2015). A data hiding scheme using pixel value differencing and improving exploiting modification directions. *Computers & Security*, *48*, 131–141. doi:10.1016/j.cose.2014.07.008

Swain, G. (2014). Digital image steganography using nine-pixel differencing and modified LSB substitution. *Indian Journal of Science and Technology*, *7*(9), 1444–1450.

Swain, G., & Lenka, S. K. (2015). A novel steganography technique by mapping words with LSB array. *International Journal of Signal and Imaging Systems Engineering*, *8*(1), 115–122. doi:10.1504/IJSISE.2015.067052

Wang, Z., & Bovic, A. C. (2002). A universal image quality index. *IEEE Signal Processing Letters*, *9*(3), 81–84. doi:10.1109/97.995823

Wu, D. C., & Tsai, W. H. (2003). A steganograhic method for images by pixel value differencing. *Pattern Recognition Letters*, *24*(9-10), 1613–1626. doi:10.1016/S0167-8655(02)00402-6

Zhang, X., & Wang, S. (2004). Vulnerability of pixel-value differencing steganography to histogram analysis and modification for enhanced security. *Pattern Recognition Letters*, *25*(3), 331–339. doi:10.1016/j.patrec.2003.10.014

Zhang, X., & Yang, S. (2006). Efficient steganographic embedding by exploiting modification direction. *IEEE Communications Letters*, *10*(11), 781–783. doi:10.1109/LCOMM.2006.060863

Chapter 7
Steganography Techniques Based on Modulus Function and PVD Against PDH Analysis and FOBP

ABSTRACT

This chapter proposes two improved steganography techniques by addressing two problems in the existing literature. The first proposed technique is modulus function-based steganography and it addresses pixel difference histogram (PDH) analysis. The modulus function is used to calculate an evaluation function and based on the value of the evaluation function embedding decision is taken. There are two variants of this technique: (1) modulus 9 steganography and (2) modulus 16 steganography. In modulus 9 steganography, the embedding capacity in a pair of pixels is 3 bits, and in modulus 16 steganography the embedding capacity in a pair of pixels is 4 bits. Both the variants possess higher PSNR values. The experimental results prove that the PDH analysis cannot detect this technique. The second proposed technique is based on pixel value differencing with modified least significant bit (MLSB) substitution and it addresses fall off boundary problem (FOBP). This technique operates on 2×2 pixel blocks. In one of the pixels of a block data hiding is performed using MLSB substitution. Based on the new value of this pixel, three difference values with three neighboring pixels are calculated. Using these difference values, PVD approach is applied. Experimental results prove that the PDH analysis and RS analysis is unable to detect this proposed technique. The recorded values of bit rate and peak signal-to-noise ratio are also satisfactory.

DOI: 10.4018/978-1-5225-7516-0.ch007

INTRODUCTION

Least significant bit (LSB) substitution is one of the oldest data hiding approaches, wherein one or more LSBs of a pixel are substituted by secret data bits. This simplest technique is detected by RS analysis (Fridrich, Goljian, & Du, 2001). Wu & Tsai (2003) exposed the fact that the edge regions in an image can conceal more amount of data as compared to the smooth regions. Based on this principle they proposed pixel value differencing (PVD) steganography. The image is partitioned into 1×2 size non-overlapped pixel blocks. For a block the difference value between the two pixels is computed and changed to a new value by hiding data in it. The PVD technique with block size of 2×2 has been proposed to enhance the embedding capacity in (Chang, Chang, Huang, & Tu, 2008; Lee, Lee, Chen, Chang, Su & Chang, 2012). In blocks of size 2×2, edges in three directions are considered to increase the hiding capacity. Chang & Tseng (2004) considered the values of 2, 3, and 4 neighboring pixels, to find the correlation among the pixels of a block, and then calculated the pixel value differences. Based on these differences embedding decision is taken.

LSB substitution techniques offer higher embedding capacity, but PVD techniques offer higher imperceptibility. Thus, PVD and LSB substitution techniques have been combined to obtain higher hiding capacity and higher imperceptibility (Wu, Wu, Tsai & Hwang, 2005; Yang, Weng, Wang & Sun, 2010). Chen (2014) proposed a PVD steganography technique using two reference tables to randomize the data embedding. Khodaei & Faez (2012) proposed a combination of modified LSB (MLSB) substitution with PVD in 1×3 pixel blocks to achieve higher embedding capacity. This idea is extended to 2×2 pixel blocks in (Swain, 2016b). This extended technique possesses higher hiding capacity, but it suffers with fall off boundary problem (FOBP). Based on pixel value differences adaptive LSB substitution has been performed in (Liao, Wen & Zhang, 2011).

The traditional PVD steganography techniques follow a static range table. Due to this some zig-zag appearance (known as step effect) is introduced in pixel difference histograms of the stego-images (Chang, Su & Chang, 2012). This is referred as pixel difference histogram (PDH) analysis. The step effect can be avoided by applying two tricks, (i) using adaptive range table and (ii) utilizing edges in all possible directions. Luo, Huang & Huang (2010) also proposed an adaptive PVD steganography with three-pixel blocks, which does not suffer from step effects. Swain (2016a) proposed two adaptive

PVD steganography techniques using vertical and horizontal edges, which does not suffer from step effects. In general, adaptive image steganography schemes possess lower embedding capacity. The edges can be predicted by some prediction functions and hiding capacity depends upon this prediction functions. If we hide in smooth regions distortion will be more. Based on the level of complexity of the edge regions, adaptive embedding can be applied (Chakraborty, Jalal & Bhatnagar, 2017). In this way capacity can be increased and chance of detection can be decreased.

Balasubramanian, Selvakumar & Geetha (2014) proposed a PVD schemes with 3×3 pixel blocks, to achieve higher hiding capacity. Darabkh, Al-Dhamari & Jafar, (2017) also proposed PVD steganography using eight directional PVD which is an extension from Wu & Tsai's PVD technique. Any PVD technique which is an extension of Wu & Tsai's technique should be tested by PDH analysis. Zhang & Wang (2006) proposed exploiting modification direction (EMD) steganography. The primary intention was to convert a group of bits to a digit in (2n+1)-ary notational system, and hide it in a pixel of the block. As the hiding capacity of this technique was very less, so Kim (2014) used an improved notational system to improve upon it. Shen & Huang (2015) measured the complexity of a block using PVD and then applied EMD to improve upon PSNR and hiding capacity. But this method is not resistant to PDH analysis. This chapter proposes two steganography techniques, (i) modulus function-based steganography, and (ii) PVD with MLSB substitution. The first proposed technique addresses the PDH analysis that exist in Shen & Huang's (2015) technique. The second proposed technique addresses the FOBP, that exist in Swain's (2016b) technique.

RELATED WORKS

Shen and Huang's PVD Based EMD

Shen & Huang's (2015) PVD based EMD steganography technique has been described in this sub-section. The image is divided into non-overlapped embedding units with two consecutive pixels, $\{P_i, P_{i+1}\}$. A difference value $d = |P_i - P_{i+1}|$ is calculated. It falls in one of the ranges, R_i of Table 1. The hiding capacity of this range is t. Now calculate $k = \log_2 t^2$. Take k bits of secret data and convert to a decimal number m in t^2-ary number system.

Compute $f = \{(t\text{-}1) \times P_i + t \times P_{i+1}\} \bmod t^2$. After hiding m in the block $\{P_i, P_{i+1}\}$, the stego-pixels are calculated using the following three cases.

Case 1: if m=f, then $P_i' = P_i$, and $P_{i+1}' = P_{i+1}$

Case 2: if m>f, then $P_i' = (P_i - (m-f) \bmod t)$, and $P_{i+1}' = \left(P_{i+1} + \frac{m-f}{t} + (m-f) \bmod t\right)$

Case 3: if m<f, then $P_i' = (P_i + (f-m) \bmod t)$, and $P_{i+1}' = \left(P_{i+1} - \frac{f-m}{t} - (f-m) \bmod t\right)$

If one of the new pixel values P_i' or P_{i+1}' is not falling in the range [0, 255], then either underflow or overflow occurs. To address this issue an alternate block $\{P_i^*, P_{i+1}^*\}$ is chosen, such that the value $\{(P_i - P_i^*)^2 + (P_{i+1} - P_{i+1}^*)^2\}$ is minimum, and the two conditions, (i) f = m, and (ii) Range of d = Range of d' should be satisfied, where, $d' = |P_i^* - P_{i+1}^*|$. Finally $\{P_i^*, P_{i+1}^*\}$ is the stego-block.

To extract the secret data from a stego-pixel block $\{P_i^*, P_{i+1}^*\}$, calculate $d' = |P_i^* - P_{i+1}^*|$. The d' value belongs to a range in Table 1 whose hiding capacity is t. Calculate the decimal value $m = \{(t\text{-}1) \times P_i^* + t \times P_{i+1}^*\} \bmod t^2$. Convert m into t binary bits. This is the extracted data.

The embedding and extraction procedures of this technique are very fine, there is no problem. But the PDH analysis can detect this technique. PDH is a curve with pixel difference value on X-axis and frequency of the pixel difference on Y-axis (Pradhan, Sahu, Swain & Sekhar, 2016). For an original image the curve shall be a smooth curve. For the stego-image if the curve shows step effects i.e. looks zig-zag in nature, then the steganography is detected. Otherwise, steganography is not detected. Figure 1 represents the PDH analysis for Shen & Huang's technique with Lena and Baboon images. There are two sub-figures in it. In each sub-figure there are two curves. The solid line curve is for the original image and the dotted line curve is for the stego-image. It is clearly evident that the step effects are there in the dotted line curves. Hence Shen & Huang's technique is vulnerable to PDH analysis.

Table 1. Range table of Shen & Huang's (2015) technique

Range, R_i	[0, 7]	[8, 15]	[16, 31]	[32, 63]	[64, 127]	[128, 255]
hiding capacity, t	3	3	4	5	6	7

Figure 1. PDH analysis of Shen & Huang's technique

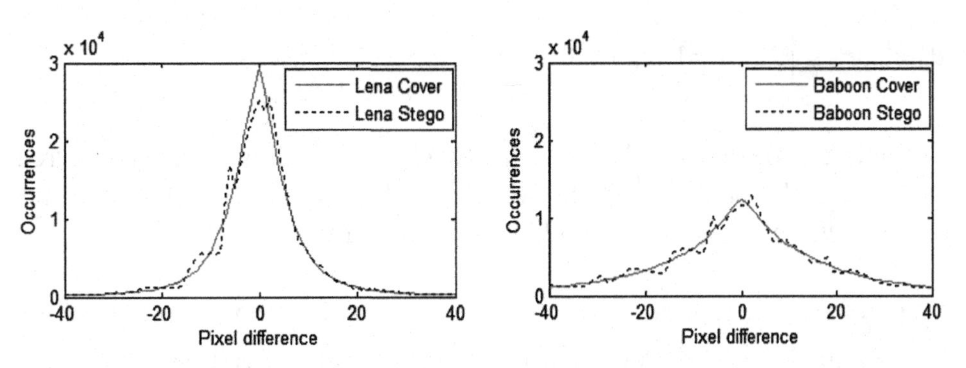

To address this problem, a modulus function-based steganography technique is proposed in section 3. The proposed modulus steganography technique exists in two variants, (i) modulus 9 steganography, and (ii) modulus 16 steganography. Both these two variants show higher PSNR as compared to Shen & Huang's technique and are undetectable by PDH analysis.

Swain's PVD With MLSB Substitution

Swain (2016b) proposed a PVD technique with MLSB substitution. Out of 4 pixels in a 2×2 non-overlapped pixel block, MLSB substitution is applied in one pixel. Considering the modified value of this pixel, 3 difference values are calculated with reference to other three neighboring pixels. Based on these three difference values, PVD is applied. Figure 2 (a) represents a 2×2 pixel block. The embedding procedure in this block is described below.

Step 1: In the pixel g_x, k-bit LSB substitution is applied, where the k value is 3. Let g_x' is the new value of g_x after applying k-bit LSB substitution. Suppose L and S are the decimal values of k LSBs of g_x and k LSBs of g_x' respectively. Now calculate a difference value, diff=L-S and optimize the value of g_x' using Eq. (1).

$$g'_x = \begin{cases} g'_x + 2^k & \text{if diff} > 2^{k-1} \text{ and } 0 \le (g'_x + 2^k) \le 255 \\ g'_x - 2^k & \text{if diff} < -2^{k-1} \text{ and } 0 \le (g'_x - 2^k) \le 255 \\ g'_x & \text{otherwise} \end{cases} \quad (1)$$

Step 2: The three neighboring pixels of g_x are g_1, g_2 and g_3. Calculate three difference values using Eq. (2).

$$d_i = \left| g'_x - g_i \right|, \text{ for i =1, 2, 3} \quad (2)$$

Table 2 is the range table. There are two rows for hiding capacity, referred as type 1 and type 2. Out of the two types, the one which will be used for embedding, the same one should be used for extraction.

Step 3: For i =1, 2, 3, the difference value d_i may fall into a range R_j of the range table, where j can be a value from 1 to 6. Let L_i and t_i be the lower bound and hiding capacity of this range. For i =1, 2, 3, take t_i bits of data, convert to decimal value DEC_i. Now calculate 3 new difference values using Eq. (3).

$$d'_i = L_i + DEC_i, \text{ for i =1, 2, 3} \quad (3)$$

Step 4: For i =1, 2, 3, two new values of g_i, namely g''_i and g'''_i are calculated using Eq. (4). One of these two values is chosen using Eq. (5), and this chosen value is g'_i. It is the stego-value of g_i. The stego-block is shown in Figure 2(b).

$$g''_i = g'_x - d'_i, \text{ and } g'''_i = g'_x + d'_i, \text{ for i =1, 2, 3} \quad (4)$$

$$g'_i = \begin{cases} g''_i & \text{if } \left| g_i - g''_i \right| < \left| g_i - g'''_i \right| \text{ and } 0 \le g''_i \le 255 \\ g'''_i & \text{otherwise} \end{cases}, \text{ for i =1, 2, 3} \quad (5)$$

Table 2. Range table of Swain's (2016b) technique

Range	R_1 = [0, 7]	R_2 = [8, 15]	R_3 = [16, 31]	R_4 = [32, 63]	R_5 = [64, 127]	R_6 = [128, 255]
hiding capacity, type 1	3	3	3	3	4	4
hiding capacity, type 2	3	3	4	5	6	6

Figure 2. (a) and (c) Original blocks, (b) and (d) Stego blocks

g_x	g_1
g_2	g_3

(a)

g'_x	g'_1
g'_2	g'_3

(b)

181	182
255	182

(c)

180	181
259	181

(d)

The data extraction from a 2×2 non-overlapped stego-pixel block, shown in Figure 2 (b), can be done by the following steps.

Step 1: The k- LSBs of g'_x are extracted and appended to extracted data stream.

Step 2: For i =1, 2, 3, three difference values, $d'_i = |g'_i - g'_x|$ are calculated. This difference value, d'_i falls into one of the six ranges R_j of Table 2, where j can be a value from 1 to 6. Let L_i and t_i be the lower bound and hiding capacity of this range.

Step 3: Now for i =1, 2, 3, calculate the decimal value $DEC_i = d'_i - L_i$.

Step 4: For i =1, 2, 3, convert DEC_i to t_i binary bits and append to extracted data stream.

Swain's (2016b) PVD with MLSB substitution suffers from FOBP. This fact is illustrated by the following discussion. Let us consider a 2×2 pixel block as shown in Figure 2 (c). The secret binary data stream to be embedded is: 1000011111001_2 . The value of pixel g_x is 181, its binary value in 8 bits is: 10110101_2 . The values of g_1 , g_2 and g_3 are 182, 255, and 182 respectively. Let us choose k=3 and type 1 of range Table 2. The 3 bits of data from the secret data stream is 100_2. After applying 3-bit LSB substitution, the binary value of g_x changes to 10110100_2, which is equal to 180 in decimal. Thus, the value of g_x' is 180. The three least significant bits of g_x are 101_2, in decimal it is 5. The three least significant bits of g_x' are 100_2, in decimal it is 4. Thus diff=L-S=5-4=1. By applying Eq. (1), the optimized value of g_x' is 180.

Now the 3 difference values are, $d_1 = |180 - 182| = 2$, $d_2 = |180 - 255| = 75$ and $d_3 = |180 - 182| = 2$. The difference value d_1 belongs to the range [0, 7], so L_1 and t_1 values are 0 and 3 respectively. The next 3 bits of data from the secret data stream are 001_2, its decimal value is 1, i.e. DEC_1=1. The new difference value d_1' is 0+1=1, as per Eq. (3). The difference value d_2 belongs to the range [64, 255], so L_2 and t_2 values are 64 and 4 respectively. The next 4 bits of data from the secret data stream are 1111_2, its decimal value is 15, i.e. DEC_2=15. The new difference value d_2' is 64+15=79, as per Eq. (3). The difference value d_3 belongs to the range [0, 7], so L_3 and t_3 values are 0 and 3 respectively. The next 3 bits of data from the secret binary data stream are 001_2, its decimal value is 1, i.e. DEC_3=1. The new difference value d_3' is 0+1=1, as per Eq. (3).

Now by referring Eq. (4), $g_1'' = g_x' - d_1' = 180 - 1 = 179$, $g_1''' = g_x' + d_1' = 180+1=181$, $g_2'' = g_x' - d_2' = 180-79=101$, $g_2''' = g_x' + d_2' = 180+79=259$, $g_3'' = g_x' - d_3' = 180 - 1=179$, and $g_3''' = g_x' + d_3' = 180+1=181$. By referring Eq.s (5), g_1', g_2', and g_3' are calculated. This is shown as Eq.s (6), (7) and (8) respectively.

$$g_1' = \begin{cases} 179, & \text{if } |182 - 179| < |182 - 181| \text{ and } 0 \le 179 \le 255 \\ 181, & \text{otherwise} \end{cases} = 181 \quad (6)$$

$$g_2' = \begin{cases} 101, & \text{if } |255 - 101| < |255 - 259| \text{ and } 0 \le 101 \le 255 \\ 259, & \text{otherwise} \end{cases} = 259 \quad (7)$$

$$g_3^{'} = \begin{cases} 179, & \text{if} \left|182 - 179\right| < \left|182 - 181\right| \text{and } 0 \leq 179 \leq 255 \\ 181, & \text{otherwise} \end{cases} = 181 \quad (8)$$

Hence, we obtain, $g_1^{'}=181$, $g_2^{'}=259$ and $g_3^{'}=181$. The stego-block is as shown in Figure 2(d). As $g_2^{'}$ value is greater than 255, so FOBP occurred. Thus, the embedding procedure of Swain's technique needs some modification. To address this FOBP, an improved PVD with MLSB substitution has been proposed in section 4.

THE PROPOSED MODULUS FUNCTION STEGANOGRAPHY TECHNIQUE

The Modulus 9 Steganography Technique

The pixels of the image are accessed in raster scan order and non-overlapped blocks are formed with a pair of consecutive pixels. The embedding in a block $\{P_i, P_{i+1}\}$ is performed by the following steps.

Step 1: The difference value of this pair of pixels, d is computed as $d = \left|P_i - P_{i+1}\right|$. The value d falls in one of the six quantization ranges, R_j of Table 3, where j can be any value from 1 to 6.

Step 2: From the secret binary data stream, 3 bits of data is taken and converted to decimal value, m.

Step 3: An evaluation function, f is calculated as in Eq. (9).

$$f = \{2 \times P_i + 3 \times P_{i+1}\} \bmod 9 \quad (9)$$

Step 4: After embedding 3 bits of data in the block, the new pixel block, $\{P_i^{'}, P_{i+1}^{'}\}$ is calculated by Eq. (10).

$$\{P_i', P_{i+1}'\} = \begin{cases} \{P_i,\ P_{i+1}\}, & \text{if } m = f \\ \{(P_i - (m\text{-}f) \bmod 3),\ (P_{i+1} + \frac{m\text{-}f}{3} + (m\text{-}f) \bmod 3)\}, & \text{if } m > f \\ \{(P_i + (f\text{-}m) \bmod 3),\ (P_{i+1} - \frac{f\text{-}m}{3} - (f\text{-}m) \bmod 3)\}, & \text{if } m < f \end{cases} \quad (10)$$

Step 5: If one of the new pixel values P_i' or P_{i+1}' does not fall in the range [0, 255], then either underflow or overflow occurs. To address this issue an alternate block { P_i^*, P_{i+1}^* } is chosen, such that the value { $(P_i - P_i^*)^2 + (P_{i+1} - P_{i+1}^*)^2$ } is the minimum, and the two conditions, (i) f = m, and (ii) Range of d = Range of d' are satisfied, where, $d' = |P_i^* - P_{i+1}^*|$. Finally { P_i^*, P_{i+1}^* } is the stego-block.

The extraction of secret bits is performed in the following manner. The pixels of the stego-image are accessed in raster scan order and non-overlapped blocks are formed with every pair of consecutive pixels. The extraction from a block (P_i^*, P_{i+1}^*) is done by the following steps.

Step 1: The decimal equivalent of the embedded data bits, m is calculated by Eq. (11).

$$m = \{2 \times P_i^* + 3 \times P_{i+1}^*\} \bmod 9 \quad (11)$$

Step 2: This decimal value, m is converted to 3 binary bits. These are the extracted bits.

Table 3. Range Table of the proposed modulus steganography technique

R_1	R_2	R_3	R_4	R_5	R_6
[0, 7]	[8, 15]	[16, 31]	[32, 63]	[64, 127]	[128, 255]

Figure 3 and Figure 4 are the flowcharts for data embedding and data extraction of modulus 9 steganography.

The Modulus 16 Steganography Technique

The pixels of the image are accessed in raster scan order and non-overlapped blocks are formed with a pair of consecutive pixels. The embedding in a block $\{P_i, P_{i+1}\}$ is performed by the following steps.

Step 1: The difference value of this pair of pixels, d is computed as d = $|P_i - P_{i+1}|$. The value d falls in one of the six quantization ranges, R_i of Table 3, where j can be any value from 1 to 6.

Step 2: From the secret binary data stream, 4 bits of data is taken and converted to decimal value, m.

Step 3: An evaluation function, f is calculated as in Eq. (12).

$$f = \{3 \times P_i + 4 \times P_{i+1}\} \bmod 16 \tag{12}$$

Figure 3. Flowchart for embedding procedure of modulus 9 steganography

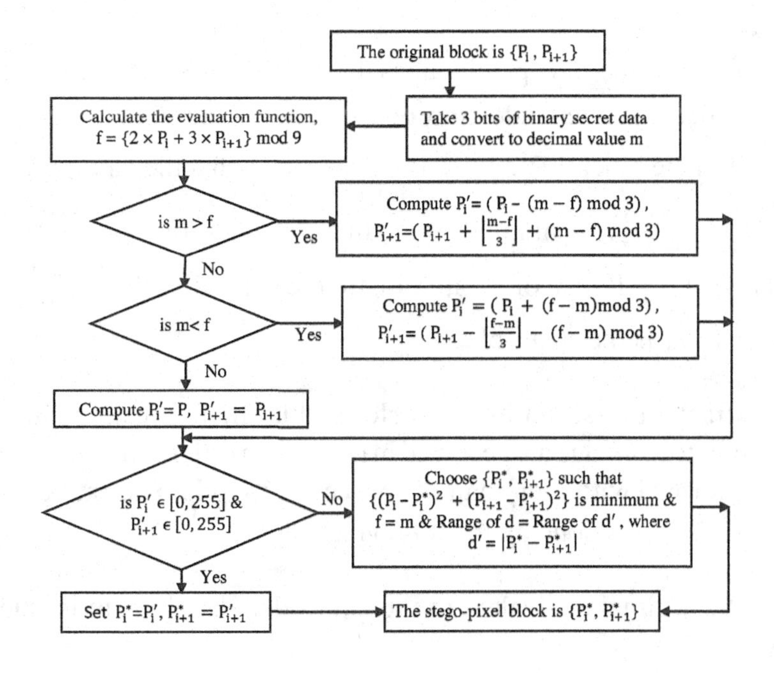

Figure 4. Flowchart for extraction procedure of modulus 9 steganography

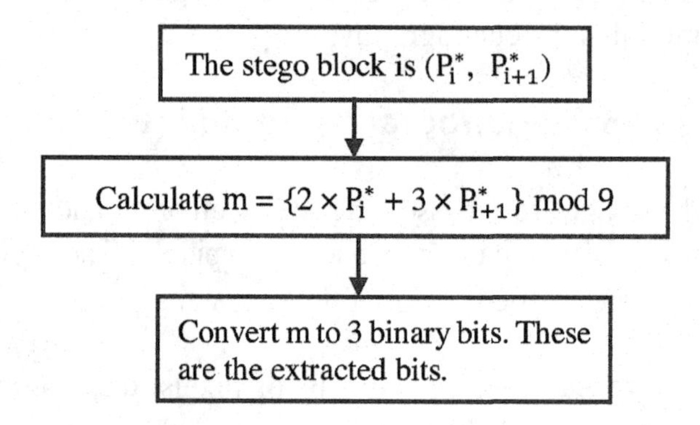

Step 4: After embedding 4 bits of data in the block, the new pixel block, $\{P_i', P_{i+1}'\}$ is calculated by Eq. (13).

$$\{P_i', P_{i+1}'\} = \begin{cases} \{P_i,\ P_{i+1}\}, & \text{if } m = f \\ \{(P_i - (m - f) \bmod 4),\ (P_{i+1} + \frac{m - f}{4} + (m - f) \bmod 4)\}, & \text{if } m > f \\ \{(P_i + (f - m) \bmod 4),\ (P_{i+1} - \frac{f - m}{4} - (f - m) \bmod 4)\}, & \text{if } m < f \end{cases} \quad (13)$$

Step 5: If one of the new pixel values P_i' or P_{i+1}' does not fall in the range [0, 255], then either underflow or overflow occurs. To address this issue an alternate block $\{P_i^*, P_{i+1}^*\}$ is chosen, such that the value $\{(P_i - P_i^*)^2 + (P_{i+1} - P_{i+1}^*)^2\}$ is minimum, and the two conditions, (i) f = m, and (ii) Range of d = Range of d' are satisfied, where, $d' = |P_i^* - P_{i+1}^*|$. Finally $\{P_i^*, P_{i+1}^*\}$ is the stego-block.

The extraction of secret bits is performed in the following manner. The pixels of the stego-image are accessed in raster scan order and non-overlapped blocks are formed with every pair of consecutive pixels. The extraction from a block (P_i^*, P_{i+1}^*) is done by the following steps.

Step 1: The decimal equivalent of the embedded data bits, m is calculated by Eq. (14).

$$m = \{3 \times P_i^* + 4 \times P_{i+1}^*\} \bmod 16 \quad (14)$$

Step 2: This decimal value, m is converted to 4 binary bits. These are the extracted bits.

An Example of the Proposed Modulus 9 Steganography Technique

An example of embedding in modulus 9 steganography is as follows. Let us consider a block $\{P_i, P_{i+1}\} = \{150, 250\}$. Then $d = |P_i - P_{i+1}| = 100$. The difference value, d belongs to range R_5 of Table 3. Using Eq. (9), we get f=6. Suppose the 3 bits of secret data to be hidden are 111_2. Then m = 7 and m > f, so using Eq. (10), we get $P_i' = 149$, and $P_{i+1}' = 251$. FOBP does not arise, so step 5 of embedding procedure is not required and the stego-pixel block, $\{P_i^*, P_{i+1}^*\} = \{149, 251\}$. Now let us extract the data from the stego-pixel block, $\{P_i^*, P_{i+1}^*\} = \{149, 251\}$. The difference value, $d' = |P_i^* - P_{i+1}^*| = 102$. It falls in range R_5 of Table 3. Using Eq. (11), m = (2×149 + 3×251) mod 9 = 7. Convert 7 into 3 binary bits, it is 111_2. This is the extracted data, same as the embedded data.

THE PROPOSED PVD WITH MLSB SUBSTITUTION STEGANOGRAPHY TECHNIQUE

The embedding and extraction procedures of the proposed PVD with MLSB substitution technique is given in sub-section 4.1, and an example is given in sub-section 4.2.

The Embedding and Extraction Procedures

The image is scanned in raster scan order and divided into non-overlapped blocks of size 2×2, as shown in Figure 2 (a). The data embedding is performed by the following steps.

Step 1: In the pixel g_x, k-bit LSB substitution is applied. The k value can be 3, 4, or 5. Let g_x' is the new value of g_x after applying k-bit LSB substitution. Suppose L and S are the decimal values of k LSBs of g_x and k LSBs of g_x' respectively. Now calculate a difference value, diff=L-S and optimize the value of g_x' using Eq. (1).

Step 2: The three neighboring pixels of g_x are g_1, g_2 and g_3. Calculate three difference values using Eq. (2). Table 4 is the range table. There are two rows for hiding capacity, referred as type 1 and type 2. Out of two types, the one which will be used for embedding, the same one should be used for extraction.

Step 3: For i =1, 2, 3, the difference value d_i, may fall into a range R_j of the range Table 4, where j can be a value from 1 to 5. Let L_i and t_i be the lower bound and hiding capacity of this range. For i =1, 2, 3, take t_i bits of data, convert to decimal value DEC_i. Now calculate 3 new difference values using Eq. (3).

Step 4: For i =1, 2, 3, two new values of g_i, namely g_i'' and g_i''' are calculated using Eq. (4). One of these two values is selected as g_i'. The selection is done by using one of the following four cases. It is the stego-value of g_i. The stego block is shown in Figure 2 (b).

Case 1: $g_i' = g_i'''$, if $g_i'' < 0$

Case 2: $g_i' = g_i''$, if $g_i''' > 255$ and case 1 is not satisfied

Case 3: $g_i' = g_i''$, if $\left|g_i - g_i''\right| < \left|g_i - g_i'''\right|$ and neither case 1 nor case 2 is satisfied

Case 4: $g_i' = g_i'''$, if none of the above three cases satisfies

The flowchart for this embedding procedure is presented in Figure 5 for better understanding by the readers.

The data extraction from a stego-pixel block, Figure 2 (b), can be done by the following steps.

Step 1: The k LSBs of g_x' are extracted and appended to extracted data stream.

Table 4. Range table of the proposed PVD+MLSB technique

Range, R_j	[0,7]	[8,15]	[16,31]	[32,63]	[64, 255]
hiding capacity, type 1	3	3	3	4	4
hiding capacity, type 2	3	3	4	5	6

Step 2: For i =1, 2, 3, three difference values, $d_i' = |g_i' - g_x'|$ is calculated. This difference value, d_i' falls into one of the five ranges R_j of the range Table 4, where j can be a value from 1 to 5. Let L_i and t_i be the lower bound and hiding capacity of this range.

Step 3: Now for i =1, 2, 3, calculate the decimal value $DEC_i = d_i' - L_i$.

Step 4: For i =1, 2, 3, convert DEC_i to t_i binary bits and append to extracted data stream.

The flowchart for this extraction procedure is presented in Figure 6 for better understanding by the readers.

Figure 5. Flowchart for embedding procedure of the proposed PVD+MLSB substitution technique

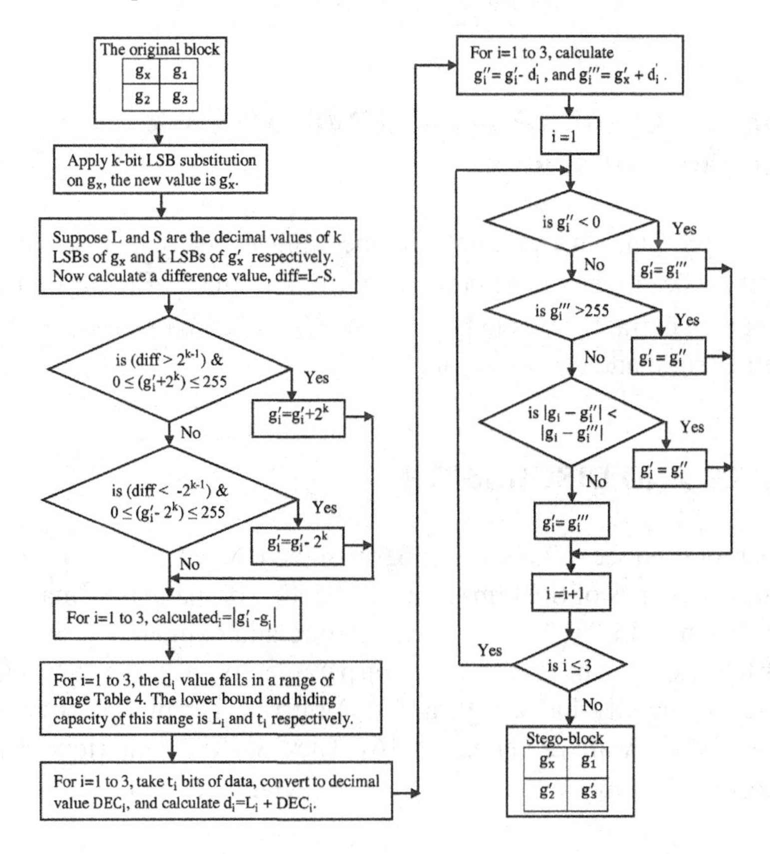

Figure 6. Flowchart for extraction procedure of the proposed PVD+MLSB substitution technique

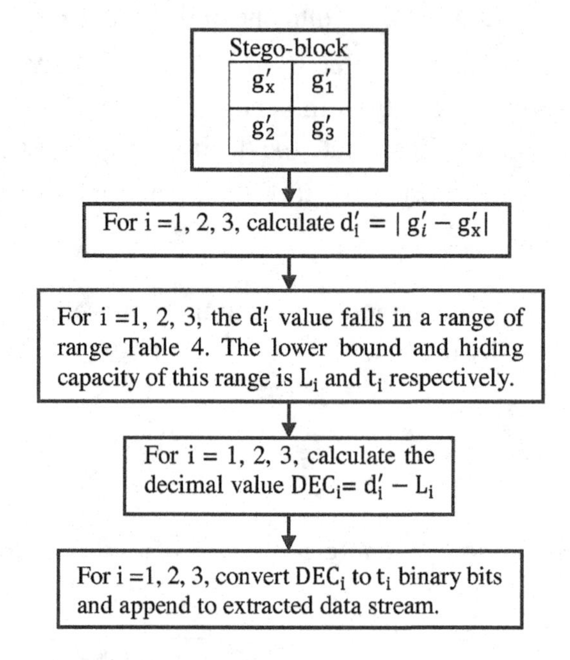

An Examples of the Proposed PVD+MLSB Substitution Technique

Figure 7 represents an example of embedding using type 1 and t=3. The secret data to be embedded is: 000010001101_2. Similarly, Figure 8 represents an example of extraction using type 1 and t=3. We can traverse these figures from left to right and top to bottom.

RESULTS AND DISCUSSION

The two proposed techniques are experimented using MATLAB, and tested with various images of SIPI image database. Out of many test images, eight images shown in Figure 9 are used for testing and comparison with related existing techniques. The four comparison parameters are, (i) PSNR, (ii) hiding capacity, (iii) quality index (Q), and (iv) bit rate i.e. bits per byte (BPB) (Pradhan, Sahu, Swain & Sekhar, 2016). The PSNR is a metric to calculate the distortion. It is measured using Eq. (15), where X_{ij} and Y_{ij} are the pixel

Figure 7. Example of embedding

Original 2×2 pixel block	*3 bit LSB substitution at g_x*	*g_x is changed to g'_x*
190 192 190 200 Original block	Value of g_x is 190. 190= $(10111110)_2$ 3 bits of data= **000** $(10111000)_2$=184	184 192 190 200 g'_x is 184
Calculate the difference values	*These differences belong to different ranges of table 4*	*Find t_i and L_i values. Calculate DEC_i values.*
$d_1=\lvert 184-192\rvert=8$ $d_2=\lvert 184-190\rvert=6$ $d_3=\lvert 184-200\rvert=16$	$d_1 \in$ [8, 15] $d_2 \in$ [0, 7] $d_3 \in$ [16, 31]	$t_1=3$ $L_1=8$ $DEC_1=2$ $t_2=3$ $L_2=0$ $DEC_2=1$ $t_3=3$ $L_3=16$ $DEC_3=5$
Calculate the new difference values	*Calculate g''_1, g''_2 and g''_3 values*	*Calculate g'''_1, g'''_2 and g'''_3 values*
$d'_1=8+2=10$ $d'_2=0+1=1$ $d'_3=16+5=21$	$g''_1=184-10=174$ $g''_2=184-1=183$ $g''_3=184-21=163$	$g'''_1=184+10=194$ $g'''_2=184+1=185$ $g'''_3=184+21=205$
For i=1 to 3, select g'_i from g''_i and g'''_i		*Stego-pixel block*
$g'_1=194$, $g'_2=185$, $g'_3=205$		184 194 185 205

Figure 8. Example of extraction

Stego-block	*Calculate the differences*	*Map to ranges in range table 4*	*Find t_i, L_i and DEC_i values*
184 194 185 205 $g'_x=184=(10111000)_2$	$d'_1=\lvert 184-194\rvert=10$ $d'_2=\lvert 184-185\rvert=1$ $d'_3=\lvert 184-205\rvert=21$	$d_1 \in$ [8, 15] $d_2 \in$ [0, 7] $d_3 \in$ [16, 31]	$t_1=3$ $L_1=8$ $DEC_1=10-8=2$ $t_2=3$ $L_2=0$ $DEC_2=1-0=1$ $t_3=3$ $L_3=16$ $DEC_3=21-16=5$
Extract 3 LSBs of g'_x	*Convert DEC_1 to 3 binary bits*	*Convert DEC_2 to 3 binary bits*	*Convert DEC_3 to 3 binary bits*
000_2	010_2	001_2	101_2
Hence the extracted bits are: 000 010 001 101_2			

values of original image and stego-image respectively. The size of the original image or stego-image is m×n. The decrease in value of PSNR implies increase in distortion. The embedding capacity represents the maximum number of bits permitted by the technique to be concealed inside the image. The average embedding capacity in a byte of the image is known as bit rate or bits per byte (BPB). The quality index (Q) is an estimation of similarity between the original image and the stego-image. The larger value of Q represents more similarity, and vice versa. It is measured using Eq. (16), where $\overline{X}$ and $\overline{Y}$ is the average pixel values of the original image and the stego-images respectively.

$$\mathrm{PSNR} = 10 \times \log_{10} \frac{m \times n \times 255 \times 255}{\sum_{i=1}^{m} \sum_{j=1}^{n} \left(X_{ij} - Y_{ij}\right)^2} \tag{15}$$

$$Q = \frac{4 \times \bar{X} \times \bar{Y} \times \left\{\sum_{i=1}^{m} \sum_{j=1}^{n} \left(X_{ij} - \bar{X}\right) \times \left(Y_{ij} - \bar{Y}\right)\right\}}{\left\{\sum_{i=1}^{m} \sum_{j=1}^{n} \left(X_{ij} - \bar{X}\right)^2 + \sum_{i=1}^{m} \sum_{j=1}^{n} \left(Y_{ij} - \bar{Y}\right)^2\right\} \times \left\{\left(\bar{X}\right)^2 + \left(\bar{Y}\right)^2\right\}} \tag{16}$$

Results of the Proposed Modulus Function Steganography Technique

The PSNR value of the proposed modulus function steganography is estimated after hiding 700,000 (seven lakhs) bits of data in the images. Four sample stego-images are shown in Figure 10. The stego-images are imperceptible. The results are compared with Shen & Huang's (2015) technique in Tables 5 and 6. From Tables 5 and 6 it can be noticed that the PSNR values of the modulus function steganography technique is higher than that of the Shen & Huang's technique. The hiding capacity of modulus 16 steganography is greater than the hiding capacity of Shen & Huang's technique. The hiding capacity of modulus 9 steganography is nearly equal to that of the Shen & Huang's technique. In between the two proposed variants, modulus 16 steganography is preferable for higher hiding capacity and modulus 9 steganography is preferable for higher PSNR. Another admiring factor is that both the proposed schemes are not detectable by PDH analysis, but Shen & Huang's technique is detectable by PDH analysis.

To check the security of these schemes, pixel difference histogram (PDH) analysis has been performed. Figure 11 shows the PDH analysis of the proposed modulus 9 steganography with Lena and Baboon images. The solid line curves are for original images and the dotted line curves are for stego-images. The dotted line curves do not show any step effects. Hence the proposed modulus 9 steganography technique is resistant to PDH analysis. Figure 12 shows the PDH analysis of the proposed modulus 16 steganography technique with Lena and Baboon images. The dotted line curves do not show any step effects. Hence the proposed modulus 16 steganography technique is resistant to PDH analysis.

Figure 9. Sample test images

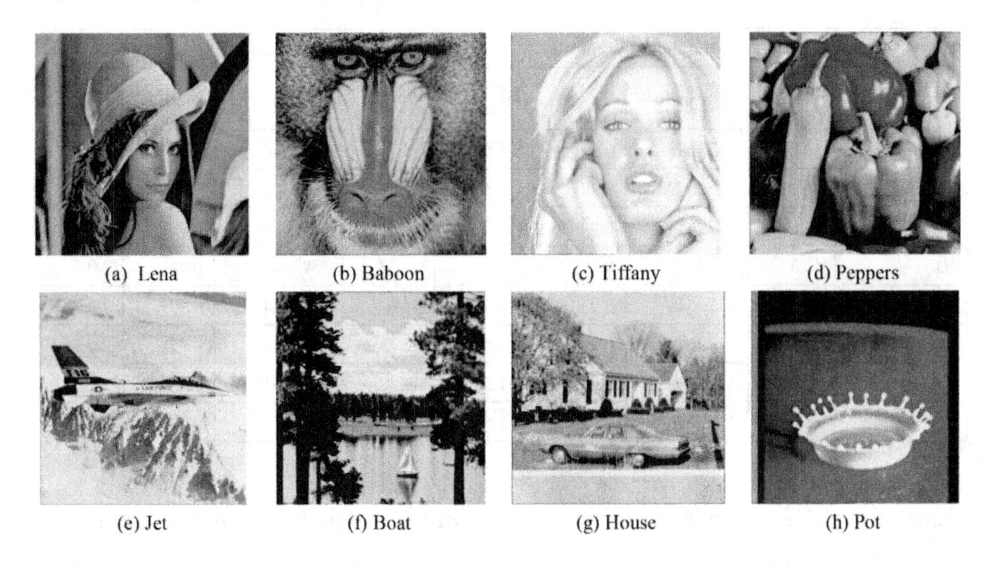

(a) Lena (b) Baboon (c) Tiffany (d) Peppers

(e) Jet (f) Boat (g) House (h) Pot

Figure 10. Stego-images of the proposed modulus 16 steganography technique

PSNR=35.72 PSNR=42.89 PSNR=43.78 PSNR=44.39

Table 5. Results Shen & Huang's (2015) technique

Images (512× 512×3)	PSNR	Capacity	Q	Bit Rate
Lena	38.01	1223062	0.998	1.56
Baboon	40.14	1343274	0.999	1.71
Peppers	41.57	1226139	0.999	1.56
Jet	43.35	1212350	0.999	1.54
Boat	41.35	1264742	0.999	1.61
House	41.75	1242081	0.999	1.58
Pot	43.38	1195641	0.999	1.52
Average	41.36	1243898	0.999	1.58

Table 6. Results of the proposed modulus 9 and modulus 16 steganography techniques

Images 512× 512×3	Modulus 9 (Variant 1)				Modulus 16 (Variant 2)			
	PSNR	Capacity	Q	Bit Rate	PSNR	Capacity	Q	Bit Rate
Lena	39.22	1179648	0.998	1.5	35.72	1572864	0.997	2.0
Baboon	46.11	1179648	0.999	1.5	42.89	1572864	0.999	2.0
Peppers	46.62	1179648	0.999	1.5	44.39	1572864	0.999	2.0
Jet	46.57	1179648	0.999	1.5	44.33	1572864	0.999	2.0
Boat	46.58	1179648	0.999	1.5	44.34	1572864	0.999	2.0
House	46.58	1179648	0.999	1.5	43.78	1572864	0.999	2.0
Pot	46.63	1179648	0.999	1.5	44.39	1572864	0.999	2.0
Average	45.47	1179648	0.999	1.5	42.83	1572864	0.999	2.0

Figure 11. PDH analysis of the proposed modulus 9 steganography technique

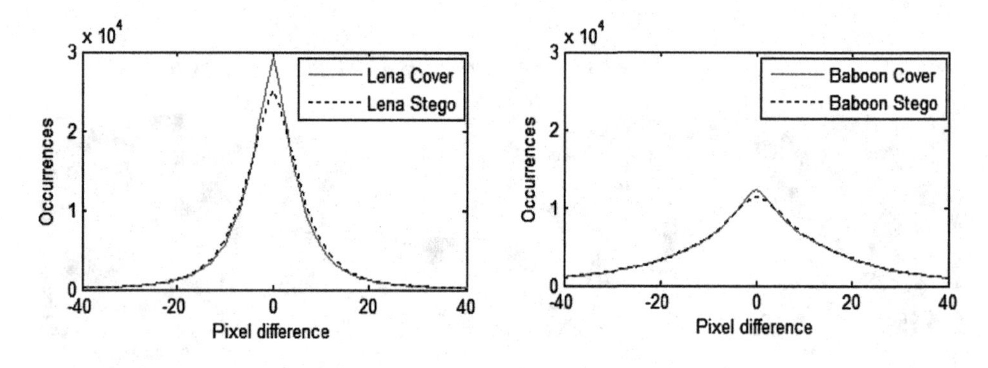

Figure 12. PDH analysis of the proposed modulus 16 steganography technique

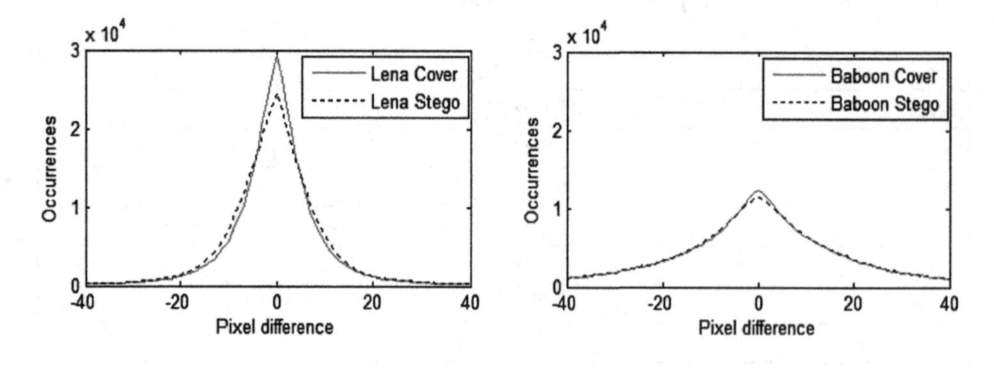

Results of the Proposed PVD+MLSB Substitution Technique

The PSNR of the proposed PVD+MLSB substitution technique is estimated after hiding 840,000 (eight lakhs and forty thousand) bits of data in the images. Four sample stego-images are shown in Figure 13. The stego-images are imperceptible. The results are compared with Khodaei & Faez's (2012) technique and Swain's (2016b) technique, in Tables 7, 8 and 9.

From Tables 7 and 8 it can be observed that Khodaei & Faez's technique and Swain's technique suffer with FOBP. The number of blocks suffering with FOBP is counted and shown. From Table 9 it can be observed that the proposed PVD+MLSB substitution technique does not suffer with FOBP, because the number of blocks suffering with FOBP is zero. Furthermore, it can be observed from these tables that in proposed technique, the hiding

Figure 13. Stego-images of the proposed PVD+ M LSB substitution technique (type 2)

PSNR=40.75

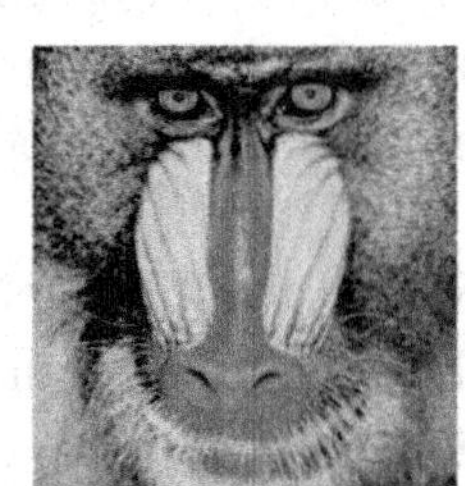
PSNR=32.16

PSNR=37.49

PSNR=41.04

Table 7. Results of Khodaei & Faez's (2012) technique

Images 512×512×3	Type 1					Type 2				
	PSNR	Capacity	Q	Bit Rate	FOBP Count	PSNR	Capacity	Q	bit Rate	FOBP Count
Lena	41.74	2375248	0.999	3.02	98	40.46	2434603	0.999	3.09	121
Baboon	37.27	2443361	0.998	3.1	12	34.19	2662080	0.996	3.38	26
Tiffany	38.7	2372396	0.997	3.01	12045	39.27	2416944	0.998	3.07	11994
Peppers	38.57	2372858	0.999	3.01	0	36.91	2435223	0.998	3.09	2
Jet	39.98	2374048	0.998	3.01	0	40.13	2418419	0.998	3.07	0
Boat	39.18	2391994	0.999	3.04	0	36.9	2504613	0.996	3.18	7
House	38.58	2387183	0.998	3.03	4	37.97	2470824	0.998	3.14	16
Pot	40.33	2366001	0.999	3.00	0	37.00	2387494	0.999	3.03	0
Average	39.29	2385386	0.998	3.03	1520	37.85	2466275	0.998	3.13	1521

Table 8. Results of Swain's (2016b) three directional PVD with MLSB substitution technique

Images 512×512×3	Type 1					Type 2				
	PSNR	**Capacity**	**Q**	**Bit Rate**	**FOBP Count**	**PSNR**	**Capacity**	**Q**	**Bit Rate**	**FOBP Count**
Lena	42.22	2361875	0.999	3.00	105	40.55	2437700	0.999	3.09	5
Baboon	34.67	2393475	0.996	3.04	22	32.09	2772545	0.993	3.52	25
Tiffany	42.02	2363192	0.998	3.00	13416	36.86	2425193	0.996	3.08	0
Peppers	39.49	2364428	0.999	3.00	1754	38.02	2447737	0.998	3.11	8
Jet	41.82	2365839	0.998	3.00	27	41.9	2443492	0.998	3.1	0
Boat	38.07	2370147	0.998	3.01	242	35.87	2539530	0.998	3.22	13
House	39.67	2366686	0.998	3.00	36	38.65	2510373	0.998	3.19	3
Pot	42.75	2364360	0.999	3.00	2206	41.17	2394782	0.999	3.04	0
Average	40.09	2368750	0.998	3.01	2226	38.13	2496419	0.997	3.17	6.75

capacity and bit rate have been slightly improved as compared to that of Khodaei & Faez's technique. Although Swain's technique possesses almost same PSNR and hiding capacity as compared to the proposed technique, but it suffers with FOBP.

This proposed technique uses MLSB substitution and PVD, so need to be analyzed by both RS analysis and PDH analysis. Figure 14 represents the PDH analysis over Lena, Baboon, Tiffany, and Jet images for the type 1 of this proposed technique. Similarly, Figure 15 represents the PDH analysis over Lena, Baboon, Tiffany, and Jet images for type 2 of this proposed technique. There are four sub-figures in Figure 14 and four sub-figures in Figure 15. In each sub-figure there are two curves. The solid line curves are for the original images and the dotted line curves are for the stego-images. In all the eight sub-figures, the curves of stego-images do not show any step effects. Hence it can be concluded that the proposed PVD+MLSB substitution technique is tolerant to PDH analysis.

The RS analysis is performed using some statistical measurements in the following way. Define a function F_1: 2n ↔2n+1 (Pradhan, Sahu, Swain & Sekhar, 2016). It defines two transformations, (i) from value 2n to value 2n + 1, and (ii) from value 2n + 1 to value 2n. Similarly, define another function F_{-1}: 2n ↔2n -1. It defines other two transformations, (i) from value 2n to value 2n – 1, and (ii) from value 2n - 1 to value 2n. The image, say M is divided into a number of equal size blocks. Suppose such a block is G, whose

Table 9. Results of the proposed PVD+ M LSB substitution technique

Images 512×512×3	Type 1					Type 2				
	PSNR	Capacity	Q	Bit Rate	FOBP Count	PSNR	Capacity	Q	Bit Rate	FOBP Count
Lena	42.06	2375979	0.999	3.02	0	40.75	2437700	0.999	3.09	0
Baboon	34.84	2483174	0.997	3.16	0	32.16	2772545	0.994	3.52	0
Tiffany	38.46	2374426	0.997	3.02	0	36.5	2425193	0.996	3.08	0
Peppers	36.02	2376797	0.998	3.02	0	36.35	2447737	0.998	3.11	0
Jet	39.86	2381768	0.998	3.03	0	40.42	2443492	0.998	3.1	0
Boat	36.13	2402514	0.998	3.05	0	35.04	2539530	0.998	3.22	0
House	37.80	2397850	0.998	3.05	0	37.49	2510373	0.998	3.19	0
Pot	41.26	2368074	0.999	3.01	0	41.04	2394782	0.999	3.04	0
Average	38.30	2395073	0.998	3.05	0	37.47	2496419	0.997	3.17	0

Figure 14. PDH analysis of the proposed PVD+MLSB substitution technique (type 1)

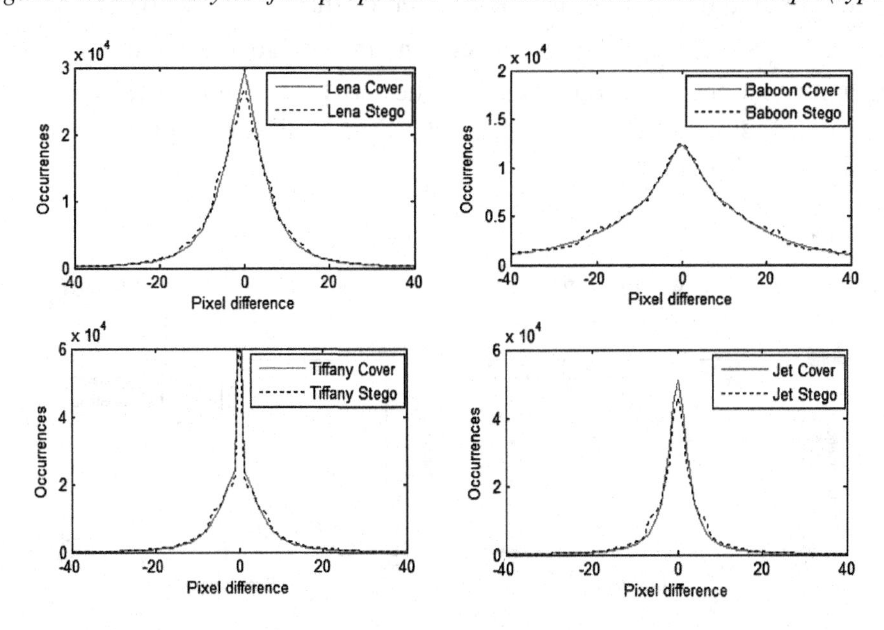

pixels are $X_1, X_2, X_3, \ldots, X_n$. Then use the function $f = \sum_{i=1}^{n-1} \left| X_{i+1} - X_i \right|$ to measure the smoothness of G. Then apply F_1 to all the blocks of M and define the two values R_m and S_m. R_m is equal to the number of blocks satisfying the condition $f\left(F_1\left(G\right)\right) > f\left(G\right)$ divided by the total number of blocks. S_m is equal to the number of blocks satisfying the condition $f(F_1(G)) < f(G)$ divided by the total number of blocks. Similarly, apply F_{-1} to all the blocks of M and define the two parameters R_{-m} and S_{-m}. R_{-m} is equal to the number of blocks satisfying the condition $f(F_{-1}(G)) > f(G)$ divided by the total number of blocks. S_{-m} is equal to the number of blocks satisfying the condition $f(F_{-1}(G)) < f(G)$ divided by the total number of blocks.

As per RS analysis, if the condition $R_m \approx R_{-m} > S_m \approx S_{-m}$ is true, then it is inferred that there is no data hidden in the image, M. But if the condition R_{-m} - $S_{-m} > R_m$ - S_m is true, then it is inferred that some secret data is hidden in image, M. The RS analysis over Lena and Baboon images for type 1 of the proposed PVD+MLSB substitution technique is shown in Figure 16 and the RS analysis over Lena and Boon images for type 2 of the proposed PVD+MLSB substitution technique is shown in Figure 17. In these two figures, for all the four cases it can be observed that the condition $R_m \approx R_{-m} > S_m \approx S_{-m}$ is satisfied. Lena is a very smooth image and Baboon is a very edged image. For the other images also, the above condition will arise. Hence it can be concluded that the proposed PVD+MLSB substitution technique is resistant to RS analysis.

Figure 15. PDH analysis of the proposed PVD+MLSB substitution technique (type 2)

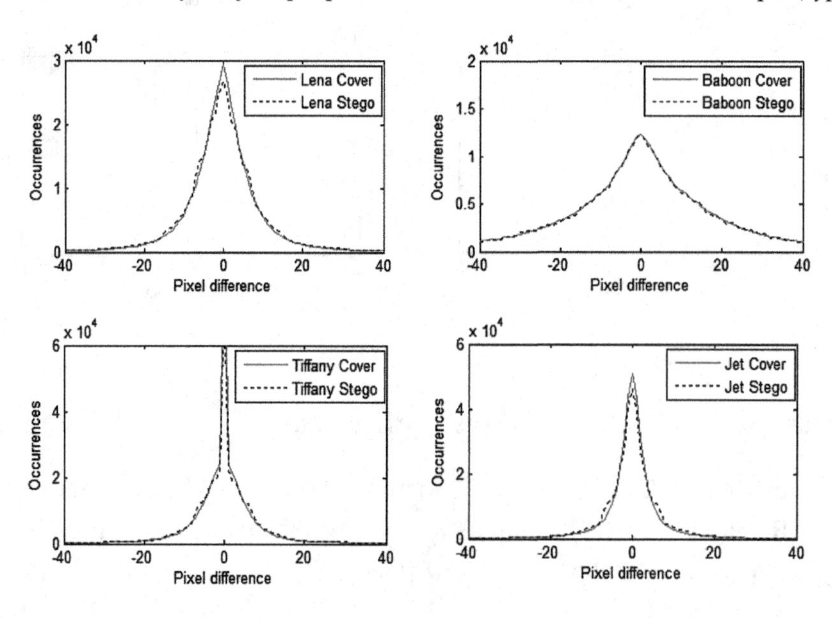

Figure 16. RS analysis of the proposed PVD+MLSB substitution technique (type 1)

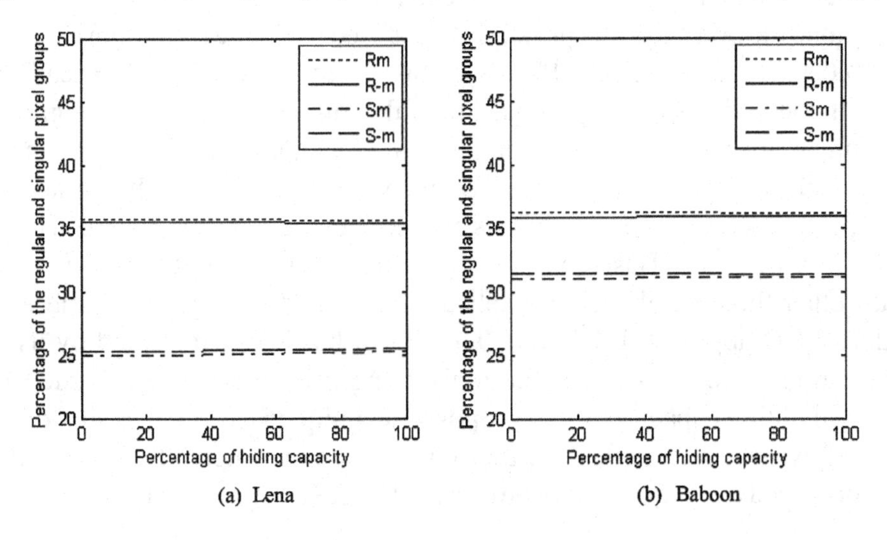

Figure 17. RS analysis of the proposed PVD+MLSB substitution technique (type 2)

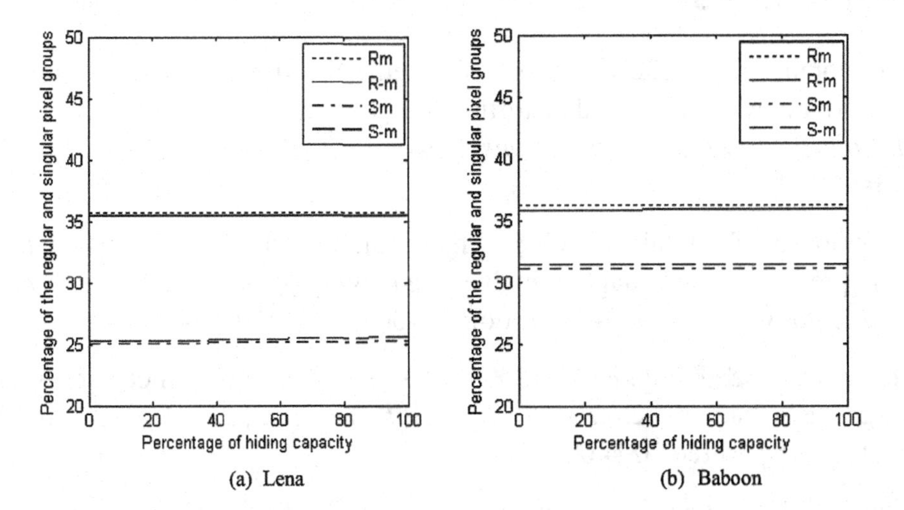

CONCLUSION

This chapter proposes two steganography techniques. The first proposed technique known as modulus function steganography. It exists in two variants, (i) modulus 9 steganography, and (ii) modulus 16 steganography. This steganography technique performs better as compared to Shen & Huang's PVD based EMD technique. Since Shen & Huang's technique uses PVD in connection with EMD, so can be attacked by PDH analysis. In the proposed technique the original PVD principle is not used to decide the hiding capacity of a block, so it is resistant to PDH analysis. Furthermore, the PSNR readings of both the variants of the proposed modulus function-based steganography technique are higher than that of Shen & Huang's technique. The second proposed technique is based on PVD and MLSB substitution. It operates on 2×2 pixel blocks. In one of the pixels of a block embedding is performed using MLSB substitution. Based on the new value of this pixel, difference values with other three neighboring pixels are calculated. Using these difference values PVD approach is applied. The FOBP has been eradicated by using suitable embedding logic in the embedding procedure. The recorded bit rate and hiding capacity of this proposed technique is as good as that of the related existing techniques. Furthermore, it is experimentally verified that this proposed technique cannot be detected by RS analysis and PDH analysis.

REFERENCES

Balasubramanian, C., Selvakumar, S., & Geetha, S. (2014). High payload image steganography with reduced distortion using octonary pixel pairing scheme. *Multimedia Tools and Applications*, *73*(3), 2223–2245. doi:10.100711042-013-1640-4

Chakraborty, S., Jalal, A. S., & Bhatnagar, C. (2017). LSB based non blind predictive edge adaptive image steganography. *Multimedia Tools and Applications*, *76*(6), 7973–7987. doi:10.100711042-016-3449-4

Chang, C. C., & Tseng, H. W. (2004). A steganographic method for digital images using side match. *Pattern Recognition Letters*, *25*(12), 1431–1437. doi:10.1016/j.patrec.2004.05.006

Chang, K. C., Chang, C. P., Huang, P. S., & Tu, T. M. (2008). A novel image steganography method using tri-way pixel value differencing. *Journal of Multimedia*, *3*(2), 37–44. doi:10.4304/jmm.3.2.37-44

Chen, J. (2014). A PVD-based data hiding method with histogram preserving using pixel pair matching. *Signal Processing Image Communication*, *29*(3), 375–384. doi:10.1016/j.image.2014.01.003

Darabkh, K. A., Al-Dhamari, A. K., & Jafar, I. F. (2017). A new steganographic algorithm based on multi directional PVD and modified LSB. *Journal of Information Technology and Control*, *46*(1), 16–36.

Fridrich, J., Goljian, M., & Du, R. (2001). Detecting LSB steganography in color and gray-scale images. *Magazine of IEEE Multimedia and Security*, *8*(4), 22–28. doi:10.1109/93.959097

Khodaei, M., & Faez, K. (2012). New adaptive steganographic method using least-significant-bit substitution and pixel-value differencing. *IET Image Processing*, *6*(6), 677–686.

Kim, C. (2014). Data hiding by an improved exploiting modification direction. *Multimedia Tools and Applications*, *69*(3), 569–584. doi:10.100711042-012-1114-0

Lee, Y. P., Lee, J. C., Chen, W. K., Chang, K. C., Su, I. J., & Chang, C. P. (2012). High-payload image hiding with quality recovery using tri-way pixel-value differencing. *Information Sciences*, *191*, 214–225. doi:10.1016/j.ins.2012.01.002

Liao, X., Wen, Q. Y., & Zhang, J. (2011). A steganographic method for digital images with four-pixel differencing and modified LSB Substitution. *Journal of Visual Communication and Image Representation*, *22*(1), 1–8. doi:10.1016/j.jvcir.2010.08.007

Luo, W., Huang, F., & Huang, J. (2010). A more secure steganography based on adaptive pixel-value differencing scheme. *Multimedia Tools and Applications*, *52*(2-3), 407–430. doi:10.100711042-009-0440-3

Pradhan, A., Sahu, A. K., Swain, G., & Sekhar, K. R. (2016). Performance evaluation parameters of image steganography techniques. IEEE international conference on research advances in integrated navigation systems, 1-8. doi:10.1109/RAINS.2016.7764399

Shen, S. Y., & Huang, L. H. (2015). A data hiding scheme using pixel value differencing and improving exploiting modification directions. *Computers & Security*, *48*, 131–141.

Swain, G. (2016a). Adaptive pixel value differencing steganography using both vertical and horizontal edges. *Multimedia Tools and Applications*, *75*(21), 13541–13556. doi:10.100711042-015-2937-2

Swain, G. (2016b). A Steganographic method combining LSB substitution and PVD in a block. *Procedia Computer Science*, *85*, 39–44. doi:10.1016/j.procs.2016.05.174

Wu, D. C., & Tsai, W. H. (2003). A steganograhic method for images by pixel value differencing. *Pattern Recognition Letters*, *24*(9), 1613–1626.

Wu, H. C., Wu, N. I., Tsai, C. S., & Hwang, M. S. (2005). Image steganographic scheme based on pixel-value differencing and LSB replacement methods. *IEEE Proceedings Vision, Image and Signal Processing, 152*(5), 611-615. 10.1049/ip-vis:20059022

Yang, C. H., Weng, C. Y., Wang, S. J., & Sun, H. M. (2010). Varied PVD+LSB evading programs to spatial domain in data embedding systems. *Journal of Systems and Software*, *83*(10), 1635–1643. doi:10.1016/j.jss.2010.03.081

Zhang, X., & Yang, S. (2006). Efficient steganographic embedding by exploiting modification direction. *IEEE Communications Letters*, *10*(11), 781–783. doi:10.1109/LCOMM.2006.060863

Related Readings

To continue IGI Global's long-standing tradition of advancing innovation through emerging research, please find below a compiled list of recommended IGI Global book chapters and journal articles in the areas of image steganography, digital watermarking, and cryptography. These related readings will provide additional information and guidance to further enrich your knowledge and assist you with your own research.

A., U. B. (2018). High Efficient Data Embedding in Image Steganography Using Parallel Programming. In P. Karthikeyan, & M. Thangavel (Eds.), *Applications of Security, Mobile, Analytic, and Cloud (SMAC) Technologies for Effective Information Processing and Management* (pp. 67-80). Hershey, PA: IGI Global. doi:10.4018/978-1-5225-4044-1.ch004

Abirami, A. M., Askarunisa, A., Shiva Shankari, R. A., & Revathy, R. (2018). Ontology Based Feature Extraction From Text Documents. In P. Karthikeyan & M. Thangavel (Eds.), *Applications of Security, Mobile, Analytic, and Cloud (SMAC) Technologies for Effective Information Processing and Management* (pp. 174–195). Hershey, PA: IGI Global. doi:10.4018/978-1-5225-4044-1.ch009

Ahmad, M., & Ahmad, Z. (2018). Random Search Based Efficient Chaotic Substitution Box Design for Image Encryption. *International Journal of Rough Sets and Data Analysis*, *5*(2), 131–147. doi:10.4018/IJRSDA.2018040107

Ahmad, R. H., & Pathan, A. K. (2017). A Study on M2M (Machine to Machine) System and Communication: Its Security, Threats, and Intrusion Detection System. In M. Ferrag & A. Ahmim (Eds.), *Security Solutions and Applied Cryptography in Smart Grid Communications* (pp. 179–214). Hershey, PA: IGI Global. doi:10.4018/978-1-5225-1829-7.ch010

Ahmed, M. (2017). Infrequent Pattern Identification in SCADA Systems Using Unsupervised Learning. In M. Ferrag & A. Ahmim (Eds.), *Security Solutions and Applied Cryptography in Smart Grid Communications* (pp. 215–225). Hershey, PA: IGI Global. doi:10.4018/978-1-5225-1829-7.ch011

Alcaraz, C., & Lopez, J. (2017). Secure Interoperability in Cyber-Physical Systems. In M. Ferrag & A. Ahmim (Eds.), *Security Solutions and Applied Cryptography in Smart Grid Communications* (pp. 137–158). Hershey, PA: IGI Global. doi:10.4018/978-1-5225-1829-7.ch008

Alohali, B., Kifayat, K., Shi, Q., & Hurst, W. (2017). A Key Management Scheme for Secure Communications Based on Smart Grid Requirements (KMS-CL-SG). In M. Ferrag & A. Ahmim (Eds.), *Security Solutions and Applied Cryptography in Smart Grid Communications* (pp. 242–265). Hershey, PA: IGI Global. doi:10.4018/978-1-5225-1829-7.ch013

AlShahrani, A. M., Al-Abadi, M. A., Al-Malki, A. S., Ashour, A. S., & Dey, N. (2017). Automated System for Crops Recognition and Classification. In N. Dey, A. Ashour, & S. Acharjee (Eds.), *Applied Video Processing in Surveillance and Monitoring Systems* (pp. 54–69). Hershey, PA: IGI Global. doi:10.4018/978-1-5225-1022-2.ch003

Aman, M. N., Chua, K. C., & Sikdar, B. (2019). Hardware Primitives-Based Security Protocols for the Internet of Things. In M. Banday (Ed.), *Cryptographic Security Solutions for the Internet of Things* (pp. 117–141). Hershey, PA: IGI Global. doi:10.4018/978-1-5225-5742-5.ch005

Amenta, V., Lazzaroni, A., & Abba, L. (2019). Emerging Social and Legal Issues of the Internet of Things: A Case Study. In M. Banday (Ed.), *Cryptographic Security Solutions for the Internet of Things* (pp. 269–295). Hershey, PA: IGI Global. doi:10.4018/978-1-5225-5742-5.ch010

Balasubramanian, K. (2018). Experiments with the Cryptool Software. In K. Balasubramanian & M. Rajakani (Eds.), *Algorithmic Strategies for Solving Complex Problems in Cryptography* (pp. 186–194). Hershey, PA: IGI Global. doi:10.4018/978-1-5225-2915-6.ch015

Balasubramanian, K. (2018). Hash Functions and Their Applications. In K. Balasubramanian & M. Rajakani (Eds.), *Algorithmic Strategies for Solving Complex Problems in Cryptography* (pp. 66–77). Hershey, PA: IGI Global. doi:10.4018/978-1-5225-2915-6.ch005

Balasubramanian, K. (2018). Recent Developments in Cryptography: A Survey. In K. Balasubramanian & M. Rajakani (Eds.), *Algorithmic Strategies for Solving Complex Problems in Cryptography* (pp. 1–22). Hershey, PA: IGI Global. doi:10.4018/978-1-5225-2915-6.ch001

Balasubramanian, K. (2018). Secure Two Party Computation. In K. Balasubramanian & M. Rajakani (Eds.), *Algorithmic Strategies for Solving Complex Problems in Cryptography* (pp. 145–153). Hershey, PA: IGI Global. doi:10.4018/978-1-5225-2915-6.ch012

Balasubramanian, K. (2018). Securing Public Key Encryption Against Adaptive Chosen Ciphertext Attacks. In K. Balasubramanian & M. Rajakani (Eds.), *Algorithmic Strategies for Solving Complex Problems in Cryptography* (pp. 134–144). Hershey, PA: IGI Global. doi:10.4018/978-1-5225-2915-6.ch011

Balasubramanian, K. (2018). Variants of the Diffie-Hellman Problem. In K. Balasubramanian & M. Rajakani (Eds.), *Algorithmic Strategies for Solving Complex Problems in Cryptography* (pp. 40–54). Hershey, PA: IGI Global. doi:10.4018/978-1-5225-2915-6.ch003

Balasubramanian, K., & Abbas, A. M. (2018). A Software Library for Multi Precision Arithmetic. In K. Balasubramanian & M. Rajakani (Eds.), *Algorithmic Strategies for Solving Complex Problems in Cryptography* (pp. 195–227). Hershey, PA: IGI Global. doi:10.4018/978-1-5225-2915-6.ch016

Banday, M. T. (2019). Security in Context of the Internet of Things: A Study. In M. Banday (Ed.), *Cryptographic Security Solutions for the Internet of Things* (pp. 1–40). Hershey, PA: IGI Global. doi:10.4018/978-1-5225-5742-5.ch001

Barik, R. C., Changder, S., & Sahu, S. S. (2019). A New Bi-Level Encoding and Decoding Scheme for Pixel Expansion Based Visual Cryptography. *International Journal of Rough Sets and Data Analysis*, *6*(1), 18–42. doi:10.4018/IJRSDA.2019010102

Bhasin, H., & Alam, N. (2017). Applicability of Cellular Automata in Cryptanalysis. *International Journal of Applied Metaheuristic Computing*, *8*(2), 38–48. doi:10.4018/IJAMC.2017040103

Biswas, R. N., Mitra, S. K., & Naskar, M. K. (2019). Preserving Security of Mobile Anchors Against Physical Layer Attacks: A Resilient Scheme for Wireless Node Localization. In M. Banday (Ed.), *Cryptographic Security Solutions for the Internet of Things* (pp. 211–243). Hershey, PA: IGI Global. doi:10.4018/978-1-5225-5742-5.ch008

C. J. P. (2017). An Overview of Text Information Extraction from Images. In N. Kumar, A. Sangaiah, M. Arun, & S. Anand (Eds.), Advanced Image Processing Techniques and Applications (pp. 32-60). Hershey, PA: IGI Global. doi:10.4018/978-1-5225-2053-5.ch002

Cao, Y., Wang, T., & Wang, Y. (2017). Enabling Publish/Subscribe Communication for On-the-Move Electric Vehicle Charging Management. In M. Ferrag & A. Ahmim (Eds.), *Security Solutions and Applied Cryptography in Smart Grid Communications* (pp. 350–379). Hershey, PA: IGI Global. doi:10.4018/978-1-5225-1829-7.ch017

Chakraborty, S., Patra, P. K., Maji, P., Ashour, A. S., & Dey, N. (2017). Image Registration Techniques and Frameworks: A Review. In N. Dey, A. Ashour, & S. Acharjee (Eds.), *Applied Video Processing in Surveillance and Monitoring Systems* (pp. 102–114). Hershey, PA: IGI Global. doi:10.4018/978-1-5225-1022-2.ch005

Chantrapornchai, C., & Preechasuk, J. (2017). Exploring Image and Video Steganography Based on DCT and Wavelet Transform. In N. Kumar, A. Sangaiah, M. Arun, & S. Anand (Eds.), *Advanced Image Processing Techniques and Applications* (pp. 61–89). Hershey, PA: IGI Global. doi:10.4018/978-1-5225-2053-5.ch003

Chen, Z., Lu, J., Yang, P., & Luo, X. (2017). Recognizing Substitution Steganography of Spatial Domain Based on the Characteristics of Pixels Correlation. *International Journal of Digital Crime and Forensics*, *9*(4), 48–61. doi:10.4018/IJDCF.2017100105

Cheng, Y., Fu, Z., Yu, B., & Shen, G. (2019). General Construction for Extended Visual Cryptography Scheme Using QR Codes. *International Journal of Digital Crime and Forensics*, *11*(1), 1–17. doi:10.4018/IJDCF.2019010101

Chetan, K. R., & Nirmala, S. (2018). An Adaptive Curvelet Based Semi-Fragile Watermarking Scheme for Effective and Intelligent Tampering Classification and Recovery of Digital Images. *International Journal of Rough Sets and Data Analysis*, *5*(2), 69–94. doi:10.4018/IJRSDA.2018040104

D, E., & M, A. (2017). Fuzzy Approaches and Analysis in Image Processing. In N. Kumar, A. Sangaiah, M. Arun, & S. Anand (Eds.), *Advanced Image Processing Techniques and Applications* (pp. 1-31). Hershey, PA: IGI Global. doi:10.4018/978-1-5225-2053-5.ch001

D, J., & D, D. (2017). Background Subtraction and Object Tracking via Key Frame-Based Rotational Symmetry Dynamic Texture. In N. Kumar, A. Sangaiah, M. Arun, & S. Anand (Eds.), *Advanced Image Processing Techniques and Applications* (pp. 267-296). Hershey, PA: IGI Global. doi:10.4018/978-1-5225-2053-5.ch013

Dass, S., & Prabhu, J. (2018). Amelioration of Big Data Analytics by Employing Big Data Tools and Techniques. In P. Karthikeyan & M. Thangavel (Eds.), *Applications of Security, Mobile, Analytic, and Cloud (SMAC) Technologies for Effective Information Processing and Management* (pp. 212–232). Hershey, PA: IGI Global. doi:10.4018/978-1-5225-4044-1.ch011

Debnath, S. K. (2019). Secure Computation of Private Set Intersection Cardinality With Linear Complexity. In M. Banday (Ed.), *Cryptographic Security Solutions for the Internet of Things* (pp. 142–180). Hershey, PA: IGI Global. doi:10.4018/978-1-5225-5742-5.ch006

Dhawale, C. A. (2017). Review and Applications of Multimodal Biometrics for Secured Systems. In N. Kumar, A. Sangaiah, M. Arun, & S. Anand (Eds.), *Advanced Image Processing Techniques and Applications* (pp. 251–266). Hershey, PA: IGI Global. doi:10.4018/978-1-5225-2053-5.ch012

Dhawale, C. A., & Jambhekar, N. D. (2017). Digital Image Steganography: Survey, Analysis, and Application. In N. Kumar, A. Sangaiah, M. Arun, & S. Anand (Eds.), *Advanced Image Processing Techniques and Applications* (pp. 324–346). Hershey, PA: IGI Global. doi:10.4018/978-1-5225-2053-5.ch015

Doraikannan, S. (2018). Efficient Implementation of Digital Signature Algorithms. In K. Balasubramanian & M. Rajakani (Eds.), *Algorithmic Strategies for Solving Complex Problems in Cryptography* (pp. 78–86). Hershey, PA: IGI Global. doi:10.4018/978-1-5225-2915-6.ch006

Gandhi, S., & Ratanpara, T. V. (2017). Object-Based Surveillance Video Synopsis Using Genetic Algorithm. In N. Dey, A. Ashour, & S. Acharjee (Eds.), *Applied Video Processing in Surveillance and Monitoring Systems* (pp. 193–219). Hershey, PA: IGI Global. doi:10.4018/978-1-5225-1022-2.ch009

Gandhi, U. D. (2017). A Novel Approach of Human Tracking Mechanism in Wireless Camera Networks. In N. Kumar, A. Sangaiah, M. Arun, & S. Anand (Eds.), *Advanced Image Processing Techniques and Applications* (pp. 297–323). Hershey, PA: IGI Global. doi:10.4018/978-1-5225-2053-5.ch014

Geetha, S., Punithavathi, P., Infanteena, A. M., & Sindhu, S. S. (2018). A Literature Review on Image Encryption Techniques. *International Journal of Information Security and Privacy*, *12*(3), 42–83. doi:10.4018/IJISP.2018070104

Gill, H. K., Verma, A. K., & Sandhu, R. (2019). An Adaptive Security Framework for the Internet of Things Applications Based on the Contextual Information. In M. Banday (Ed.), *Cryptographic Security Solutions for the Internet of Things* (pp. 244–267). Hershey, PA: IGI Global. doi:10.4018/978-1-5225-5742-5.ch009

Guo, T., Jiao, J., Liu, F., & Wang, W. (2017). On the Pixel Expansion of Visual Cryptography Scheme. *International Journal of Digital Crime and Forensics*, *9*(2), 38–44. doi:10.4018/IJDCF.2017040104

Hallaq, B., Nicholson, A., Smith, R., Maglaras, L., Janicke, H., & Jones, K. (2017). CYRAN: A Hybrid Cyber Range for Testing Security on ICS/SCADA Systems. In M. Ferrag & A. Ahmim (Eds.), *Security Solutions and Applied Cryptography in Smart Grid Communications* (pp. 226–241). Hershey, PA: IGI Global. doi:10.4018/978-1-5225-1829-7.ch012

Hamdane, B., Boussada, R., Elhdhili, M. E., & El Fatmi, S. G. (2018). Enhancing Security and Trust in Named Data Networking using Hierarchical Identity Based Cryptography. *International Journal of Systems and Service-Oriented Engineering*, *8*(1), 1–20. doi:10.4018/IJSSOE.2018010101

Hatamlou, A., Erfannia, A., & Mahalleh, F. (2017). Watermarking of Digital Images With the Substitution of Low-Value Bits to Increase Capacity. *International Journal of Computer Vision and Image Processing*, *7*(4), 41–50. doi:10.4018/IJCVIP.2017100104

Hemalatha, J., KavithaDevi, M.K., & Geetha, S. (2018). A Recent Study on High Dimensional Features Used in Stego Image Anomaly Detection. In P. Karthikeyan, & M. Thangavel (Eds.), Applications of Security, Mobile, Analytic, and Cloud (SMAC) Technologies for Effective Information Processing and Management (pp. 49-66). Hershey, PA: IGI Global. doi:10.4018/978-1-5225-4044-1.ch003

Hu, W., Kaabouch, N., Guo, H., & ElSaid, A. A. (2018). Location-Based Advertising Using Location-Aware Data Mining. In P. Karthikeyan & M. Thangavel (Eds.), *Applications of Security, Mobile, Analytic, and Cloud (SMAC) Technologies for Effective Information Processing and Management* (pp. 196–211). Hershey, PA: IGI Global. doi:10.4018/978-1-5225-4044-1.ch010

Karopoulos, G., Ntantogian, C., & Xenakis, C. (2017). Privacy-Preserving Aggregation in the Smart Grid. In M. Ferrag & A. Ahmim (Eds.), *Security Solutions and Applied Cryptography in Smart Grid Communications* (pp. 80–97). Hershey, PA: IGI Global. doi:10.4018/978-1-5225-1829-7.ch005

Khaire, P. A., & Kotkondawar, R. R. (2017). Measures of Image and Video Segmentation. In N. Dey, A. Ashour, & S. Acharjee (Eds.), *Applied Video Processing in Surveillance and Monitoring Systems* (pp. 28–53). Hershey, PA: IGI Global. doi:10.4018/978-1-5225-1022-2.ch002

Kirmani, M. S., & Banday, M. T. (2019). Digital Forensics in the Context of the Internet of Things. In M. Banday (Ed.), *Cryptographic Security Solutions for the Internet of Things* (pp. 296–324). Hershey, PA: IGI Global. doi:10.4018/978-1-5225-5742-5.ch011

Krishnamoorthy, K., & Jeyabalu, M. (2017). A New Image Encryption Method Based on Improved Cipher Block Chaining with Optimization Technique. In N. Kumar, A. Sangaiah, M. Arun, & S. Anand (Eds.), *Advanced Image Processing Techniques and Applications* (pp. 133–149). Hershey, PA: IGI Global. doi:10.4018/978-1-5225-2053-5.ch006

Kumar, M. S., & Prabhu, J. (2018). Recent Development in Big Data Analytics: Research Perspective. In P. Karthikeyan & M. Thangavel (Eds.), *Applications of Security, Mobile, Analytic, and Cloud (SMAC) Technologies for Effective Information Processing and Management* (pp. 233–257). Hershey, PA: IGI Global. doi:10.4018/978-1-5225-4044-1.ch012

Ladjailia, A., Bouchrika, I., Harrati, N., & Mahfouf, Z. (2017). Encoding Human Motion for Automated Activity Recognition in Surveillance Applications. In N. Dey, A. Ashour, & S. Acharjee (Eds.), *Applied Video Processing in Surveillance and Monitoring Systems* (pp. 170–192). Hershey, PA: IGI Global. doi:10.4018/978-1-5225-1022-2.ch008

Li, J., Wang, J., Yu, S., & Luo, X. (2019). A Reversible Watermarking Algorithm Resistant to Image Geometric Transformation. *International Journal of Digital Crime and Forensics, 11*(1), 100–113. doi:10.4018/IJDCF.2019010108

Lopes, Y., Fernandes, N. C., Bornia de Castro, T., Farias, V. D., Noce, J. D., Marques, J. P., & Muchaluat-Saade, D. C. (2017). Vulnerabilities and Threats in Smart Grid Communication Networks. In M. Ferrag & A. Ahmim (Eds.), *Security Solutions and Applied Cryptography in Smart Grid Communications* (pp. 1–28). Hershey, PA: IGI Global. doi:10.4018/978-1-5225-1829-7.ch001

M, V., & Thirugnanam, M. (2017). Shape Determination of Aspired Foreign Body on Pediatric Radiography Images Using Rule-Based Approach. In N. Kumar, A. Sangaiah, M. Arun, & S. Anand (Eds.), *Advanced Image Processing Techniques and Applications* (pp. 170-181). Hershey, PA: IGI Global. doi:10.4018/978-1-5225-2053-5.ch008

Maglaras, L., Janicke, H., Jiang, J., & Crampton, A. (2017). Novel Intrusion Detection Mechanism with Low Overhead for SCADA Systems. In M. Ferrag & A. Ahmim (Eds.), *Security Solutions and Applied Cryptography in Smart Grid Communications* (pp. 160–178). Hershey, PA: IGI Global. doi:10.4018/978-1-5225-1829-7.ch009

Masoodi, I. S., & Javid, B. (2019). A Review of Cryptographic Algorithms for the Internet of Things. In M. Banday (Ed.), *Cryptographic Security Solutions for the Internet of Things* (pp. 67–93). Hershey, PA: IGI Global. doi:10.4018/978-1-5225-5742-5.ch003

Mishra, S., Mohapatra, S. K., Mishra, B. K., & Sahoo, S. (2018). Analysis of Mobile Cloud Computing: Architecture, Applications, Challenges, and Future Perspectives. In P. Karthikeyan & M. Thangavel (Eds.), *Applications of Security, Mobile, Analytic, and Cloud (SMAC) Technologies for Effective Information Processing and Management* (pp. 81–104). Hershey, PA: IGI Global. doi:10.4018/978-1-5225-4044-1.ch005

Mohan, K., Palanisamy, P. B., Kanagachidambaresan, G., Rajesh, S., & Narendran, S. (2018). Role of Security Mechanisms in the Building Blocks of the Cloud Infrastructure. In P. Karthikeyan & M. Thangavel (Eds.), *Applications of Security, Mobile, Analytic, and Cloud (SMAC) Technologies for Effective Information Processing and Management* (pp. 1–23). Hershey, PA: IGI Global. doi:10.4018/978-1-5225-4044-1.ch001

Muñoz, M. C., & Moh, M. (2017). Authentication of Smart Grid: The Case for Using Merkle Trees. In M. Ferrag & A. Ahmim (Eds.), *Security Solutions and Applied Cryptography in Smart Grid Communications* (pp. 117–136). Hershey, PA: IGI Global. doi:10.4018/978-1-5225-1829-7.ch007

Nafi, N. S., Ahmed, K., & Gregory, M. A. (2017). Modelling Software-Defined Wireless Sensor Network Architectures for Smart Grid Neighborhood Area Networks. In M. Ferrag & A. Ahmim (Eds.), *Security Solutions and Applied Cryptography in Smart Grid Communications* (pp. 267–286). Hershey, PA: IGI Global. doi:10.4018/978-1-5225-1829-7.ch014

Nagarajan, S. K., & Sangaiah, A. K. (2017). Vegetation Index: Ideas, Methods, Influences, and Trends. In N. Kumar, A. Sangaiah, M. Arun, & S. Anand (Eds.), *Advanced Image Processing Techniques and Applications* (pp. 347–386). Hershey, PA: IGI Global. doi:10.4018/978-1-5225-2053-5.ch016

Parkavi, R., Priyanka, C., Sujitha, S., & Sheik Abdullah, A. (2018). Mobile Cloud Computing: Applications Perspective. In P. Karthikeyan & M. Thangavel (Eds.), *Applications of Security, Mobile, Analytic, and Cloud (SMAC) Technologies for Effective Information Processing and Management* (pp. 105–123). Hershey, PA: IGI Global. doi:10.4018/978-1-5225-4044-1.ch006

Pramanik, P. K., Pal, S., Brahmachari, A., & Choudhury, P. (2018). Processing IoT Data: From Cloud to Fog—It's Time to Be Down to Earth. In P. Karthikeyan & M. Thangavel (Eds.), *Applications of Security, Mobile, Analytic, and Cloud (SMAC) Technologies for Effective Information Processing and Management* (pp. 124–148). Hershey, PA: IGI Global. doi:10.4018/978-1-5225-4044-1.ch007

Pudumalar, S., Suriya, K. S., & Rohini, K. (2018). Data Classification and Prediction. In P. Karthikeyan & M. Thangavel (Eds.), *Applications of Security, Mobile, Analytic, and Cloud (SMAC) Technologies for Effective Information Processing and Management* (pp. 149–173). Hershey, PA: IGI Global. doi:10.4018/978-1-5225-4044-1.ch008

Qian, Z., Wang, Z., Zhang, X., & Feng, G. (2019). Breaking Steganography: Slight Modification with Distortion Minimization. *International Journal of Digital Crime and Forensics, 11*(1), 114–125. doi:10.4018/IJDCF.2019010109

Raj, A. N., & Mahesh, V. G. (2017). Zernike-Moments-Based Shape Descriptors for Pattern Recognition and Classification Applications. In N. Kumar, A. Sangaiah, M. Arun, & S. Anand (Eds.), *Advanced Image Processing Techniques and Applications* (pp. 90–120). Hershey, PA: IGI Global. doi:10.4018/978-1-5225-2053-5.ch004

Ramaiah, M., & Ray, B. K. (2017). A Technique to Approximate Digital Planar Curve with Polygon. In N. Kumar, A. Sangaiah, M. Arun, & S. Anand (Eds.), *Advanced Image Processing Techniques and Applications* (pp. 150–169). Hershey, PA: IGI Global. doi:10.4018/978-1-5225-2053-5.ch007

Rathee, G., & Saini, H. (2018). Authentication Through Elliptic Curve Cryptography (ECC) Technique in WMN. *International Journal of Information Security and Privacy, 12*(1), 42–52. doi:10.4018/IJISP.2018010104

Rawat, D. B., & Chatfield, B. A. (2017). Detecting Synchronization Signal Jamming Attacks for Cybersecurity in Cyber-Physical Energy Grid Systems. In M. Ferrag & A. Ahmim (Eds.), *Security Solutions and Applied Cryptography in Smart Grid Communications* (pp. 68–78). Hershey, PA: IGI Global. doi:10.4018/978-1-5225-1829-7.ch004

Reddy, V. L. (2017). Improved Secure Data Transfer Using Video Steganographic Technique. *International Journal of Rough Sets and Data Analysis, 4*(3), 55–70. doi:10.4018/IJRSDA.2017070104

Roy, P., Patra, N., Mukherjee, A., Ashour, A. S., Dey, N., & Biswas, S. P. (2017). Intelligent Traffic Monitoring System through Auto and Manual Controlling using PC and Android Application. In N. Dey, A. Ashour, & S. Acharjee (Eds.), *Applied Video Processing in Surveillance and Monitoring Systems* (pp. 244–262). Hershey, PA: IGI Global. doi:10.4018/978-1-5225-1022-2.ch011

Roy, S. (2017). Denial of Service Attack on Protocols for Smart Grid Communications. In M. Ferrag & A. Ahmim (Eds.), *Security Solutions and Applied Cryptography in Smart Grid Communications* (pp. 50–67). Hershey, PA: IGI Global. doi:10.4018/978-1-5225-1829-7.ch003

Roy, S., Ahuja, S. P., Harish, P. D., & Talluri, S. R. (2018). Energy Optimization in Cryptographic Protocols for the Cloud. In P. Karthikeyan & M. Thangavel (Eds.), *Applications of Security, Mobile, Analytic, and Cloud (SMAC) Technologies for Effective Information Processing and Management* (pp. 24–48). Hershey, PA: IGI Global. doi:10.4018/978-1-5225-4044-1.ch002

S. P. S., T, R., & N, B. (2017). An Image De-Noising Method Based on Intensity Histogram Equalization Technique for Image Enhancement. In N. Kumar, A. Sangaiah, M. Arun, & S. Anand (Eds.), Advanced Image Processing Techniques and Applications (pp. 121-132). Hershey, PA: IGI Global. doi:10.4018/978-1-5225-2053-5.ch005

Saad, A. H., & Ali, A. A. (2017). An Overview of Steganography: "Hiding in Plain Sight. In N. Dey, A. Ashour, & S. Acharjee (Eds.), *Applied Video Processing in Surveillance and Monitoring Systems* (pp. 116–144). Hershey, PA: IGI Global. doi:10.4018/978-1-5225-1022-2.ch006

Saraf, K. R., & Jesudason, M. P. (2019). Encryption Principles and Techniques for the Internet of Things. In M. Banday (Ed.), *Cryptographic Security Solutions for the Internet of Things* (pp. 42–66). Hershey, PA: IGI Global. doi:10.4018/978-1-5225-5742-5.ch002

Saranjame, R., & Das, M. L. (2018). Securing Digital Image from Malicious Insider Attacks. *International Journal of Computer Vision and Image Processing*, *8*(2), 49–58. doi:10.4018/IJCVIP.2018040103

Sarkar, A., & Kumar, R. (2017). Study of Various Image Segmentation Methodologies: An Overview. In N. Dey, A. Ashour, & S. Acharjee (Eds.), *Applied Video Processing in Surveillance and Monitoring Systems* (pp. 1–27). Hershey, PA: IGI Global. doi:10.4018/978-1-5225-1022-2.ch001

Sevugan, P., Purushotham, S., & Chandran, A. (2017). Expert System through GIS-Based Cloud. In N. Kumar, A. Sangaiah, M. Arun, & S. Anand (Eds.), *Advanced Image Processing Techniques and Applications* (pp. 387–398). Hershey, PA: IGI Global. doi:10.4018/978-1-5225-2053-5.ch017

Shet, S., Aswath, A. R., Hanumantharaju, M. C., & Gao, X. (2017). Design of Reconfigurable Architectures for Steganography System. In N. Dey, A. Ashour, & S. Acharjee (Eds.), *Applied Video Processing in Surveillance and Monitoring Systems* (pp. 145–168). Hershey, PA: IGI Global. doi:10.4018/978-1-5225-1022-2.ch007

Singh, R. K., & Shaw, D. K. (2018). A Hybrid Concept of Cryptography and Dual Watermarking (LSB_DCT) for Data Security. *International Journal of Information Security and Privacy*, *12*(1), 1–12. doi:10.4018/IJISP.2018010101

Sowmyarani, C. N., & Dayananda, P. (2017). Analytical Study on Privacy Attack Models in Privacy Preserving Data Publishing. In M. Ferrag & A. Ahmim (Eds.), *Security Solutions and Applied Cryptography in Smart Grid Communications* (pp. 98–116). Hershey, PA: IGI Global. doi:10.4018/978-1-5225-1829-7.ch006

Sultan, I., & Banday, M. T. (2019). Addressing Security Issues of the Internet of Things Using Physically Unclonable Functions. In M. Banday (Ed.), *Cryptographic Security Solutions for the Internet of Things* (pp. 95–116). Hershey, PA: IGI Global. doi:10.4018/978-1-5225-5742-5.ch004

T, P., & Nair, J. (2017). Diophantine Equations for Enhanced Security in Watermarking Scheme for Image Authentication. In N. Kumar, A. Sangaiah, M. Arun, & S. Anand (Eds.), *Advanced Image Processing Techniques and Applications* (pp. 205-229). Hershey, PA: IGI Global. doi:10.4018/978-1-5225-2053-5.ch010

Toor, G. S., & Ma, M. (2017). Security Issues of Communication Networks in Smart Grid. In M. Ferrag & A. Ahmim (Eds.), *Security Solutions and Applied Cryptography in Smart Grid Communications* (pp. 29–49). Hershey, PA: IGI Global. doi:10.4018/978-1-5225-1829-7.ch002

Ul-Haq, A., & Azhar, M. (2017). Feasibility Study of Renewable Energy Integrated Electric Vehicle Charging Infrastructure. In M. Ferrag & A. Ahmim (Eds.), *Security Solutions and Applied Cryptography in Smart Grid Communications* (pp. 313–349). Hershey, PA: IGI Global. doi:10.4018/978-1-5225-1829-7.ch016

Urrea, C., & Solar, G. (2017). Evaluation of Image Detection and Description Algorithms for Application in Monocular SLAM. In N. Kumar, A. Sangaiah, M. Arun, & S. Anand (Eds.), *Advanced Image Processing Techniques and Applications* (pp. 182–204). Hershey, PA: IGI Global. doi:10.4018/978-1-5225-2053-5.ch009

Urrea, C., & Uren, V. (2017). Technical Evaluation, Development, and Implementation of a Remote Monitoring System for a Golf Cart. In N. Dey, A. Ashour, & S. Acharjee (Eds.), *Applied Video Processing in Surveillance and Monitoring Systems* (pp. 220–243). Hershey, PA: IGI Global. doi:10.4018/978-1-5225-1022-2.ch010

Urrea, C., & Yau, A. (2017). Design, Construction, and Programming of a Mobile Robot Controlled by Artificial Vision. In N. Kumar, A. Sangaiah, M. Arun, & S. Anand (Eds.), *Advanced Image Processing Techniques and Applications* (pp. 230–250). Hershey, PA: IGI Global. doi:10.4018/978-1-5225-2053-5.ch011

Vasavi, S., Jyothi, T. N., & Rao, V. S. (2017). Moving Object Classification in a Video Sequence. In N. Dey, A. Ashour, & S. Acharjee (Eds.), *Applied Video Processing in Surveillance and Monitoring Systems* (pp. 70–101). Hershey, PA: IGI Global. doi:10.4018/978-1-5225-1022-2.ch004

Veerapathiran, N., & Anand, S. (2017). Reducing False Alarms in Vision-Based Fire Detection. In N. Dey, A. Ashour, & S. Acharjee (Eds.), *Applied Video Processing in Surveillance and Monitoring Systems* (pp. 263–290). Hershey, PA: IGI Global. doi:10.4018/978-1-5225-1022-2.ch012

Verma, P. (2019). A Secure Gateway Discovery Protocol Using Elliptic Curve Cryptography for Internet-Integrated MANET. In M. Banday (Ed.), *Cryptographic Security Solutions for the Internet of Things* (pp. 181–210). Hershey, PA: IGI Global. doi:10.4018/978-1-5225-5742-5.ch007

Wang, Z., Yin, Z., & Zhang, X. (2019). Asymmetric Distortion Function for JPEG Steganography Using Block Artifact Compensation. *International Journal of Digital Crime and Forensics, 11*(1), 90–99. doi:10.4018/IJDCF.2019010107

Yahyaoui, I., Ghraizi, R., Tadeo, F., & Segatto, M. E. (2017). Smart Energy and Cost Optimization for Hybrid Micro-Grids: PV/ Wind/ Battery/ Diesel Generator Control. In M. Ferrag & A. Ahmim (Eds.), *Security Solutions and Applied Cryptography in Smart Grid Communications* (pp. 287–312). Hershey, PA: IGI Global. doi:10.4018/978-1-5225-1829-7.ch015

Yahyaoui, I., Tadeo, F., & Vieira Segatto, M. E. (2017). Smart Control Strategy for Small-Scale Photovoltaic Systems Connected to Single-Phase Grids: Active and Reactive Powers Control. In M. Ferrag & A. Ahmim (Eds.), *Security Solutions and Applied Cryptography in Smart Grid Communications* (pp. 380–404). Hershey, PA: IGI Global. doi:10.4018/978-1-5225-1829-7.ch018

Yan, X., Lu, Y., Liu, L., Wan, S., Ding, W., & Liu, H. (2017). Exploiting the Homomorphic Property of Visual Cryptography. *International Journal of Digital Crime and Forensics, 9*(2), 45–56. doi:10.4018/IJDCF.2017040105

Zhang, S., Yang, L., Xu, X., & Gao, T. (2018). Secure Steganography in JPEG Images Based on Histogram Modification and Hyper Chaotic System. *International Journal of Digital Crime and Forensics*, *10*(1), 40–53. doi:10.4018/IJDCF.2018010104

Zhong, P., Li, M., Mu, K., Wen, J., & Xue, Y. (2019). Image Steganalysis in High-Dimensional Feature Spaces with Proximal Support Vector Machine. *International Journal of Digital Crime and Forensics*, *11*(1), 78–89. doi:10.4018/IJDCF.2019010106

Zhu, J., Guan, Q., Zhao, X., Cao, Y., & Chen, G. (2017). A Steganalytic Scheme Based on Classifier Selection Using Joint Image Characteristics. *International Journal of Digital Crime and Forensics*, *9*(4), 1–14. doi:10.4018/IJDCF.2017100101

Zhu, J., Zhao, X., & Guan, Q. (2019). Detecting and Distinguishing Adaptive and Non-Adaptive Steganography by Image Segmentation. *International Journal of Digital Crime and Forensics*, *11*(1), 62–77. doi:10.4018/IJDCF.2019010105

About the Author

Gandharba Swain is a Professor by profession. He is a voracious reader, a prolific writer, and a passionate thinker. Presently he is working in the Department of Computer Science and Engineering at Koneru Lakshmaiah Education Foundation, Vaddeswaram, Andhra Pradesh, India. Previously he had worked at GMR Institute of Technology, Rajam, Andhra Pradesh, India and at IACR Engineering College, Rayagada, Odisha, India. He received B.Sc (Hons) degree from Berhampur University in 1995, MCA degree from VSS University of Technology (VSSUT), Burla, in 1999, M.Tech (CSE) degree from NIT, Rourkela, in 2004 and PhD degree from SOA Deemed to be University, Bhubaneswar in 2014. He has more than 20 years of teaching experience and more than 10 years of research experience. He has authored more than 65 research articles in international journals and conferences in the areas of Networks, Security and Digital Image Steganography. Some of his articles are published in reputed journals owned by reputed publishers like Elsevier, Springer, Wiley, Hindawi, and Inderscience. As on 4 April 2019 his h-index is 14, i-10 index is 19 and his google scholar citation count is 535. He taught several subjects like Object Oriented Analysis & Design, Computer Networks, TCP/IP protocol suite, Digital Logic Design, Computer Organization & Architecture, Advanced Computer Architecture, C & Data Structures, Object Oriented Programming through C++ and Java, Design & Analysis of Algorithms, Artificial Intelligence, Multi-Agent Systems, Software Testing Methodologies, Simulation and Modeling, and Secure Programming to undergraduate and post graduate engineering students. He has authored a book entitled "Object Oriented Analysis and Design through Unified Modeling Language", published by Lakshmi Publications, New Delhi.

Index

Printed in the United States
By Bookmasters